T0354939

Remembering
George Town East

Julianne Venditto

iUniverse, Inc.
Bloomington

Remembering George Town East

iUniverse books may be ordered through booksellers or by contacting:

iUniverse
1663 Liberty Drive
Bloomington, IN 47403
www.iuniverse.com
1-800-Authors (1-800-288-4677)

ISBN: 978-1-4502-8011-2 (pbk)
ISBN: 978-1-4502-8012-9 (cloth)
ISBN: 978-1-4502-8013-6 (ebk)

Library of Congress Control Number: 2010918792

Printed in the United States of America

iUniverse rev. date: 12/15/2010

Introduction

While writing this book, I couldn't help but think of those from my generation, children of middle-class families who grew up in the 1970s and '80s. In the process of writing this memoir, my closest childhood friend and I had a blast as we reminisced about the good old days of playing on what seemed to be endless hot summer days, and watching shows like *Donny & Marie* or *Happy Days*. We looked back on what felt like simpler times, spending leisurely days riding our bikes around, going to the movies, roller-skating, and talking on the phone (before portable phones and caller ID were invented). We began wondering who else out there remembers those days of just being a kid in the 1970s, growing up without a care in the world except for school, summer vacations, and holidays, and then becoming a teenager in the awesome '80s. My generation will never forget hanging out with friends or falling in love for the first time and getting their hearts broken. I hope this book will help my contemporaries remember their first love or crush, their prom, close friends, and awkward teenage moments. This is not a tribute to the '70s and '80s, though. This is simply my story.

Acknowledgments

I'd like to thank my husband, Steve, for listening to me constantly talk about George Town, for giving me support, and for helping me navigate my way around the computer. I'm also grateful to my parents for choosing an awesome neighborhood, and for making financial sacrifices in order to raise me there. Thank you to all my childhood friends for giving me great memories. Thank you, Elena, for always being there, and RoseMary, for your support. I also extend my gratitude to my writing group colleagues, Gordon, Brian, Janine, and Dave, for their support and guidance.

Part One

I spent the first five years of my life living near the airport in Norfolk, Virginia. My parents, Audie and Dennis Nesby, rented a small brick house on the corner of Terry Drive and Gamage Drive. Our green, grassy corner lot was huge, leaving plenty of room for me and my friends to run around. Across the street lived my first and best friend, Teddy Jeffries. Some people teased Teddy, calling him "Dennis the Menace" because of his mischievous ways. Teddy was always getting into trouble for pulling pranks on people. He was a cute little boy with short sandy-blond hair and sparkling blue eyes. I'll never forget the cat-that-ate-the-canary grin he wore whenever he was thinking up a practical joke or one of his prankster schemes. He would throw rocks at passing cars and then run away, me right at his heels. One time he took a can of black spray paint from his dad's garage. Every time our friend Ben would turn his back, Teddy would look at me with that wide grin and spray the back of Ben's shirt. Poor Ben was always unsuspecting. I wonder to this day what Ben's mom must have thought when she found the painted shirt. Like a lot of neighborhood parents, she probably suspected Teddy.

Teddy and I were inseparable. My first years of trick-or-treating were spent with him. I'll never forget the December evenings when we would walk around looking at houses decorated with Christmas lights. We spent birthdays together, hunted for Easter eggs together, and during the winter months, we had snowball fights and made lots of snowmen. During the summer months, we played in the sprinkler, taking turns jumping over the spraying water, stomping on the grass and turning it into mud. Countless times we climbed up the tall pines in my backyard, finding locust shells or collecting acorns to decorate our mud pies with. My simple life back then seemed like it would never change. My only challenge was my recurring nightmares, fueled by my active imagination. There were many nights I would wake up terrified after dreaming about headless people in my closet chasing me down the hall. When I was only five years old, I didn't know if these nightmares were real or not. I remember playing in my room in the middle of the day. Any sound I heard coming from my closet made me run out of my room. I thought it was the headless people coming to get me. They were normal looking dressed people except with no heads. I imagined them as attractive, if they had their heads back. One of the monsters was a lady who wore a red floral dress with matching high heels. I used to ask myself, *What happened to their heads?* I was too scared to tell my parents about the dreams, for fear of the headless people claiming my parents, if they decided to go after the monsters.

I can recall one particular dream like it was just yesterday. I woke up in the dark, hearing the sliding wooden doors of my closet being pushed open by the monsters. I knew I would have to run. The covers wouldn't protect me. The headless people would grab me if I stayed in my bed. My knees shook and I began to sweat from fear. I hoped I could make it down the hall to the kitchen table, where I knew my dad would be reading the newspaper. As I ran down the hall, I could feel the hairs on the back of my neck starting to rise. The monsters were right behind me! The hallway seemed to double in length as I ran toward my dad. I screamed for help. I was almost there. My dad was still reading the newspaper, not hearing my desperate cries for help. I was getting closer, but the headless people weren't giving up. Their arms were outstretched, reaching for me. I could hear their footsteps. There must be three or four of them this time. "Help!" I screamed again. This time my dad heard me and looked up. The monsters disappeared. I woke up. It was sunny outside. Golden rays poured through my bedroom window. *Thank God*, I thought. Someday I would have to ask my dad about how these monsters got in my closet.

When I found out my dad had wanted to move to a different neighborhood (because "It's time to buy a house," he had said), I became worried. Terry Drive and Teddy Jeffries were my world. I had a nice swing set, teeter-totter, and sandbox in the backyard that I would have to leave behind as well. Would my new home have all that? Would the headless people move with us? I wondered.

Our real-estate agent was a tall, older man with gray hair, Mr. Gentry. He wore a mustard-gold jacket with an emblem on its breast pocket reading CENTURY 21. He showed us several houses in various neighborhoods. There was one house I particularly liked, a sprawling brick ranch settled back in a cul-de-sac. I liked the bedroom that would have been mine, with its plush red carpet and brown paneled walls. The room's closet door didn't slide open; it was a regular swinging door with a knob. *I could get a lock put on it*, I thought. I was getting excited about the possibility of moving into that house when my dad announced he'd found another one he liked better.

"This one is in a bigger neighborhood, and there is a nice school, close enough to walk to," he explained to me with enthusiasm.

That sounded a little intimidating to me. A *big* neighborhood and *walking* to school. Would I get lost? I had never walked to school before.

I remember sitting in the back seat of the car heading down a long, narrow road called Providence Road. Mr. Gentry told us about two different neighborhoods that linked together. One was called George Town Colony, and the other George Town East. There was another planned neighborhood not yet built that would be called George Town Point. As I sat in the back of my parents' car staring out the window, I saw lots of brick ranch homes surrounded by tall pine trees. We came upon a large field. In the field sat an elementary school with two windows per classroom.

"That's where you'll be going to school, Junie," my dad said, pointing to it as we drove by.

I wondered if the school would be nice.

George Town East

I remember our making a left-hand turn into our new neighborhood that spring morning back in 1973.

On either side of the street (which was called Dunbarton Drive, the entrance of the neighborhood) stood four-foot-high, curved white-brick walls. On the wall on the left, black wrought-iron letters spelled out GEORGE TOWN, and the right wall it read EAST. Yellow daffodils were planted all along the bottom of the walls, below the lettering. The elementary school was on the left of us surrounded, by a large, grassy field.

"We're looking for a street called Crown Crescent," my dad said as we drove slowly.

"There it is!" my mom said, pointing to a blue street sign.

"Okay, it's the third house on the left," my dad said out loud, trying to remember the location. Our new house was a rectangular brick ranch, bigger than the house that we had been renting. All the houses were beautiful—long, brick ranch homes with immaculate, sprawling lawns. The lots were all landscaped with tall pine trees, boxwood shrubs, and dogwood trees with pink and white blooms. Our house had a little Japanese plum tree in the front yard. The porch was mid-sized, with brick steps. The house was trimmed in white with black shutters.

"Our house has three bedrooms and two bathrooms," my dad announced as we entered.

"Wow, there's two living rooms and a separate dining room" my mom said, standing in the living room gazing around. I could tell she had decorating ideas running through her head already. The kitchen was small, with a window over the sink looking into the backyard.

The utility room was off the kitchen, and led to the garage. The utility room also had a door leading out back and a door leading upstairs to an unfinished room over the garage. The stairs were wooden and unfinished. The room over the garage was spooky, but had a window giving a view of the neighboring roofs. The backyard was large, with a cluster of pine trees in the corner. There was a sidewalk that wrapped around one side of the house, leading from the driveway to the back cement patio. All the neighbors' yards connected, without any fences dividing them.

Our dishes and things were still in boxes for a couple of days, leaving us eating meals from Burger King while sitting by the fireplace, using it as our kitchen table. This is a good memory I have of my mom and dad. We were absolutely thrilled about the new place. My dad was happy as well, even if eating dinner in an empty den was out of character for him. He was a firm believer in home-cooked meals, served at the dinner table, 5:30 sharp, every evening. Our new den was dark, with chocolate-colored linoleum flooring and dark, wood-paneled walls. Even the fireplace's bricks were a deep, dark red. There was a door that led onto the patio, its windows letting light in.

My dad had rented a yellow moving truck from Ryder. I rode with him after a day of loading and unloading furniture from our old house into the new one. Dad had a couple of friends from the navy help us move. I'll never forget Moose, who was a tall fellow with broad shoulders and muscular arms. Moose actually picked up our refrigerator and carried it into the moving truck all by himself!

As we were heading back to the old house for our last load, I noticed my dad's face as he came to a stop at a red light on the highway. He seemed happy. He had an eased look, a small smile on his face.

Out of the blue, I decided to ask my silly question. "Dad, will the headless people that live in my closet move with us?"

He looked at me quizzically. "Headless people?"

"Yeah. They live in my closet and chase me down the hall at night."

"Oh no, they're all gone, all gone. Don't worry about them anymore." He must have known I had nightmares or a big imagination, because his reaction was intuitive and effective.

As we pulled up into our old driveway, I looked at the last few pieces of furniture on the lawn, waiting to be loaded into the moving truck. I felt a sadness in my heart that slid all the way down into my gut. I was going to miss Teddy, I really was. I was going to miss living on Terry Drive as well.

We got settled into our new home with beige walls and Dutch blue carpeting. I laid awake the first night with my double canopy bed facing the sliding wooden doors of my closet. It looked just like my closet back in Norfolk. I remembered what my dad had said. *They're gone, all gone.* My old nightmares of headless people slowly faded away. I started thinking about my mom telling me how I would like the windows in the new house.

"The new windows are low enough to where you can stand at them to see out, Junie. Unlike in Norfolk, where the windows were high up near the ceiling causing you to have to pull up a chair to peer out."

I looked out my new window facing the backyard. I could see the night sky. I watched tiny airplanes flying over. My mind filled with thoughts. I wondered how much further I must be from the Norfolk airport, which we used to live by. I wondered how Teddy felt about me not living across the street from him any longer. Did he miss me when he woke up in the morning, knowing he couldn't walk over and knock on my door? I wondered about the brick house behind ours now. Who lived there? Were they nice? My eyes grew heavy and I drifted off to sleep, listening to the lonely sound of a distant train's moaning horn.

I only had a month and a half left in first grade. Mom had to wake me up extra early now that we lived further away from school in order to get me there on time. My school was a small brick building with only one corridor. The classrooms had stained glass windows of pink, red, green, and blue, filling the rooms with colors when the sun shone through them. I would stare at the windows completely enthralled, wishing my bedroom had the same stained glass. When I finished first grade, I felt a little uneasy. Not because I would miss the stained glass windows, but because I would be attending a new school after summer vacation.

My parents soon had the new house in order. I remember sitting on the front porch, watching kids walking by, staring at me. Some pointed as they spoke, their voices sounding cheerful, although I couldn't make out what they were saying. I was too shy to speak. I did the same routine each day after dinner. I sat on the porch with my face resting in my hands, elbows on my knees. Sometimes I would wave. Some kids would wave back, but they never spoke or came over.

"No one will ever come over to meet me, I'll never have friends," I whined one day, feeling hopeless.

"Take our cat, Samantha, out on the porch with you along with her kittens, and just play with them," my dad suggested. "You'll have all kinds of friends then."

So after dinner the next day, I brought Samantha and the kittens out with me. They were *so* cute with their little blue eyes, brown fur, and black faces. They were chocolate point Siamese kittens. Back in Norfolk, a neighbor had had a cat the same breed as Samantha, and we had let the cats mate.

I looked up when I heard the voices of three girls crossing my lawn. They all resembled each other. I guessed they were sisters.

"Oh, how adorable!" the oldest looking girl said, staring at the kittens lovingly.

"Can we hold one?" the youngest girl asked.

"Sure. Please be gentle though, they're still young," I said.

The girls all had long, beautiful, thick brown hair. The oldest girl reminded me of the singer Marie Osmond. "I'm Katie. What's your name?" the oldest asked.

"I'm Junie." I was so happy to be meeting some of the new neighbors finally.

"These are my younger sisters, Kelly and Krissy," she said, picking up a kitten and kissing it on the nose.

"How old are you?" the youngest asked.

"I'm six, but I'll be seven August 22," I replied.

"I'm five, but I'll be six August 23rd."

"Wow, how about that? Something in common, Krissy," Katie said, setting her kitten down and picking up another one.

As we started chatting about the kittens and my moving from

Norfolk, my dad came out to meet my new friends. Katie asked if she could have one of the kittens, if her parents approved.

"Sure," my dad replied, delighted at the thought of finally giving one of the kittens away.

"We live right over there," Katie said, pointing to the house across the street, on the corner lot of the cul-de-sac and our street. They had a large lawn, and a nice brick ranch that was a little bigger than ours. "Come over tomorrow some time, Junie," Katie added as she gently set her kitten down. Kelly and Krissy did the same. "Krissy would be glad to have a new friend to play with."

As the girls turned to head home, they all waved good-bye with flashy white smiles.

"One more thing! I babysit, if you ever need me," Katie called back from the edge of our yard.

"Sounds good," my dad replied, sounding delighted once again.

Katie later returned to say she wasn't allowed to have a cat.

New Friends Who Would Shape My Life

The next morning after waking up and getting dressed (my summer shorts and a summer blouse with frilly short sleeves) I quickly ate a bowl of Lucky Charms before heading over to Krissy's house.

Krissy answered the door with a large smile. "Hi, Junie! I'm glad you came over."

A petite lady with short brown hair cut like my mom's entered the foyer. "So you're the new girl! Welcome to the neighborhood."

Being shy, "Thank you" was all I could manage in response.

"Follow me," Krissy said, heading down the hallway. As I followed, I noticed their hallway's unique carpeting. It was striped in colors of blue, red, violet, and beige. The only part of the carpet that was shag was the beige part.

"This is my room," Krissy announced from the doorway where she had stopped. Her room was small, with a large window facing the front yard. Barbie dolls were scattered all over her bedroom floor. I thought about my Barbies at home, and how I kept them scattered all over my bedroom floor as well.

"Do you like to play Barbies?" Krissy asked as she opened the sliding door of her Barbie camper.

"Yes, I love Barbies."

"Let's take them outside."

"Okay." I started helping her put the dolls in the camper.

We spent the afternoon getting acquainted and playing Barbies outside in the green grass under the tall pine trees. I liked the sound of the pines swaying in the breeze. It was a beautiful day.

A girl came around the corner of Krissy's house. When she spotted us, she started walking over toward us. She had shoulder-length red hair and wore a blouse just like mine, except hers was light blue. Her shorts were dark blue. Something was wrapped around her left thigh. *Was her leg broken?* I wondered.

"Hi, Joanie," Krissy said.

"Hi," the new arrival said.

So Joanie was her name. She stopped and looked down at me.

"What's your name?"

"I'm Junie."

Krissy went ahead and introduced us, not forgetting to be polite. "Have a seat, Joanie."

I was trying not to stare at the strange brown leather straps tied around Joanie's thigh. The bottom part of her leg appeared to be false, made of wood perhaps. She seemed to sit down with no problem, though.

"Are you the new girl that moved in a while back?" Joanie asked me.

"Yeah."

"I remember riding my bike by your house while you were sitting on the front porch."

I remembered seeing Joanie before just as she said that. She had gone by slowly on her bike, staring at me. Her nose had been crinkled, with her eyes sort of squinting to see me better. She had had her red hair tied back in a ponytail that day. I had noticed the freckles across her nose, too. When I had waved to her, she hadn't waved back. She just kept riding past slowly, staring.

Joanie told me a bit about herself. She was adopted, and had an older brother named Morris, who wasn't adopted. She explained that she had been friends with Krissy and her sisters for a long time. Then she told me about her leg. "I was born with no leg below my knee, so I wear this wooden one to help me walk."

"Oh." I felt bad that she only had half a leg, but I didn't feel sorry for her, seeing how well she got around. *Why was she born that way?* I wondered.

My first summer in George Town turned out to be a busy one, which made me happy. After such skepticism at first, sitting on my front porch doubting I would ever make any friends, I was soon thrilled to have more friends than I ever could have imagined. I had even more kids to play with than I had had back in Norfolk. I still missed Teddy, though. We spoke on the phone every now and then. Krissy and I became best friends right away. We both liked roller-skating around the cul-de-sac, playing Barbies, and dress-up. We were typical little girls with big imaginations. We attended vacation bible school together, and by midsummer we were taking ballet lessons at the local rec center. For our recital, our moms got together and made us giant egg costumes out of cardboard. I don't remember what the recital was about, but I do remember Krissy and I having fun dancing around on stage with our proud moms watching.

We had sleepovers a lot. When I stayed over at Krissy's house, her sisters would wash our hair for us in the double sink bathroom. We would wrap towels around our heads to let our hair dry. Krissy's mom told us bedtime stories about when she was little and lived in India for awhile, because Krissy's grandfather had taken a job over there. Mrs. Coddle would always start off her stories by saying "India has lots of snakes everywhere."

Krissy's dad was a dentist in the navy, and the family had moved around to different places. Krissy was born in the Philippines. Most of their house was decorated with interesting things from there. They had high-backed wicker chairs and dark stained bamboo tables with lamps that had decorative carvings on their bases, images of monkeys etched into the bamboo. I loved watching the fish in the seventy-five-gallon fish tank that sat on a deep red stained bamboo table in their living room.

Krissy's oldest sibling, Dean, was a straight-A student. I remember him always having a book in his hand or sitting at his desk writing with his emerald-green desk lamp giving him light. Dean had short brown hair, and was tall and thin. He had the worst case of acne. He had his own special soap, a gold-colored translucent bar. Whenever I had to use their bathroom, I would carve the word "jerk" into the special soap with my fingernails. Then I would set it back in the soap dish where I found it. Dean always yelled at Krissy if he could hear us playing in her room, which was next to his. One day while we were playing Barbies, Dean barged in yelling at *me.*

"*You...* quiet now!" He had his finger pointing right in my face.

I wasn't sure if he was serious or not, and giggled, thinking he had a goofy look on his face. I covered my mouth with my hand when I realized he was actually angry. Dean didn't like the fact that I had laughed. He raised his hand and smacked me hard enough to make a sound. My hair was strewn across my face.

"Quiet! Do you *understand?*"

I nodded my head, shocked. The following day, he apologized to me after Krissy told their mom what he had done. I told him I accepted his apology. I didn't forget his action, though.

The next afternoon, when all of the neighborhood kids were playing out in the street as usual, Dean came out to tell Krissy to go in for dinner. Right as he spoke, a ball of fire went shooting across of the sky, making a whistling sound. It burned out before hitting the ground, thankfully.

"What was that?" someone asked.

"Was it an airplane?" another kid wondered.

"The atmosphere stopped it from hitting the earth," Dean said, still looking up at the sky where the fireball had been.

"What?" Michael Clark asked.

"It was a meteor, a large rock from space. We were lucky to have witnessed that."

I put my hands on my hips and glared at Dean. "Well, smarty-pants, my dad can explain that better than you can. He's smarter than *you!*" I said before stomping away from know-it-all Dean.

I told my dad about the meteor during dinner. He explained how meteors hit the earth all the time, and how it must have been a good sized one if it made it close enough to the earth for us to see and hear.

I enjoyed sitting on the front porch of our house, watching people passing by, taking their evening walks or riding bicycles down our street. It was the end of a hot July day, and I could hear the crickets starting to chirp. First one cricket, and then another, and then the whole chorus joined in. All of a sudden, I heard a familiar yelling start again. Things had been pleasant for a whole two weeks or so, but now my parents were back to their typical routine of evening fights. I started getting nervous as I heard the screaming and the profanity. I had to get away from it! I ran to the side of the house and pulled my bike out of the garage, hoping not to hear any more. I tore off down the street, my heart racing and my palms sweating. My parents never cared if I was in the room or not when they had one of their meaningless fights. I would get angry with them for it, and feared for my mom's life. I would get even angrier with her for egging my dad on. Sometimes I thought she would scream just loud enough to make sure that I could hear her, wherever I was. I loved my parents, but hated them at the same time. I know they loved me as well. They were just a really odd pair.

As I rode away from my house, I was glad the neighborhood was big and full of long, intertwining streets. I was getting to know my way around pretty well. It was soon dark. Lightning bugs were appearing, and I knew I needed to get home, even though I didn't want to return. The streetlights were starting to come on. I noticed them blinking, first with a pinkish color and then white. I was supposed to go straight home when the lights came on, or else! *Hopefully things would be calm now, and I can just go in and play in my room a while before bedtime*, I thought as I pedaled back. It was scary pulling up into the driveway.

I jumped when I heard my dad's booming voice yell "Junie!" He stood on the front porch. I could see his white T-shirt in the darkness. "Where the hell have you been?"

Sometimes I couldn't believe they didn't actually expect me to run off for good when they fought. "Just for a bike ride! It got dark *so fast,*" I said nonchalantly, hoping to calm his anger. I found my mom in the guest bedroom, pulling out the ironing board.

"Get in the tub and take a bath," she snapped, as if I had done something wrong. I didn't argue. I didn't want to fuel the fire that had been started.

I sat in the tub, watching the tiny white bubbles pop and make little fizzling sounds. I heard more profanity and prayed the yelling wouldn't start again. It would be hard for me to get out of the tub and run out without having to pass through the midst of the fight. I eyed my clothes lying on the floor, just in case I had to get dressed real fast to run out. I heard my dad go to bed. Everything was quiet again. I couldn't wait for a new day to come so I could run out and play with my friends.

With my dad being in the navy and working aboard the ship, he would sometimes have to spend the night on board for work. I would picture him sitting at his desk, talking on his black phone, smoking, cigarettes and writing with his black-and-silver pen. Everything else aboard ship was gray: his desk, the hallways, the walls, all of it was gray. It was noisy, too. He once told me that he had been woken up by the "deafening sound of silence. There is a lot of noise in an aircraft carrier and when the electric system shut down one time, it seemed ghostly how quiet it got."

My mom and I enjoyed our evenings together. Things were a little more on the casual side when my dad wasn't home. We would eat her delicious tuna casseroles (that my dad detested) while sitting on the couch watching *Laverne & Shirley* or *Happy Days*. I'll never forget our first night alone in our new house.

"Let's go for a bike ride," Mom said out of the blue.

"Okay!" *What a fun idea*, I thought. Even though it was 8:30 in the evening, I didn't feel like going to bed anytime soon. I went into the garage after getting out of my pajamas and putting on clothes and shoes. I saw my mom gathering up scissors and a flashlight, putting them in the baskets that straddled the back tire of her bike.

"What are you doing?" I asked with curiosity.

She would get funny ideas sometimes. One time, when my dad had forbidden her from hanging a heavy picture in my bedroom, out of fear of the picture damaging the wall; my mom got the bright idea of gluing it on. When she realized the glue wasn't strong enough, she got the bright idea of using super glue. They almost had to repair the wall after that ordeal, once the picture was furiously ripped off by my dad.

"I thought I'd just ride down to that nice house nobody is living in yet and cut some of the carpet rolled up in the garage."

We had ridden our bikes during the day, and had gone by the house in question to see if we could get inside, just to look around. The home was empty, with a FOR SALE sign out front. We were able to get in the side garage door, but the door leading into the house was locked. My mom and I walked around, peering inside the windows. This place had the same floor plan as our house, even though it was located just outside of George Town East on a somewhat busy road.

"You have to be quiet now as we go," my mom told me, brushing her short black hair out of her eyes to the side. Mom had a good tan, unlike me. She looked cute, wearing her white shorts, pink sleeveless shirt, and sandals. "Actually, you should stay here," she decided.

"No Mom! I'm too scared to stay alone, and you shouldn't go up there alone either."

"Well, okay. But ride on the back of my bike. We don't need to be on separate bikes this time of the night."

I straddled the back fender with one foot in one side basket and the other foot in the other basket. If I sat, my weight would make the fender hit the tire, which made a funny *whirr* sound. So I had to stand up to let the fender off the tire. But then I would get tired and would have to sit back down. *Whirr*, the sound of the tire went again. I looked like I was riding a horse. I got a glimpse of our silly-looking shadow on the street as we went under a streetlight. It gave me the giggles. My mom even started laughing a little. As we approached Providence Road, we had to wait for traffic to go by. It was a hot summer night, and people were out and about. Some cars pulled up next to us, waiting for the traffic to clear as well. Some of the people in the cars looked at us which made me start laughing again, knowing how goofy we must have seemed. I straddled my mom's bike while she kept fussing at me to stop laughing, though she was laughing too. Finally the road cleared. As we started to cross, I had to start sitting up, then down, up, then down, to give the tire a rest. The thought of how silly I looked continued to make me giggle. I must have looked like an idiot.

The house was just up on the right. As my mom pedaled up the driveway, I jumped off the bike, startling her. *This was fun*, I thought. I wondered if it was legal. We pulled around to the side garage door. The door was hidden in the darkness of the night and in the shadows of the pine trees.

"I'm scared," I said. I grabbed the back of my mom's shirt, burying my face in it.

"You wait out here and keep watch," she said. She slowly opened the door, turning on her flashlight. I decided to stand just inside the door and keep watch from within. I looked up at the pine trees. The wind was making them sway. My mom crossed the cool, empty garage and unrolled one of the carpet stacks. The moonlight shown through the big garage door's windows, giving us light without using the flashlight. My mom cut out carpet squares as quickly as she could. I kept watch, seeing an occasional car go by, headlights on. My mom wanted to get enough carpet squares to put around her sewing machine upstairs.

"Start putting some of the stacks I've got cut in the baskets," she said as she rolled out another carpet to cut. We ended up walking home while my mom pushed the bike. I couldn't sit on the back with the baskets full. We crossed Providence Road, this time with no traffic. After we got home and put the bike back in the garage, we carried the burgundy, dark blue and dark olive green squares of carpet up to the tiny room over the garage. We placed them around the sewing machine and under it, where my mom's feet would rest whenever she decided to sew. It all looked silly, especially knowing the unnecessary trouble we went through to get them.

Crown Crescent looked like a schoolyard almost every day during the summer. Cheery voices and laughter from children rang through the neighborhood. A lot of kids from George Town came to our street to play. I remember feeling as if days would last forever and the fun would never stop. I loved running out across my lawn to join a group of girls playing jump rope or jacks.

On some afternoons, we would all roller-skate around the cul-de-sac wearing our metal-wheeled skates, which were designed for outdoors only. Our skates beating the pavement could be heard from all around as we raced one another. We had many sunny afternoons of playing dodgeball or kickball. Some of the boys would strike me hard with the ball, which made me not want to play. They would usually talk me into playing again, promising to be gentler. I was very coordinated and could even walk along a chain-link fence, but I quickly learned that baseball wasn't for me after getting hit very hard in the shins a couple of times by the ball. I decided to stay away from sports like that for a while, joining the girls who watched from curbside. I was brave enough, however, to play flag football behind the Ceavers' house with the boys. All the lawns connected behind the houses, giving us a perfect, fence-free football field. Paul, Mick and James Ceaver, Michael Clark, and Morris would let me fill in if they were short a player. I was fast and agile, and gave them a real challenge. One afternoon we had a torrential rainfall sneak up on us. Even though it was hard to see and the ball was slippery, we continued playing, embracing the challenge while getting soaked and muddy. Usually, Mick, who lived right across the street, would knock on my door to let me know they were getting together for a game. That meant I would go and knock on Paul's door, while Mick went to get Morris and so on down the line. We would all meet behind Mick's house or at the elementary school's field.

One day when I knocked on Paul's door, a chubby little girl with dark, curly hair answered. I'd never seen her before.

"Is Paul home?" I asked, looking past her, hoping he'd come to the door.

"No, he went outside."

"Do you know where outside?"

"Naha ... What's your name?"

"I'm Junie."

"What's yours?"

"Neana."

"Okay, Neana. Tell him I stopped by."

"Do you want to play?"

Neana looked too young for me to be playing with. "How old are you?" I asked.

"I'm three."

"Okay, well, nice meeting you, Neana. Don't forget to tell Paul I stopped by."

"Okay."

Over the next few days, when I would go to get Paul for a game, he was never there. We had Keith fill in for him. Keith was a big kid, not fat, but tall with round, broad shoulders. He was good-looking and knew it. He usually irritated everyone by imitating pro-wrestlers when he talked, and could get quite arrogant.

Neana was always the one who answered the door when I went over looking for Paul, and she always asked me to play. One day I accepted her invitation so that I could wait around for Paul. Their parents seemed very friendly. They were in the living room watching *The Dating Game* on TV. They both smiled at me after asking my name and where I lived. I met Neana's little brother, Jake, who had black curly hair like hers and Paul's. I sat on the pretty red shag carpet in Neana's room, humoring her as she showed me her baby dolls one by one. After an hour or so, I was tired of waiting for Paul to come home.

"It's time for me to go home, Neana."

"Why?"

"Because my parents might be looking for me."

"Why?"

Oh brother, I thought. I didn't want to hurt this kid's feelings. "I'll see you another day, okay?" I said getting up to leave.

"Okay."

Good, she didn't ask me "why" again. I later learned that Paul was always out mowing lawns or washing cars to earn money of his own. Even at the age of nine, he was mindful of making and saving money.

Roses Shopping Center was packed with shoppers scurrying around, filling their carts with supplies needed for school, the beginning of which was only a week away. My mom and I met up with Krissy and her mom so we could shop together. I had just turned seven and was nervous about attending second grade in a new school. I was relieved that Krissy was attending the same school. Krissy was going into first grade, and was excited that we could walk to school together.

While standing in the long checkout line, I took inventory of the items in our cart. I had picked out little cardboard pencil boxes, paper, a composition notebook, and saddle shoes. As I looked at the Elmers glue bottle, I thought about how I liked pouring the glue into the palm of my hand and letting it dry so I could peel it off like dead skin after a sunburn. I picked up the crayon box and sniffed it. For some reason, I liked the way the waxy paper smelled. Krissy and I had picked out matching lunch boxes that had pictures of Holly Hobby on them. We liked Holly Hobby's giant blue bonnet and patchwork dress.

On the first day of school, Krissy and I and our moms all walked to school together. It was a short walk just down our street, left on Dunbarton, and then a short distance down to the large field on the right-hand side where the school sat. As we entered the building, all of the first grade classrooms were on the left, and a cafeteria with a wooden stage was on the right. The corridors were loud, as voices echoed with the excitement of the first day. Krissy waved good-bye to me as she and her mom went into her classroom to meet her new teacher.

"Bye, Krissy! See you after school!"

My mom continued to walk with me down the hall to where it intersected with another corridor. This part of the back corridor was carpeted, which helped muffle the clatter of footsteps and loud voices. The hall was crescent-shaped. My classroom was the first door on the right. Mrs. Brown was my teacher's name—she was a black woman. I thought her skin looked brown, matching her name. She was short and wore glasses on a chain, like older ladies wore to keep.

"Sit wherever you like," she told me after asking me my name and checking it off on her clipboard. The desks were arranged in pairs. I made my way over and sat in the closest one to Mrs. Brown. I heard my mom tell Mrs. Brown how shy I was. It was true—I could be really shy at times, and would cling to my mom in public places around people I didn't know. I also heard my mom tell Mrs. Brown that she would love to participate in being a room mother.

Children started filing in one by one. A frail-seeming little boy, with black, shiny hair parted on the side over his pale face, sat next to me. He seemed familiar to me, but I couldn't place where I had seen him before.

"Hi, I'm Randy," he said, plopping down his school bag on his desk before pulling out his chair to sit.

"I'm Junie."

"Do you live on Crown Crescent?"

"Yeah, I do."

"I thought you looked familiar. I've seen you riding your bike around; you ride it a lot. I see you go by my house all the time."

It all of a sudden occurred to me where I had seen Randy. He lived about eight houses down from me on the opposite side of the street. Randy was the kid who was always hanging out in his front yard. Whenever I passed him on my bike, we would notice each other but never speak. Maybe he was shy like me.

"How come you never come out and play with all the kids?" I asked.

"I don't know. I'm not into sports and I can't ride a bike, but I did just learn to roller-skate!" His voice became high-pitched with enthusiasm.

"Oh, I love to roller-skate too," I told him, not feeling as shy. I was glad Randy was going to be my classmate *and* my neighbor.

At lunch time I couldn't sit with Krissy, because the rule was that we had to sit only with our own class. Randy and I sat together during lunch, not really knowing anybody else in our class.

One Friday afternoon, as Randy and I made our way across the school's field toward our homes, he asked if I would like to go skating with him on the following Saturday afternoon.

"Sure, just let me ask my mom first," I answered.

"Give me your phone number though, because my mom will have to speak with your mom before she lets me do anything." Randy was already digging in his school bag for a pen and paper.

"Okay, give me yours too, just in case I need it."

He wrote my info down in his notebook as I recited the numbers.

"Four ... two ... zero ... dash—"

Randy giggled in his high-pitched voice. "You don't have to say 'dash.' I know to write that after the first three numbers!"

"Oh, sorry. It's just some dumb habit I have when I give out a phone number," I said, somewhat embarrassed. My mom had had me recite our phone number over and over until I'd memorized it. Saying "dash" after the first three digits somehow helped me remember it better.

Randy wrote down his number and ripped the page out of his blue spiral notebook.

"Thanks," I said putting the page in my book bag. We continued walking across the field toward Dunbarton. All of the neighborhood's streets led to Dunbarton. We didn't go toward the main crosswalk, where there was always a crossing guard after school let out. We felt we were big enough to cross by ourselves further down. Dunbarton wasn't a very busy street anyway.

After having my after-school snack, I took off my shoes and red button-up sweater and retreated to my room. I filed through the tie-dye record box that held all of my 45s. LP albums were too big to fit in the box, so I kept them stacked on a shelf. I put on "That's Rock 'n' Roll" by Shaun Cassidy. I thought he was *so* cute as I looked at the poster of him on my wall, a picture of him wearing a light blue satin jacket. I loved his bright white smile. This was one of my favorite songs. As it played, I danced around my room, holding my hairbrush up to my mouth, pretending it was a microphone. I imagined I was on the stage at school giving a rock concert. I pretended to play the guitar, and imagined everybody in the audience cheering me on. When the song ended, I took a bow and then another as the crowd cheered. I heard my name being called.

"Junie?"

I took another bow.

"Junie?"

I looked up and realized I was in still in my room.

"Juuunie!"

I turned and saw my mom standing in the doorway.

"Oh!" I said, surprised to see her. I quickly realized it was her that had been calling my name.

"Randy's mom just called and said that if you want, you can go skating with him tomorrow afternoon."

"Oh goody!" I said, jumping up with zeal at the thought of skating.

"They will be here tomorrow at 1:45 to pick you up, and so I can meet them."

Saturday afternoon arrived. My mom walked me out to Randy's parents' brown station wagon parked in front of our house. His mom was very nice, but also seemed very strict. Randy's older sister sat up front with their mom. His sister seemed irritated at my mere existence. At College Park Skating Rink, we paid our $4 admissions fee, plus a $1 rental fee for the skates. After lacing up our ugly, used, beige skates, which were designed for indoor use only, I held Randy's hand to help keep him from falling. He was still a little unstable on skates. He seemed impressed with my skating. When it came time to play "limbo," Randy decided to watch from the sideline. He beamed at me as I went under the limbo stick. After the skating session was over, we unlaced our skates and complained about the blisters on our toes and heels. We did have a lot of fun, though. Spending Saturday afternoons skating became a routine for Randy and me.

My dad was a Senior Chief in the navy when we moved to George Town. I loved going aboard ship with him for a meal or on family days.

One evening, my mom and I followed him up the long gangway. I could see the choppy water below through the grating of the gangway as we climbed up. It was dark green and seemed like it would be quite cold if I fell in. The *Nimitz* was tied to the dock with huge cables. I remember seeing one of the anchors and being in awe of its enormous size. It was bigger than a car! The ship was about the length of a couple of football fields.

On board, some of the sailors would salute my dad, calling him "Sir," while my dad would salute others, calling them "Sir" in turn. All the sailors wore uniforms and were clean-cut. We were invited to eat in the formal dining room, with a white tablecloth and stemware on each table. The tables were laden with formal settings of silverware, including soup spoons and salad forks. I thought the tablecloths looked elegant as did the white dishes and cloth napkins folded into triangular shapes set on each plate. There were water goblets and wine glasses set in front of each of the plates. I thought it was odd how each of the tables was bolted to the floor. I guess things got rocky when the ship went over huge swells out at sea. We were served oyster stew with iced tea, and soft bread rolls with butter. For the main course we had steak, lobster, and a salad.

When it was time to leave, my dad offered a shipmate a ride home. I can't remember his name or why he didn't have his own car, but I'll never forget how nice he was—and how handsome. He had on his dress blue uniform, topped with a black-brimmed white cap with a gold emblem on it. He had brought me a little doll as a gift. She looked like a queen, with golden brown hair fixed in a bouffant style, with tiny gold leaves as an accessory. Her dress was burgundy laced with gold. She seemed regal. I made plans to set her amongst my Barbies as their queen when we got home.

My dad was very intelligent, above the average, which enabled him to swiftly climb the ranks in the navy. I was proud of him and the aircraft carrier he worked on. The *Nimitz* had a huge flight deck that carried all kinds of fighter planes. The planes were so loud—they screamed as they flew overhead, flying faster than the speed of sound.

"Sailors handle all different sections of the ship," a navy guide told us on the family day tour. "There are personnel to handle missiles and tend the ship's armory, engineering personnel to maintain and operate their equipment as well. We also have cooks that make food twenty-four hours a day, seven days a week."

He further explained the deck departments and the many different parts of the crew. My dad was in charge of the electronics in what was called the OE Division. He had lots of men working under him at that time. My dad had a lot of responsibility, and was very good at what he did.

I'll never forget how my dad would leave each morning at 5:00 AM sharp to drive through heavy traffic to the Norfolk navy base when the ship was in dock. He would go out to sea a lot, too. His job was tough, but he enjoyed it, and made a good career out of it.

My two favorite seasons were summer and fall. After school one fall day, I took my usual bike ride around the block. What a perfect autumn day it was! It was bright, sunny, and around seventy degrees. As I rode down the street, I breathed in the smoky smell in the air, and stared at all the leaves that were turning bright red, orange, and yellow. Neighbors had pumpkins set out on their porches and Halloween decorations in the windows. Some had scarecrows in their yards. I turned right onto another street; this one was lined with much bigger homes. A lot of them were two-story homes on lots larger than my house and yard. There was an empty lot with some hilly trails on it. Oh, how I loved coasting down those hills on my bike. Whenever I was on my bike, I felt free, as if I could explore the whole world if I wanted to. The wind was rustling the leaves above me as I rode. I wished my bike could take off and fly.

I had an awesome bike my dad had found at a yard sale. The bike was probably made in the 1950s, but it was in mint condition. It was dark purple, with wide handlebars and tires. Its black seat was comfortably cushioned.

Sometimes Krissy and I would cut straws in half and put them on our spokes as decorations and noisemakers. My dad had a great idea one day—attaching a playing card to my spokes with a clothespin, so when I rode the spokes flipped the card, making a motor sound.

As I rode around the block, I began to feel a little lonely. So I decided to find a friend to ride around with me. Krissy wasn't home when I knocked on her door. Neither was Joanie. I noticed their family cars weren't in the driveways, either. I decided to go down into the cul-de-sac to Paul's house, but no luck there. I looked across the street and noticed Michael Clark's mom's car in the Clarks' driveway. I parked my bike, putting down the kickstand and went up to the door. Michael appeared.

"I'm riding my bike around. Do you want to go with me?"

"Sure!" he said, suddenly exuberant. He grabbed his light blue jacket.

His mom yelled from the doorway after he had pulled his bike from the garage. "Don't be late for dinner!"

"Okay Mom!" he yelled back.

We both had dinner hours around 5:30. I had my digital watch on to keep track of the time.

"Come on!" I said, starting to pedal faster. "I've got to show you something cool!"

Michael Clark was my age and in the same grade, but we had different teachers. He had brown hair cut above the ears, a round, pudgy face, and gray eyes. He pedaled faster to keep up with me. I took him to the hilly dirt trails. It was a lot of fun standing at the top of a hill, looking down at the trail.

"Go ahead," I urged him. "It seems scary at first, but once you go down it's exciting. Watch!"

Whoosh down the hill I went, gracefully maneuvering around the tree that sat in the middle of the trail. I coasted up an incline before stopping to look back at Michael. He followed my example.

"Wow that was so cool!"

After zooming up and down the hills, I looked at my watch: 5:25. It was time to go.

"We need to head back. It's almost dinner time."

As we pedaled hard to get back on time, Michael was still enthralled by the whole experience.

"That was so much fun. We'll have to go back after dinner!"

"Okay, come and get me, or if I'm done eating first, I'll come and get you!" I shouted back as he turned left down the cul-de-sac.

"See ya!"

I turned into my driveway, jumping off my bike and letting it crash in the yard. I ran in through the front door. I didn't want to be late; I might get in trouble and not be allowed to go back out after dinner. I could hear steaks sizzling on the stove. They smelled great. I actually had an appetite tonight. My mom had made baked potatoes, along with a salad. My dad cooked the steaks. He always cooked them rare. He was an excellent cook, and would backseat-drive my mom whenever she cooked. He forbade her to make any of her recipes, which is why she would get up at 2:00 AM to make her cakes or casseroles.

I quickly cleaned my plate. After eating, I asked if I could go back out after helping my mom clear the table.

"I suppose," my mom said.

"Come home no later than seven, so you can do homework," my dad boomed. He had a loud, commanding voice that could be startling at times.

"I will," I hurriedly answered, eager to go get Michael.

When I knocked on Michael's door, he was less ebullient than I was. "My mom says it's getting late, and I have to stay in because it's a school night." His voice was muted, and disappointment was in his eyes.

"Okay, we'll go tomorrow," I said, trying to cheer him up.

His eyes lit up. "Okay, see ya."

"See ya." I turned to hop on my bike. *I bet my mom would go with me if I asked her to*, I thought. I went straight home.

My mom was just finishing up the dishes. I decided to help her put them away.

"Mom, will you go for a bike ride with me?"

"Oh, I suppose so."

I helped her pull her dark green bike with back-wheel baskets from the garage. We rode all the way down to where the hilly bike trails were.

"You ride way down that hill?" she asked.

"Yeah! Watch!"

Whoosh down I went, showing her how I could go around the tree and up the other side.

"Come on, Mom, try it!"

"Well, I don't know," she said reluctantly.

"Just swerve around the tree at the bottom and you'll be fine. It's easy."

So down she went. But instead of going around the tree, she smacked right into the tree *with her face*! I rode down quickly to see if she was okay. She was cut severely on her jawbone. She put the kickstand down on the bike and started walking around aimlessly.

"Mom, we need to get you home! You need a band-aid."

"No, your dad will get mad if he sees me." She wasn't thinking straight, which worried me even more. "Help me find some leaves or something to put on my cut, I'll be okay." She pulled back the skin around the cut, and I actually saw her jawbone!

"Stay right here, Mom. I'm going to get you a band-aid, don't worry." I jumped on my bike, pedaling as fast as I could. My dad was where he always was this time of day after work and dinner. He was on the couch watching TV. "Where's your mom?"

"Oh … she's coming."

I was trying to sneak band-aids into my pocket quickly so I could get back out to my mom. My dad suspected something.

"Okay, tell me where your mother is." It was getting late. I worried. I pictured my mom wandering aimlessly down there alone, so I told my dad what happened.

"Damn it!" he shouted, getting up from the couch. "Where is she?"

We got in the green pickup truck and drove down to get her. I was surprised to find her actually riding her bike back. After putting the bike in the bed of the pickup truck, we drove home. My dad examined her jaw.

"You need stitches, Audie." He put a white cloth over her wound. "Hold this."

My mom held the cloth to her cut as she sat on the edge of their bed. My dad called Katie to come babysit so he could take Mom to the doctor. Fortunately, Katie was able to come right over. I felt bad. It was my fault. I should have never let my mom go down that hill.

Good Old Days of the Seasons and Holidays

One of my favorite holidays was Halloween. In 1973, I was seven years old and still believed that witches flew around on brooms, vampires lurked in George Town's tall pine trees, and mummies roamed the streets on All Hallows' Eve. Excitement was in the air. While walking home after school in the month of October, kids exhibited a newfound attentiveness to things they otherwise would never notice. Black cats roaming the neighborhood that never received any special attention previously became something to point at with excitement and fear. Trees swaying in the night breeze seemed alive.

"Maybe they'll grab us," I would say to Krissy as we walked over to her house at night. One of my favorite parts of Halloween is the tradition of carving the jack-o'-lantern. My dad would carve the face in the pumpkin perfectly, while Krissy, Joanie, and I would scoop out the flesh and seeds from inside, squishing the pumpkin innards between our fingers. The smell was delightful, especially when my dad toasted the pumpkin seeds in the oven. My dad was a big fan of popcorn caramel balls, which he made himself along with candied apples. I enjoyed watching him making treats. I never asked to help because he was such a perfectionist. I would get yelled at if I made the slightest mistake. So I just sat watching, amused.

For that Halloween, I decided to dress up as a black cat, which excited my mom because it gave her the chance to make something on her sewing machine (and she enjoyed Halloween herself). She made me a black tail and black ears out of felt. I wore my black leotard, black stockings, and black ballet slippers. I attached the tail on my back with a large safety pin. Krissy dressed up as a pirate.

Our moms followed with flashlights as we trick-or-treated around the neighborhood among many different groups of kids, each one dressed in their costume of choice. Some wore store-bought costumes with a plastic mask held on by an elastic band. Most costumes were homemade like mine.

On the far edge of the neighborhood was an old yellow farmhouse that was built back in the 1920s or '30s, when George Town was a large dairy pasture. I loved the old farmhouse, which had its own personality. The old bungalow had large, wide windows, wide front steps, and a huge wooden porch. Jack-o'-lanterns were set on each step, all aglow as we walked up to say "Trick or Treat!" and collect our loot. At the end of the street on a large corner lot was a two-story house set way back off the road, hidden by large pine trees. This house was dark and spooky even when it wasn't Halloween. Neighborhood kids often teased each other, saying only the ghosts of a murdered family lived there. Krissy and I decided to bypass that house. When it was time to head back home, we had covered most of George Town and could feel a late-night chill in the air nearing. We looked in our bags to see how much candy we had obtained. At home, my dad checked each piece to make sure it was safe to eat. The needle-in-the-apple rumor always remained in my memory after Teddy Jeffries said he had bit into one and had to be rushed to the hospital with the needle stuck in his neck. *Silly old storyteller.*

After the excitement of Halloween passed, my mom enrolled me in Brownies. Most of the neighborhood kids had an after-school activity of some sort. Some took ballet or piano lessons, played sports, or scouted—Girl Scouts, Boy Scouts, Cub Scouts, or Brownies. It was lonesome in the neighborhood when all the other kids were attending their after-school activities. Krissy took piano *and* ballet lessons. My mom thought that it would be helpful to keep me socially active and that joining Brownies might bring me out of my shyness.

I wore a brown jumper dress, a chocolate brown beanie, and brown socks to match. Where did they get the name *Brownies*? Brown, yuck! It was my least favorite color, but brownies were my favorite thing to eat. Maybe that's how they got started. They used to be known for making fudge brownies. I found my Brownie meetings boring. We never made brownies. We didn't even go camping, or anywhere else, for that matter. We just had meetings at a small church on Providence Road once a week. The meetings lasted one hour, starting off with paying dues—twenty-five cents. I volunteered to be treasurer. My job was collecting the quarters, placing them in a box, and checking off a roll of who had paid and who owed. One day we mostly made cupcakes, spreading different pastel-colored frosting on top and dashing on some sprinkles. Another day we made crafts, using popsicle sticks along with assorted colored pieces of yarn to make a rainbow-colored cross, which could be used as a wall hanging. "Whoop-diddy-doo," I used to say before going to my Brownie meetings. They were a drag. I would have rather been at home playing with my dolls on my bedroom floor.

"Hey, why don't you take piano lessons with me?" Krissy asked one day, likely tired of my complaining about Brownie meetings.

"No way," I said, picturing myself sitting completely dumbfounded at a piano, staring at all those keys.

"C'mon, please, please?" she begged, jumping up and down.

"I could never learn how to do something like that."

"Sure you can. It's easy! You just start out slow."

"Sorry, Krissy. Maybe another time." I thought about trying the piano later, but still found it too intimidating.

One thing I did like about Brownies was the uniform. I could wear it to school, making me feel important. Some of the kids seemed impressed that I was a Brownie. I felt like the uniform made me look smart, and I fitted in with the other groups of children that wore their uniforms to school. I usually got teased at school. I was a scrawny, pale-faced little girl with stringy hair, very self-conscious. My uniform gave me a little confidence. Michael Clark and I walked home from school together feeling a little bit taller when we were in our respective uniforms—Cub Scouts for him, Brownies for me. I was envious after listening to him describe all about the neat stuff the Cub Scouts got to do.

"We get to go camping, make campfires, and set up tents."

"You're so lucky, Michael. I make cupcakes and collect quarters."

When older students walked by us wearing Girl Scout or Boy Scout uniforms, they appeared so mature to us.

November arrived, with the leaves taking on darker shades of red, orange, and yellow. The evening air was smokier than in October, because more people were burning wood in their fireplaces now that the evenings were getting colder. Days were getting a little shorter, and I enjoyed the orange sunsets from my bedroom window while I was supposed to be doing homework. The smell of dinner cooking drifted into my bedroom, making me hungry after a long day at school. Our green yard was turning brown and no longer required mowing. During the summer months, my dad would mow the lawn every Saturday morning. My mom would sweep up the grass, putting it in the tin garbage can that I would later set out by the road for garbage day pick-up.

"Time to eat!" my mom called, always the same words, part of the family ritual. This night was fried pork chops with mashed potatoes and gravy. Yum! My parents would talk usually about things that went on aboard ship or people my parents were friends with. I sometimes listened to them chat. Other times I just ate, thinking about playing with my friends after dinner while there was still a little daylight left. Often times my parents argued at the dinner table; my dad would bang his fist on the table, causing food to spill. They always argued over meaningless things not worth fighting about. I didn't understand it. They never considered how terrifying it was for me.

Usually after dinner, I would play at Krissy's for a while or ride bikes with Michael. We would both rush home when the streetlights came on. A hot bath at the end of a cold day was the best. I enjoyed bubble baths so much that my mom would have to make me get out before I got water-logged. I would take my dolls in the bath with me, or I would try to see how long I could hold my breath under water. After I got out, dried, and bundled up in a warm bathrobe, I would watch *Happy Days* or *Laverne & Shirley*. Tuesday nights was *Little House on the Prairie*. I used to wonder what it would have been like being Laura Ingalls, growing up without electricity. I would miss my lava lamps and black lights. After my dad retired early to bed around 8:00 PM, my mom would bake cookies or make instant cherry Jell-O. I loved swooshing Jell-O between my teeth while watching *Donny and Marie*. When *Hawaii Five-0* or *The Rockford Files* came on, that was my cue to go to bed.

My bedtime was 9:00 PM, but I could never fall asleep. My mom usually joined me for a while, sitting on the foot of my bed and telling me interesting stories from her childhood in Florida. She had four brothers and four sisters, but her oldest sister had drowned when my mom was three. She remembered pacing and crying on the edge of the lake, too small to save her thirteen-year-old sister.

"My last memory of her was seeing her hand reaching up above the black water," my mom told me.

That must have been horrific. She told me other stories of how she and her sister Nora were chased up a tree by a large bull, and how they had to sit up there until their brothers came by on horses looking for them.

Mom must have been exhausted at the end of the day, but she didn't let it stop her from cooking, cleaning, or watching TV. Many nights I would wake up hungry or thirsty. Some nights I awoke from bad dreams and would go into the living room, where I could always find her watching TV late into the early-morning hours. Sometimes she would let me eat cheese and crackers with a drink of water before I went back to bed.

I get tickled remembering my mom changing the furniture around in the middle of the night. You never knew what the living room would look like in the morning. I enjoyed that. Mom was the cleanest housekeeper on the block, along with being the best interior decorator. Many nights, the smell of chocolate cake and cookies or the sound of the blender would lure me into the kitchen. Midnight was my mom's time to relax and be herself.

For Thanksgiving, our tradition was just the three of us at a large baked-turkey-and-ham dinner, sitting around our formal dining table, dressed up for the occasion. My parents had bought an expensive, elegant dining set from Ethan Allen after we moved into the new house. Along the dining room's back wall stood a dark, shiny wooden cabinet. Its wood-framed glass doors encased glass shelving on the inside, which held all of my mom's white porcelain plates and crystal stemware. There was even a light inside the cabinet to show off the porcelain if desired. Our new long, oval dining table matched the cabinet—the table had come with ten chairs! Two of the chairs had arms. We placed those chairs against the wall on either side of the china cabinet. The chairs' cushions were a gold-colored velvety material. My dad sat at one end of the table, while my mom and I sat in the middle across from one another. The table was too long for my mom to sit at the far end opposite my dad. My mom could always set the most beautiful table. She set out a white linen tablecloth with a Thanksgiving-themed runner down the middle. We had real silver silverware only used for holidays. I would help my mom polish the special silverware once or twice a year. We used white linen napkins, which were set out with sterling silver napkin rings. My dad had bought most of this in China when he had sailed to port over there. He said he bought it all for almost nothing, compared to what it would have cost in America.

My mom always began Grace with the phrase "Our dear heavenly father." I would keep my head bowed during the prayer, but always peeked up at the food on the table. My dad made the best gravy, simmering the giblets on low for a long time before adding their juices to the turkey gravy. We had candied yams, stuffing, and sliced cranberry jelly that was served on a little rectangular crystal dish. I would drink apple juice out of crystal so thin and fine that I was scared that if I bit down even the slightest amount I would bite my glass in half. My dad usually let me have a small glass of bubbly champagne with dinner. I liked the taste of it. Our cat, Samantha, never strayed too far from the dinner table, especially on Thanksgiving Day. She loved turkey so much that she would howl while it was baking in the oven.

It was great not having school during the holidays. I recall waking up excitedly to watch the Thanksgiving Day parades on TV, followed by dinner and hanging out with my friends. Dinner was served around between 2:00 and 3:00 PM, which was convenient because it left more time for me to visit with my friends afterward. We would play in the cul-de-sac, all stuffed from the holiday dinner. Pumpkin pie and whipped cream along with leftover turkey sandwiches were favorites among us kids. Some of the boys decided to go back inside to watch football. They were all Redskins fans.

As I rode my bike around the cul-de-sac, I saw Michael Clark riding out of his garage on his blue ten-speed. Some of the kids were headed out of town to go visit relatives. Other kids stayed inside their warm homes.

"Hey," Michael said as he approached me on his bike.

"Hi."

"I hate Thanksgiving. It's so *boring*."

"Really?" I never heard a kid complain about a day when we didn't have to go to school. "At least we get out of going to school."

"Yeah, I guess you're right."

We were riding in circles as we spoke. It was a gray, overcast Thanksgiving Day, with a slight breeze carrying a chill through the air.

"I dare you to throw a rock at the next car that goes by without getting caught," Michael said.

"Oh, I know how to not get caught." I took his dare, remembering Teddy and I running from cars after pegging them with rocks. Teddy even gave me advice on how to look innocent. Michael and I parked our bikes in his driveway and walked to the end of the cul-de-sac where it met Crown Crescent. We hid behind the boxwood shrubs that lined the corner of Krissy's yard along the street. Her family wouldn't see us, they were out of town. We had gathered rocks from the street's surface and curbsides. A brown station wagon went by.

"Don't throw rocks at anyone we know," I whispered, as if the car could hear us.

"Here comes one!" Michael stood up and threw a rock.

We could hear the rock's loud tap on the back window. The car came to a stop. When Michael saw the red tail lights come on, he took off, sprinting into the cul-de-sac. He tried dodging behind a bush a couple of lawns down. The driver followed him and quickly caught up.

"Son, tell me where you live."

Michael knew he couldn't outrun a car, so he told the man. I got out from behind the shrubs and sat nonchalantly on the curb. Later, the man drove by me, totally unaware that I was an accomplice. I just sat looking around like I had no clue as to what had happened—just how Teddy had told me to act. Michael Clark's mom put him on restrictions for three days.

Later, when Michael asked why I didn't run off with him, I told him my secret. "Because I know how not to get caught."

"Cool," he said, realizing why I didn't run.

Directly across the street from my house was a nice brick ranch home that had black shutters with white wooden eagle shapes on them. I never liked the shutters very much. I thought the wooden eagles looked gaudy. I don't remember when the Donaldson's moved in exactly, but it was shortly after we had moved in. Mr. Donaldson was in the navy. Mrs. Donaldson was a stay-at-home mom like mine. She had three sons: David, who was fourteen; Kevin, who was around ten; and little Stephen, who was four. They all looked different, not like brothers. David had short, thick black hair. Kevin had short brown hair with big brown eyes. Stephen had blond hair and blue eyes. I found it odd how they had moved to Virginia from Louisiana but didn't have Southern accents. They had the silliest little dog, a black-and-white boxer. I'll never forget how stupid that dog (named Sally) was. She would run across the street the minute I turned on the hose in our yard. She would stand there and let water pour down her throat while she gagged. Samantha would chase stupid Sally back into her yard if the dog got too close to her kittens. Samantha was the toughest animal in the neighborhood, except for Tish, a red Doberman pinscher who constantly terrorized the local children and pets. Samantha got chased up a tree quite a few times by that dog. My dad would shoot Tish with his BB gun, but the dog couldn't help giving chase whenever she saw a little kid or an animal out in the yard. One afternoon, Stephen was in his front yard, saw Tish, and panicked. Steven held his jacket out in front of him like a matador, using it as a shield. He started screaming. Tish took off like a bullet, heading straight for Stephen.

"Don't show her you're scared! She'll leave you alone!" I shouted, words I have been told but never really believed. As soon as Tish heard my voice, she darted across the street after me. I ran into the house. *At least I saved Stephen*, I thought as I watched him going inside his house safely behind my living room window.

Mrs. Donaldson and my mom became good friends. I remember Mrs. Donaldson as being very kind. She was tall, thin, and attractive. Her sandy blond hair was short cut in a bobbed style. My mom and she would take me out with them in the forest near the highway, which had long hiking trails. I'll never forget how the pine trees were so very tall and swayed in the breeze as Mom and Mrs. Donaldson collected pine straw, putting needles in large black garbage bags before heading across the highway on the dirt road to the nursery. The forest was full of blackberries in the summer, and we would pick them to use in waffles or tea cakes. We had dug up boxwood shrubs to plant around our house. There were clear running streams with white sandy bottoms that I loved wading in. I would wade along, imagining pretending I was the princess ruler of an alien planet. I didn't need to be entertained—I could amuse myself all day.

On one cool November day, it wasnt warm enough for me to pull my shoes off and wade in the water. So I helped my mom and Mrs. Donaldson gather branches and pinecones. The stuff we were collecting would be used for making wreaths and other pieces of home décor. Mrs. Donaldsons love for this kind of thing drew in my mom; the two of them were constantly making decorations. My mom even signed up for a horticulture class at the local community college with Mrs. Donaldson. The class was twice a week in the evenings. My dad didnt mind too much as long as my mom was home to make dinner.

One evening, I started to worry because mom was out later than usual—it was after dark. There was a Redskins football game on TV we were watching. When 9:00 PM rolled around, my dad sent me to bed. I could tell he was angry because his voice got louder and louder as he shouted at the game on TV. After a while, his screaming became so loud it made my heart jump. I could picture him on the couch at the end of the hall as I lay in bed trying to sleep. He was yelling so, so loud that I thought maybe he was trying to keep me awake just to punish my mom by making me sleepy the next day when she was trying to get me off to school. I would be slow and grumpy from sleep deprivation. Or maybe he was just blowing off steam. I wasn't sure why he was acting so bizarre.

"Dad, can you stop yelling? I'm trying to sleep."

He just sat there staring at the TV, ignoring me. I knew he'd heard me because he quieted down for a few moments. But right when I started drifting off to sleep, he started yelling at the top of his lungs again.

"Go, go, go, you bastard! Ruuun!"

I never knew someone could yell so loud. I wanted to get up and shut my door but I was too scared of the dark.

Again, I asked him to be quiet. "Dad, can you stop yelling? I can't sleep."

"Shut your door," he said, matter-of-factly.

Finally I got up and closed my door, leaving my dresser lamp light on. My mom came in shortly after, saying the professor's lecture had run late. My dad forbade her to take any more classes. Things were different for women in the 1970s.

December was another time of year when all of us kids in the neighborhood were full of excitement. Christmas was coming. The school corridors were decorated with glittery holiday decorations students had made. There was a Christmas tree at the end of the hall with multicolored lights strung around it, draped with silver tinsel and topped with a lighted silver star. Mrs. Brown put up a little tree in our classroom with silver garland and multicolored lights. When the tree was lit up, there seemed to be an aura of peace. Classmates were friendlier to one another. One day, a couple of the room mothers brought in clothespins with round tips. We spent an entire afternoon painting little faces on the pins, transforming them into little toy soldiers with painted-on red coats. Some pins were made into angels by gluing wings on and dusting them with sprinkles of silver glitter. Randy and I sat together while making our angels and soldiers. He decided to put gold glitter instead of the silver on his angel.

"My mom likes gold," he said holding up the angel looking at it. The room mothers tied strings around each ornament so we could take them home to hang on our Christmas trees. I couldn't wait to take mine home to show Mom.

After school, Krissy and I skipped home together singing "Jingle Bells" out loud, not caring who heard us. We definitely had the Christmas spirit. I went to Krissy's house after dropping off my school bag and showing my mom the little soldier and angel ornaments I had made.

"I love these! We'll have to hang them on our tree," she had said, taking the ornament from me to look at.

Mrs. Coddle made us bologna sandwiches with potato chips and cherry Kool-Aid. Krissy's oldest sister Katie laughed at us, because we had red Kool-Aid stains around our mouths when we finished lunch. Katie and Kelly were sitting on the floor around the coffee table, watching the little black-and-white TV. *Gilligan's Island* was coming on and they started singing the opening song along with the TV. Katie and

Kelly were never without a smile; they always seemed cheerful, which made me like being around them.

Katie and Kelly opened plastic bags, pouring little silver and gold bells out onto the coffee table.

"What are you doing?" Krissy asked.

"We're going to put these on our tennis shoes to wear to cheerleading practice," Katie replied.

"Come sit with us and we'll put some on your tennis shoes, too." Kelly invited.

So we joined them, taking off our tennis shoes and unlacing them in order to string up the bells. I felt special, sitting with the most popular high school cheerleaders as if I was part of their family. I wished I was as beautiful as they were. They never seemed to care that I was a scrawny dork. They treated me the same as they treated everyone else. As Krissy and I walked back over to my house, we giggled at our jingling shoes and giddily sang Christmas carols out loud into the pink and yellow sunset sky.

The next day after school, while Krissy was at ballet class, I rode my bike down to Randy's, feeling happy and relieved that I had quit my boring Brownie troop. We still skated Saturday afternoons at the College Park skating rink. Randy's oldest sister, who was a heavyset girl with short blond hair unlike Randy's, answered the door.

She let me in but teasingly announced "Hey, Randy! Your weird girlfriend is here!"

I found Randy in their living room with his little brother Robert and their father, sitting on the floor in front of the TV. They weren't *watching* TV. They were *controlling* what was on it! I had never seen anything like it before.

"Wow that's *neat!*" I said, staring at the screen.

"Have a seat, Junie. It's a video game we hooked up to our TV. Want to try it?"

"Sure! How do you play?"

Randy handed me the controls. "Just turn the knob and hit the ball when it goes to your side of the screen. You're on the left."

Boop, boop, beep—those were the game's sounds. It was tricky at first, but I got the hang of it. After a while, I beat Randy at a round of it. "What's the name of this?" I asked.

"*Pong.* They just came out in the stores not long ago."

"I want one of these."

"Yeah, it's one *bad* game," Randy said.

Later that evening, I spoke so fast at the dinner table about *Pong* my dad could barely understand me.

"Slow down. What's it called?"

"*Pong.*"

The day before Christmas vacation began, there was a surprise at school. After we finished lunch, we lined up single file as usual to walk back down to our classroom. Our teacher was in front of us, leading the way. As we approached our classroom's door, Mrs. Brown stopped and held up her index finger in front of her lips.

"Shh. We have a surprise today, but I need you all to remain quiet."

Instantly, some of the kids started giggling and whispering. Our little seven-year-old hearts were full of excitement. Mrs. Brown stuck her head inside the classroom.

"Are we ready yet?"

She turned to us smiling, and motioned for us to go in.

As we entered, our faces lit up with awe. Our classroom had been transformed into a festival of Christmas decorations. Shiny garlands of silver, red, and green hung from the overhead lights along with Christmas lights. Soft Christmas music was playing. On each of our desks was a little stocking filled with notepads, bouncy balls, and longer-than-average pencils that were striped like our candy canes. The erasers on the end of the pencils were smiling elf heads or Santa and reindeer heads. Our room mothers must have put a lot of thought into that day. I was glad to see my mom in the room with the other room mothers, experiencing all the excitement. Mom had been a part of planning all of this. One long table was covered with a red-and-white tablecloth. The table was covered in Christmas treats—all kinds of sugar cookies covered in red and green sprinkles. There were also cupcakes adorned with little plastic Christmas wreaths or Santa faces. The large punch bowl in the middle of the table looked familiar. My mom had brought it in, and made the punch.

After we enjoyed our little Christmas party, we had to clean it all up.

Randy and I went around the room picking up paper plates, cups, and napkins, and threw them in the large garbage can that was set out in the middle of the room. The school bell rang, sending loud, cheery voices from the classrooms into the corridors. No school for two weeks! As my mom and I walked down the hall, I noticed it was noisier than usual from all the holiday excitement. I rode home in the car with my mom, thinking about how much fun Christmas vacation was going to be. No getting up early, no homework, and I could hang out with my friends playing all day. But most importantly, Santa was coming! There were going to be presents under the tree, and my stocking would be bulging with Christmas gifts handcrafted by none other than Santa's elves.

Later on, Krissy came over to announce that Mrs. Ainsworth was gathering up neighbors for a Christmas caroling group on Sunday night.

"That sounds like fun," Mom said. "I'll give Mrs. Ainsworth a call."

"My mom is going too!" Krissy said.

Sunday evening came, and we all gathered in my front yard for Christmas caroling. Mrs. Ainsworth had made up several little songbooks to follow the words of the carols. She gave Joanie, Krissy, Katie, Kelly, and I little bells, like the ones Krissy and I wore on our shoes, to play while singing "Jingle Bells." It was fun to ring a house's doorbell and then see the surprised look on a neighbor's face when they answered their door. We would start with "Silent Night" or "Deck the Halls." As we got around to the end of the cul-de-sac and arrived at Paul and Neana's house, I felt a little odd. Paul had explained to me one day that his family was Jewish. I remembered not knowing exactly what that meant. He explained that they didn't celebrate Christmas, but instead observed a holiday called Hanukkah. I felt sorry for them at the time. But they were very nice when we finished our song.

"Thank you, that was beautiful!" Mrs. Simons called out as we headed to the next house.

After dinner on Monday, my mom and I dragged out the large box that contained our artificial tree, which we had to assemble. We also pulled out several boxes filled with Christmas ornaments. It was a tradition for my mom and me to put up the Christmas tree. My dad would relax in front of the TV, watching Jim Kincaid, our local evening news broadcaster. When we were done decorating, I would call Dad in to see the results. My mom had sewn little white doves out of felt to hang on the tree. We carefully dug out our red, blue, green, gold, and silver ball ornaments to hang, along with silver tinsel. I tucked into the tree's branches the little queen doll that my dad's navy friend had given me. Her gold sequins sparkled under the multicolored Christmas lights we had strung. Our cat Samantha sat on the couch watching us, appearing amused. We put the tree up in our formal living room, right in front of the window so the neighbors could see. I hung my little clothespin toy soldier and angel, wondering if everybody else from school was hanging theirs too. It looked so nice when we were done. We sat back on our new gold-colored velvet sofa with the side-table lamps turned off. I loved how the lights from the tree cast a glow on the ceiling and walls. Each evening after dinner, I would sit (sometimes my mom would join me) to gaze at our tree, enjoying the peacefulness it seemed to emit into the room.

My dad pulled the ladder out one sunny afternoon and hung red and green Christmas lights around the roof of our house—the lights were perfectly straight. I was proud of my dad, of how he always did things precisely. We placed matching plastic candles in each of the windows. Mrs. Coddle, Krissy, my mom, and I bundled up one evening and walked around the neighborhood, admiring the Christmas lights of all the houses. Some yards had large plastic Frosty the Snowman figurines, angels, or Santa's, all giving off a cheerful glow. I smiled at Frosty as we walked by one such yard. He was holding his black top hat in one hand and a corncob pipe in the other, with a wink in his eye and a smile on his face. I felt jovial, remembering when Teddy and I had stopped to stare at the glowing Nativity scene in a neighbor's yard back in Norfolk. Christmas evenings like this made me feel the world was at peace.

On Christmas Eve, I laid awake in bed staring up out my bedroom window. My mom had rearranged my room *again*, so the head of my bed was back against the wall, which gave me a view of the night sky, instead of facing down the hall. As I watched the silent airplanes flying west, I noticed the little red blinking lights on them. I let my imagination carry me away, thinking the light was Rudolph the Red-Nosed Reindeer.

When I woke up the next morning, I was full of joy and buoyancy. My stocking! It was full! Santa thought I was a good, well-behaved little girl. I got up and dumped the stocking out on my bed. There were tangerines, walnuts, all kinds of Barbie dresses, a ball and jacks, a jump rope, candy canes, and a little pair of pink footie socks. I sprinted down the hall, through the living room, and into the kitchen. The coffee pot was percolating as usual. When I was younger I would say the pot was snoring.

"*Merry Christmas!*" I said. "When can we open gifts?"

"When the coffee is finished brewing," my dad told me. "What did Santa put in your stocking?"

I ran back to my room and grabbed everything, bringing it back into the kitchen to show my parents.

"Look, I got fruit and some toys!" I held my goodies up to show them.

"Uh-huh. I guess Santa thought you've been pretty good," my dad said, getting up to check the coffee. It had finished brewing, and Mom went over to pour herself a cup. Mom had made me hot chocolate with tiny marshmallows floating in it. We all carried our hot beverages into the formal dining room to open our gifts. I sat on the floor right next to the tree. I was still in my pajamas, light blue with the feet attached so I didn't need slippers. My mom was already snapping pictures. Dad had bought bedroom slippers for me to give to my mom, and my mom had bought socks for me to give to my dad. There were many other gifts we opened, from relatives or from my friends. I had bought Krissy, Katie, Kelly, and Joanie small perfume bottles that had little teddy bears holding onto their lids. One of my favorite presents was the large Barbie house that came with Barbie furniture. The house folded up and had a handle on the top so I could carry it around. I thought about showing it to Krissy later. When we were all through, we sat back and watched Samantha attacking the torn wrapping paper scattered all over the floor. She would jump up and then pounce down, disappearing under it.

"Silly old cat," I said.

"Wait, there's one more thing," Dad said with a surprised look on his face. "What's that over there?" He pointed to the chair. Behind it I found a box wrapped in red paper with Santa faces all over it.

"Go open it," he said.

I picked the box up and ripped the paper off it. I was surprised to find the video game *Pong*.

"Thank you!" I cried with delight. "Wow, my own *Pong*! Wait until you see us play this, Mom! It's so *futuristic*."

Later, while my dad hooked *Pong* up to the TV, I played with my Barbie house. The smell of our Christmas ham baking in the oven filled the house.

For the rest of our vacation, lots of kids flocked to my house to check out *Pong*. Morris, Joanie, Keith, and Michael played all day one day. Another day, Mick and James came over. I definitely had the grooviest Christmas toy of the year.

New Year's Eve was spent at the Donaldsons' house. I fell asleep on their sofa as neighbors drank mixed drinks and chatted while waiting for the ball to drop in Times Square in New York on TV. My mom woke me up a few minutes before the countdown.

"*Happy New Year!*" everyone shouted at midnight. Everyone toasted one another, blowing horns while wearing their shiny silver and gold party hats. As "Auld Lang Syne" played on the TV, Mrs. Donaldson scooped up little Stephen and started dancing around while holding him on her hip.

"I remember dancing with you like that when you were little," my mom told me as we watched comfortably from the sofa.

After the holiday season passed, we were back to the same old routine of getting up early to walk to school carrying lunchboxes and books. Winter seemed to drag. Winters in Virginia could be gloomy and drizzly. We never got a lot of snow. We lived about twenty minutes from the beach and the Chesapeake Bay, which was nice in the summer time. We all missed summer during those winter months. The trees were bare and chimneys emitted smoke into the cold air. In the evenings after dinner, my dad would build fires in our fireplace. We had stacked wood out back. I loved sitting next to the hearth watching the embers burn yellow, bright orange, and red.

"If you see a *blue* flame, you'll know that's the hottest out of all of them," my dad explained.

Sparks would fly up when one of my parents moved the wood

around with the poker. Sometimes I felt so hot sitting next to the fire I would have to move away to cool off.

I was relieved when spring arrived. In late March, the weather was warm enough that we could ride bikes or skateboard again without heavy coats and hats. Daffodils started blooming, smelling wonderful.

Mom went in for a private meeting with my teacher Mrs. Brown one afternoon after school.

"Honey, go to the library and find a couple of books to check out while your mother and I chat," Mrs. Brown instructed.

The library was right outside my classroom's door, in an open area. It was extremely quiet without any kids in the building. The librarian was an older woman that kids called an "old biddy." We didn't like her very much. She was always fussing condescendingly about something. I quietly looked at books, mainly ones with pictures in them. I didn't like reading, even though I could read at my grade level. I just preferred to play. I found a book that had interesting pictures of a doll and a teddy bear. I didn't mind reading this book, because its pictures were intriguing. I checked it out of the library, along with another book with a mysterious cover. My mom came out of the room, motioning for me to go with her. When we got home, I was put on restrictions for a week, no playing after school, because I wasn't doing any of my homework. My grades were not high enough to pass second grade unless I completed lots of extra-credit assignments that Mrs. Brown had sent home with my mom. Each evening after dinner, I had to sit at the dinner table to work on stacks of extra-credit papers with my mom sitting right there to monitor me. I hated writing assignments because of my poor spelling.

"Why can't you be like normal children and do what you're supposed to do?" my mom asked.

"I don't know," I answered with honesty. I didn't know why it was so unusual to not want to do homework each day when I could just run out and play.

"You just don't know anything, do you?" my mom retorted. "You know, Mrs. Brown said you'll have to stay back in second grade if you don't do these assignments! I bet I could get *Neana* to come down here and do them for you."

Neana was three years younger than I. I stared down at my assignment, humiliated. I was staring at a cluster of words, unsure which one was spelled correctly. I tried writing the words out several times, and finally guessed at the right one.

One Saturday morning, I had to get dressed up. I put on a dress with white pantyhose, black shiny dress shoes, and white gloves. My mom wore a suit, and my dad had on his dress white uniform. We drove to Pier Twelve at the Norfolk navy base and sat in bleachers outside along the pier awaiting the arrival of President Gerald Ford. Lots of navy families poured in, filling up the tall bleachers behind me. I was amazed at all the people. The *Nimitz* had sailors in their dress white uniforms lining the entire ship. The men looked regal and important. There were flags strung up along the ship signifying every country. The biggest flag waving in the breeze was the American flag. Everyone cheered when President Ford appeared on the stage and shook hands with an admiral and other high-ranking naval men. I didn't understand everything in the president's speech, which seemed to go on forever. I thought he had an unusual way of speaking. Everyone stood up and cheered when the speech was over. The president's face and eyes seemed to be kind.

I followed Mom and Dad up the gangway to the giant hangar deck on the ship. There was a huge cake that must have been eight feet long, a replica of the *Nimitz*. Later, the president came in and was handed a sword to cut the first piece of cake before being whisked off to another part of the ship. We stood in line to get pieces of cake. I picked up a little gray-and-black piece that had white filling. After sitting and eating, it was time to leave. When I told my friends I had seen the president, they didn't believe me until my parents confirmed it.

Spring flew by, and I managed to get through the second grade. After all the extra-credit assignments were finished, I made sure I did my homework for the rest of the year. I had Joanie help me with hard assignments sometimes. She was really smart, usually maintaining a 4.0 average, and she was three years older than I. On the last day of school, we all said our farewells to Mrs. Brown.

"Bye, Mrs. Brown," I said as I headed out of the classroom.

"Have a nice summer now," she told me. *Summer* ... a word I loved to hear.

It was June, summer at last!

Good-bye, Randy. I'll Always be Your Friend.

Summer was a time of freedom to grow and to be myself. I could hang out with my friends, and we could kick back, laugh, joke around, and enjoy life as much as we wanted. Hot weather only lasted about three to four months in Virginia. We all did what we could to capture every moment of it. My mom had bought me new shorts with matching short-sleeved shirts and a bathing suit for the summer. As the days grew longer, we stayed out later. Morris, Joanie, Kevin Donaldson, Krissy, Mick Ceaver, Michael Clark, and I would play hide-and-seek even after the sun went down. My front porch or Joanie's porch would be used as home base. I usually helped out by running in Joanie's place because of her wooden leg. She couldn't run all that fast. Mosquitoes were bad when the sun went down. We would all be sweating from running, which attracted the little parasites even more. I would get bites on my legs bigger than quarters, and often scratched them until they bled. The itching was maddening. Bug repellant washed off after we started sweating. The sound of crickets excitedly chirping all around and the streetlights blinking before turning on were my warning signs that it was almost time to go home. Michael Clark had the same rule. I was having so much fun as we sat on Joanie's porch, chatting and catching our breaths from running around. I didn't really want to go home yet.

"The streetlights a-a-re on, y-you have to go," Morris told me.

"She can stay out longer if she wants to," Joanie argued.

"Nuh-uh, she'll get in trouble. Her dad w-w-will yell."

Sure enough, I could hear my dad standing on my porch yelling my name.

"*She's coming!*" everyone yelled back for me.

I chuckled. "Bye, see ya tomorrow," I said before I ran home.

"See ya."

I ran real fast, turning to do a hand-spring when I reached my yard.

In the morning, my mom drove Joanie, Krissy, and I to the indoor pool on the naval base. It had a nice outdoor area with a wading pool for little kids and a sunbathing area, which is where my mom stayed while we swam in the Olympic-sized pool. Joanie had to remove her wooden leg. She held my hand as she hopped down to the steps leading into the water. Once she was in, she was fine. We swam down to the deep end, and took turns diving off the diving board. After a couple hours, the three of us were worn out and hungry. We went through the McDonald's drive-through on the way home. Once we arrived at home, Joanie and Krissy headed back to their houses to change clothes. I put on a T-shirt and cutoff blue jean shorts before heading outside to get my bike. As I rode around the block, I noticed a family moving furniture into the house in between mine and Joanie's! A girl about my age, with short brown hair, was carrying in a box.

"Okay Dad," she said as a man asked her to get something else from the truck parked in their driveway. The couple that had lived there prior to this family kept to themselves and had moved out only about a month earlier.

I told my parents about the new neighbors as we ate dinner on the back patio that night. My dad had grilled hamburgers on the charcoal grill. Mom had made baked beans, potato salad, and sun tea. They had bought two wrought-iron patio tables with matching chairs. Mom also bought green pads for the chairs and a green vinyl tablecloth.

"Hopefully we'll have enough money saved by the end of summer to get a fence put up," my dad said, sounding cheery.

I wasn't sure if I liked the idea of a fence around our yard. I liked running straight across to my friends' houses from my backyard. We could see if someone was outside or not without having to knock on the front door. Plus no fences gave us more running-around room for our hide-and-seek games.

My parents set up a badminton net in the backyard, which was popular with the neighborhood kids. We saved *Pong* for rainy days.

I still spent Saturday afternoons skating with Randy at the rink. Morris and Joanie would come along too sometimes. Morris loved to speed-skate, winning every race. His prize was a free large Coke. I tried racing a couple of times, but would get slowed down turning the corners and come in only third or fourth place. My dad took me skating one afternoon and showed me how to use the toe stopper to slow around the corners, which really helped. I remember skating to the song "Rock the Boat," with my dad skating right behind me. He was a good skater.

About three weeks into summer, my mom needed to go to the grocery store while I was playing dolls at Krissy's house. My mom called the Coddles to ask that I come home. Mrs. Coddle answered the phone in the kitchen.

"Oh no, the girls are having fun, go ahead and shop. I'll keep Junie with us," Mrs. Coddle said. "Oh no, she's no trouble at all," I heard her say before hanging up.

"Junie, your mom is just running up to the grocery store. You can stay here until she gets back."

"Okay." I didn't mind hanging out with Krissy while my mom was running errands. It somehow made me feel more like part of their family. My dad was spending the night aboard ship. Krissy's mom would always keep an eye out for me when my dad was away. My mom would do the same for her when Krissy's dad was away.

The phone rang again. "Okay, uh-huh, be right there. Okay girls; let's hop in the station wagon to pick up Katie and Kelly from cheerleading practice."

Krissy and I sat in the far back of the station wagon, facing the rear window. As we were about to cross Providence Road, Mrs. Coddle put on the brakes. We turned around to see why. A black two-door sports car went whizzing by. Its driver was speeding, big time.

"Whoa, fella, slow down" Mrs. Coddle said as the black car flew down the street ahead, kicking up dust behind it.

One week later I walked down to Krissy's house and rang her

doorbell. No one answered. Their cars weren't in the driveway. So I headed down to Randy's to see if he wanted to hang out. Along the way I ran into Morris, Joanie, and Jack, standing together, talking in hushed tones.

"Hi," I said as I walked past, thoughts of playing a good game of *Pong* with Randy on my mind.

"Hey!" Morris shouted as he jogged after me. "Where a-a-a-are you going?"

"Over to Randy's. Why?"

"Tell her!" Joanie said, sternly looking at Morris.

"No!" Morris shouted back.

"Tell me what?" I asked.

"She was Randy's girlfriend, Morris," Jack said mistakenly. Randy was just a friend. I was too young for boyfriends.

"Randy is just a good friend of mine, Jack," I corrected. "Is he in trouble or something?" I pictured Randy's mom and how strict she could be.

"No, he was killed," Jack said, his voice lowering as he said "killed."

This can't be. I just saw him a week ago. "Are you teasing me?"

They all just stared at me. They were not playing around. I could see that in their eyes, on their sullen faces.

"He's only eight years old," I said. I headed home in shock and disbelief. I was speechless. I didn't know how to make sense of what I was feeling. I didn't know how to respond. I could feel hot tears welling up in my eyes. I had sensed something was off because Randy hadn't called all week. I could hear Morris' footsteps running up behind me, and then his arm was around my shoulders.

"A-a-are you oh-okay?"

"Yeah, I just dont ... I just dont know." I was trying to say something, but didnt know what. I just looked down at the road.

"I'm s-s-sorry. I didn't want to tell you, but Jack thought y-y-you should know. I am sorry, Junie."

"It's okay. I know you meant well."

"See ya later," Morris said before turning to call Jack an asshole. The three of them resumed arguing as I trudged home.

I walked in through the front door and called for my mom.

"I'm in the kitchen," she replied.

I stopped in the doorway to the kitchen. My mom was wringing out a mop over a bucket.

"Don't walk on the floor. It's wet," she said, resuming her mopping.

"Did you know … did you know Randy is dead?" I asked flatly, trying not to break out in tears. Hearing myself say the word "dead" out loud made my chest ache all of a sudden.

She kept mopping, not saying anything.

"I don't know how it happened, but Jack just told me he got killed."

"Well … I know. I didnt know how to tell you. Remember that day I went to the store and you stayed with Krissy?"

"Yeah?"

"The dark sports car you told me you saw go speeding by was the car that hit and killed Randy. He and Jack were walking along Providence Road. I pulled over to see if I could help, but a group of people were gathered around him and told me to not walk up. I only saw Randy's black hair blowing in the wind as he laid there in the grass."

"How did you know it was Randy?"

"I didn't until I read it in the paper. Jack said that they were walking along when the car sped out of nowhere and swerved erratically up on the lawn, hitting Randy before swerving back on the road. Apparently, the guy driving was strung out on drugs. Jack explained some of what happened to the police as he was crying, the paper had said. His funeral is Sunday. Family members only. I called his mom to let her know that we're here if she needs anything. She didn't say much except to tell you thank you for being his friend and that you made him happy, especially skating with him."

I will always remember Randy and his cute smile as he watched me play Limbo at the skating rink. It would be years before I could go skating there again. I laid in bed that night, looking up at the stars out my bedroom window.

"Im still your friend, Randy. Ill always be your friend," I said, before drifting off to a restless sleep.

The Chesapeake Bay and Green, Grassy Lawns: What Playgrounds

I woke up one morning to the sound of machinery coming from out back. I got up to look out my window.

Is that what they call a steam shovel? I asked myself. A big machine was digging up loads of dirt out of our neighbor's lawn, piling it almost in our backyard.

Mom came in my room. "Do you see that? They're putting in a pool!"

I got excited at the idea. *A pool ... wont that be nice on a hot day?*

"Do you think they'll invite us over to swim?" I asked.

"I'm sure they will. They already asked your daddy if they could borrow his pickup truck to haul rocks in for the landscaping around the pool's sidewalk. They said we were welcome over any time."

As I watched, I noticed a pretty blue slide being brought out to go with the pool.

After eating Captain Crunch cereal and watching *Speed Buggy* on TV, I put on a T-shirt along with my favorite blue jean cut-offs. I brought my bike out of the garage and rode out of my driveway for my usual ride. I loved riding around the neighborhood, surveying to see if anyone was out. It was only 9:00 AM, and the grass was wet with dew still and the humidity was rising. Not a cloud in the sky; it was going to be a hot one. I noticed my next-door neighbor Janie standing by her mailbox, flipping through some outgoing letters. I don't remember exactly when I'd first met her over the summer. She had two younger brothers and an older sister. The family had moved down from Maine.

Her dad was in the Navy like mine. Janie was very prim, proper, and polite.

"Hi, Junie!" she said when I stopped next to her on my bike.

"Hi! Would you like to go bike-riding with me? I can show you around the neighborhood."

"Oh. Sorry, I don't have a bike yet."

"My mom has a bike if you want to borrow hers. She won't mind. She never rides it."

"Oh really? That would be really nice of you and your mom. Should we ask her first, or something?"

"Yeah, we can. I know she won't mind though."

"I'll come and get you. Just let me tell my mom where I'm going, okay?"

"Okay."

I was happy at the possibility of making another friend. As I was explaining to my mom about the new girl next door, Janie rang our doorbell. Mom answered.

"Hi, my name is Janie. I live next door. Junie said that perhaps it would be okay if I borrow your bike so we can go bike-riding?"

"Nice to meet you, Janie. I don't mind if you borrow my bike. Just make sure Junie puts it back in the garage when you're done."

"Okay, will do."

We rode down our street, and I showed Janie a couple of ways to go around the block, demonstrating how each route lead back to our street. I told her who lived where, and where the hilly bike trails were. When we headed back home, Janie thanked me for showing her around.

"I would have been extra lost if you hadn't," she said. Janie had her brown hair cut right at her jaw line and the tips curled under. Her nose was kind of pointy, and she had thin lips. I liked the fact she was fair-skinned like me. I felt less self-conscious about how white my skin was in the middle of summer.

"When we are all outside this evening, I'll come get you, to introduce you to everyone," I said.

"Oh thanks! I have met Joanie and Morris, and my sister Ruth is friends with Donna, who lives behind you. I'll see you later, Junie."

"See ya."

When I went back inside, my mom was packing sandwiches and

iced tea in a yellow plastic beach bag. "It's going to be in the upper 90s today, so I thought we could go to the beach. Go get the beach towels out of the pantry," she said.

I loved going to the beach: nothing was better than playing in the ocean's waves. I went to my room and put on my bathing suit, a two-piece bikini that was in style in 1975, but not practical for me. It was made out of a heavy, velvety material that was a golden rust color. The suit had brass diamond-shaped sequins across the middle of the bottom piece. The silly top would sag when it got wet because of the heavy material. My skin was a pasty white and I hated that. I took after my dad, who had a lot of Irish in his family tree. My mom had English and German heritage, but enough Cherokee Indian in her to help her tan nicely. My legs were getting hairy. I didn't understand why I had such hairy legs at my age. Oh well. Who cares? I was going to the beach, where my troubles would all be washed away.

We put towels down over the beige vinyl seats of the car because they were scalding hot from the sun shining through the windows. My mom turned on the air conditioner and the radio as we drove off. As we headed down the highway looking for the exit onto the interstate, "The Streak" came on the radio. This was a funny song about a streaker running around town. It would get my mom laughing, which I enjoyed as much as the music.

We had several options for beaches. There was the Chesapeake Bay, Sand Bridge, or Virginia Beach, which my mom didn't care for because it was always a hassle to find a parking spot. There was also the Duck Inn, which was further in along the bay and didn't have very good waves. The Officers Beach was nice, but a bit longer of a drive. We settled on Fort Story Beach, which was on an army base right on the Chesapeake Bay. This beach was more secluded for being on a base. We had to have a military sticker on the windshield of our car to be allowed in.

Mom and I trudged through the sand, which felt hot. We found a good spot close to the water; the ocean's breeze felt welcoming. Mom opened up her lounge chair and set it in the sand.

"Let me get suntan lotion on you," she said, knowing I was prone to bad sunburn. She rubbed the coconut-smelling lotion all over my back and arms, and dabbed some on my nose. I always found the picture on the suntan lotion bottle (a dog pulling a little girl's bikini down) silly. "Okay," Mom said. She knew I was anxious dive into the ocean's waves.

Oh, how wonderful to hear the waves and smell the salt water! I could entertain myself all day at the beach. When a swell would come, I jumped, letting it carry me. Other kids and grown-ups were doing the same as I. Some lounged on rafts, letting the swells gently carry them up and down. Others had boogie boards to ride the waves back to shore. I felt one with the ocean. I remember opening my eyes under the salty, green water to see sunlight filtering through. Sometimes I would see silver fish swimming by. I spent all my energy jumping up, holding my nose, and then letting myself fall to the ocean's floor. I would hold onto the sand, feeling the tug of the waves being sucked back out. I did handstands in the water, letting the swells pick me up upside down. What a great playground. After a while, once I could feel the burning of the saltwater in my eyes, I headed in to take a break. I could see my mom standing up, motioning for me to come in. I bodysurfed my way in, and ran through the wave that had just crashed ashore. *Fun,* I thought.

"You've been out there over an hour. Don't you want to rest a while and have some lunch?"

I *was* hungry. I plopped down on the warm towel. I was waterlogged and felt a slight chill in the ocean breeze. I put on my white terrycloth beach cover-up while my mom dug around in the cooler for a tomato sandwich. I was famished, and took large bites as my mom poured sweet tea from her thermos. Mom would walk down every so often to the water, but never went in past her waist. She had a fear of water, unlike me. I loved the ocean, though I wasn't a fan of crabs and jellyfish. I had a blue crab clamp down on my toe once. When I tried pulling it off, it wouldn't let go. I had to shake it off, which hurt. I had been stung by jellyfish a few times as well. I would rub sand on my bites to get the sting out.

"No swimming for at least thirty minutes, until your food is digested," my mom said when I was done eating.

I didn't understand exactly what was meant by *digested*, but I obeyed. We walked along the shore searching for seashells. Every time we found a shell that had an interesting shape, we would place it in the plastic pail my mom carried. I saw a large white shell that was in perfect condition. The ocean's foamy waves started pulling it back. I chased it, getting down on my hands and knees, desperately feeling for it. The next wave crashed on shore, splashing water into my face. I closed my eyes and felt around for the shell. I felt something hard and opened my eyes.

"I got it!" I said, jumping up to show my mom.

"That's a good one. Put it in the pail and let's find another one," she said, as if we were finding diamonds or something of great value.

We walked way down the shore before heading back to our spot on the beach. I could see our abandoned towels and lounge chair waiting for us. We made a sand castle, using our plastic cups to dig a moat.

"It's about time to pack it up and head home," my mom announced. "I have to start dinner before your dad gets home."

"Can't we just stay a little longer?"

"Well, I'll give you thirty more minutes if you want to swim one more time."

"Okay!" I jumped up, covered in sand from my knees down. I ran straight into the water and dove headfirst through a wave. I swam out to where the water felt cold and was over my head. I floated on swells a while before heading back to shore. One thing I learned early in life was that you can't rinse off your feet in the ocean and then put on flip flops without getting sand stuck all over you by the time you reached your car. The best thing is to let yourself dry off a little and then wipe the sand off with a towel. Showers hadn't been installed yet, nor was there a walkway to the parking lot. The beach was still pristine, with sand dunes and tall sea grass. We drove home with the car windows down, the breeze blowing on my wet hair. The air passing through the car's windows caressed my face. I turned on the radio. Captain & Tennille's latest song, "Love Will Keep Us Together," was playing.

When we arrived back at the house, I helped my mom get the sandy towels and beach bag out of the car. She grabbed her folded-up lounge chair. She also turned the cooler upside down in the grass to let it drain. I shook out the towel, hearing sand spray our lawn. I rinsed off in my parent's shower. Their blue bathroom had a good-sized shower stall with a frosted glass door instead of a shower curtain. I used my mom's "Gee, Your Hair Smells Terrific" shampoo. The shampoo was in a bright pink bottle. I loved its spicy, flowery scent. I scrubbed my arms, torso, and legs with my mom's pink Dove bar soap. I stood in the shower a little longer to let the sand wash off. I watched the sand go down the drain.

I went in my room, closed my door, and put on a 45 record— "Magic" by Pilot. It was my favorite song other than "The Streak." I fell asleep face down on my bed. I was completely worn out. When I awoke, the sun was still shining. I could hear children's laughter coming from outside. I got up to see who was out. I looked through my bedroom window and saw Janie and her brother Tommy kicking a soccer ball back and forth in their backyard next door. I started down the hall to go out and join them, but my mom called from the kitchen.

"Junie?"

She must have heard me get up. "What?" I answered impatiently, wanting to go out and play.

"It's almost dinner time. We're just waiting for the charcoals to get hot."

"I'll just be next door." My parents would be able to see me from our back patio, where we ate in the summertime.

"I need you to set the table first."

I hurried in and picked up everything my mom had set out on a tray. I carried the tray, walking backward with my elbow hitting the latch on the door so I could get out without knocking the tray. I put the tray down on the steps and set out three plates and the flatware, not really remembering the proper place setting.

"Hi, Junie! Whatcha doin'?" Janie asked.

"We're about to eat dinner, but I have a few minutes to play first."

"We're just kicking the ball around," Tommy said.

He kicked the soccer ball in my direction, and I kicked it back, aiming at his feet. After a while, I was called back to my yard for dinner.

"See ya later" I said before running off.

"See ya," the siblings responded.

My dad had burgers on the grill and was toasting hamburger buns. My mom had sliced huge, red garden tomatoes along with onions. Pickle spears were piled on a separate relish tray.

"I found us a fence to put up by the end of summer," my dad said, pleased with the idea.

"What kind?" I asked, thinking of a chain-link fence.

"It will stand six feet tall and it's made of cedar. I'll have a gate put in by the garage, with a latch handle and a lock. Won't that be nice? We'll have privacy out here, and won't have to worry about the neighbor's dogs crapping in the yard all the time."

"It sure will," my mom replied.

As I ate, I tried to picture the fence that would soon surround our yard. I guessed the privacy would be nice. Tish the mean Doberman pinscher wouldn't be able to catch Samantha. The cat would be able to hang out in the backyard without worrying.

After dinner, I placed as much stuff as I could on the tray to carry back inside. My mom had dishwater ready, soap bubbling up in the sink.

"Just place that right next to the sink" she told me. We didn't have an automatic dishwasher.

"Can I go play now?"

"Sure, go," she said, lighting a cigarette before getting up to do the dishes.

I got my bike out of the garage and rode into the street. I noticed Morris, Joanie, Jack, Michael, Mick, and Janie playing a good game of kickball in Janie's front yard. I parked my bike on the curb to observe.

"J-J-Junie's here now! We'll h-h-have eight players as soon as Tommy comes back outside. G-g-go into the outfield!" Morris instructed.

I ran to the so-called outfield, which was Morris' front yard. Mick Ceaver and Morris were the same age, but had opposite personalities. Morris was hotheaded, always ready for a fight, always bossy. His dark brown hair was cut in sort of a shag, and he had big brown eyes. Mick was laid-back, calm, and cool. He had golden blond hair cut in the same shag style as Morris, and blue eyes. Mick's older brother James bore a strong resemblance to Mick, except for his big ears, just like their father's. I liked their North Carolina accents, especially when they said "Yes, ma'am" or "Yes, sir." We all had slight Southern accents, but not the kind with a *long* drawl, just Virginia accents.

Darkness fell upon us quickly. Michael Clark had to go home.

"Let's play hide-and-seek!" Joanie suggested.

"Junie's it!" Mick teased.

"No, *you're* it!"

"Okay, everybody make a fist," Janie said, holding her hand out.

We all made fists and put them together. Janie waved her hand over ours, chanting "Bubble gum, bubble gum, in a dish, how many pieces do you wish?"

She landed on my hand.

"Six!"

She started making the rounds again until one fist was left.

"Morris is it!"

"Hey, since its dark out y'all, let's use my front porch as base, so my parents won't call me in yet," I suggested.

Everyone walked over to my porch. Morris started counting as we all hid. As the hour grew late, the mosquitoes started biting. We all sat on my front porch to catch our breaths. My mom came out, carrying a tray with glasses of ice-cold lemonade.

"Oh, thank you," everyone said as they picked up a glass.

"Nothin' better than cold lemonade on a hot, humid summer's night," Mick said, taking a glass.

"Thanks, Mom," I said.

After we drank the lemonade and put the glasses back on the tray, I carried the tray back inside the house and set it on the kitchen counter. I could smell cigarette smoke coming from the living room. My parents were watching *The Lawrence Welk Show* on TV. Mom had put on her pink bathrobe and slippers and was curled up in the black leather lounge chair.

"Make sure you just stay out front," she said before I went back outside.

"I will!" I yelled over my shoulder as I headed out the front door. I sat down on the front steps next to Joanie and Janie. Lightning bugs were starting to appear.

"Hold on, I'll be right back," Mick said, heading for his house.

"Where are you going?" I asked.

"To get a jar."

As soon as he disappeared into the darkness, Mr. Ainsworth called for Morris and Joanie to go home.

"We'll see ya tomorrow," they said walking toward their house.

Ruth, Janie's older sister, came out a moment later. "Janie, Mom says it's time to come in," she announced.

"Okay, be right there," said Janie.

"Well, our evening ended abruptly." I thought to myself.

"Let's hang out tomorrow, okay?" I asked.

"Sure Junie! See ya."

Janie disappeared into the darkness, leaving a swirl of lightning bugs behind her. I sat a moment listening to the chorus of crickets and night frogs wondering where those creatures were. *It's funny how you never see them*, I thought. Mick came running back across my lawn carrying a couple of mason jars.

"Where'd everybody go?"

"They all got called in about the same time right after you left."

"Damn, that was quick."

We tried to catch as many bugs as possible, and eventually just sat on the steps to observe their glow.

"I wonder what would happen if we lit one on fire," Mick said, looking at the bugs.

"No! That would be mean. They're so pretty."

"They're just little bugs."

"They're way too pretty."

"Yeah, I guess you're right," Mick agreed.

We heard a crash from inside the house, followed by profanity.

"Damn, what was that?" Mick asked.

"Oh, they're just yelling again."

"They sound really mad."

We heard louder shouts of profanity from the living room.

"They like to fight all the time. I don't know why. They don't even care we're sitting right out here where we can hear them," I lamented.

"They're really mad. What are they so mad about?"

"I don't know. Probably nothing in particular."

"Do you want to let the lightning bugs go?" Mick asked, trying to ignore the fighting.

"Yeah, let's set them free."

He opened the jar and shook them out into the lawn. Some flew away and some sat on the ground, still glowing. The yelling was getting hard to ignore.

"Mick?" I heard a woman's voice calling from across the street through the darkness.

"Yeah, I'm here."

"Come home pretty soon."

"Okay Mom."

"Sounds pretty rough in there. Do you want to come over to my house?"

"No, I better not."

"Okay. I've got to go, but come over anytime or call me and I'll come over and get you."

"What's your number?" I asked, thinking I might take him up on the offer. I memorized the number, never forgetting it. He headed home and I turned to go inside. Scary.

Florida, Grandma, and Fire Ants

By the end of that week, I was packing for our usual summer trip down to Florida. I was so excited! I enjoyed spending time with my aunts and uncles.

My mom came from a big family. She was raised on a farm in north Florida. All her siblings still lived down there. My aunt Nora was married to Uncle Rex. He was a nice guy, a typical Floridian: always tan, smiling, wearing white short-sleeve shirts and khaki shorts. He loved playing golf. Aunt Nora was the first lady to become an interstate road planner in Florida. I'm not sure what Uncle Rex did. All of my relatives had good jobs, drove nice cars, and seemed to smile a lot.

I packed my baby dolls in a little beige suitcase that zipped up. I packed my Barbies as well, of course, telling them "We're going on vacation." Mom had bought me a one-piece bathing suit that didn't sag like my heavy bikini. This swimsuit was rust-orange with gold, red, and chocolate brown stripes across the top. Sometimes my dad would make the trip with us. He lightened up around my mom's family, and showed his sense of humor. Other times, my dad would stay behind because of his job. I remember flying down to Florida a few times, staring at the clouds, thinking the plane could just land on one if it needed to, instead of crashing.

I was *so* sleepy after my mom woke me up to get ready for the twelve-hour drive down to Florida. My dad was staying home on this trip, so my mom would be doing all the driving. I put a pillow and a blanket in the back seat, but sat up looking out at the morning fog on the grassy countryside. I was too excited to fall back to sleep. It was going to be a quiet trip without my parents arguing the whole way.

This trip was going to be a little different, because we were driving to Louisiana as well for a couple of days. My half-brother Tim and his wife Sheila had just had a baby. I was an awfully young aunt. I had met my brother once when I was four. They drove one of their friend's RVs all the way up to Norfolk one summer. I cried when they left. I thought they were the nicest couple. When they drove away in the RV that summer morning, I hopped on my bike with tears streaming down my cheeks. I thought about the song "Daniel" by Elton John. I felt all alone as I pedaled my bike down the street. But then I noticed my dad riding up behind me, smiling. He knew I was saddened by Tim leaving and wanted to keep me company. Tim was eighteen when I was born. We have different dads.

It takes a lifetime to drive from Virginia to Florida, according to a seven-year-old. I couldn't color or try to read because I would get carsick. I just stared out the window or napped. As we passed the "Welcome to South Carolina" sign, I asked how much longer we had to go.

"I don't know," Mom answered. She had to concentrate on the road. It was easy for her to get confused, take some random exit off the highway, and get us lost for a while. Usually she would stop and ask someone in a gas station for directions. She was always told to just stay on the highway until she reached Florida. When we made it out of South Carolina and into Georgia, we stopped to have lunch at a Stuckey's truck stop. After eating, I looked around in the gift shop while Mom paid. I came across a small Indian drum that I thought was very unique. I bet the Indians had made it! I held it up.

"Mom, can I have this?"

She walked over and stared at the price. "I guess so." As she paid the sales lady, she told me "Hurry up and get in the car. I don't want to arrive late on account of you!"

We finally hit the Florida border around 5:30 in the evening. We drove out into the country toward the little town called Mayo where my mom had grown up. As we pulled up the dirt driveway, I could see the little white house up ahead. We were surrounded by very tall pine trees that had been planted in perfect rows. My grandma came running out from behind the screen door, letting it slam behind her. She ran straight toward us.

"I'm so glad to see you," she said, giving me a strong hug. I was surprised how strong she was for an old lady. She was kind of thin and had completely white hair.

We went inside, placing our suitcases in the tiny bedroom on the right. She had a tiny three-bedroom house with a huge garden out back. I thought she was the best cook and enjoyed the fresh garden vegetables in her Southern dinners. I would eat anything if she made it. I sat on the olive-green tweed couch while she and my mom talked. I pulled out two of my baby dolls and their little pink gingham blankets to play for a while. As the evening went on, I could hear all kinds of frogs and crickets outside. The air was fresher there, even though it was much more humid. My mom helped me pull out my pajamas to put on, and then she tucked me into the soft double bed. I loved the fresh, clean smell of the sheets. The room was very cool thanks to the window air conditioner. I liked the soothing hum, which muffled my mom and grandma's conversation in the living room. It was so nice stretching out in bed. I fell right to sleep.

I woke up to the smell of bacon being cooked along and friendly-sounding voices coming from the kitchen. I rose from bed and changed into shorts and a T-shirt.

"Well, look who's here!" a cheery voice exclaimed as I went into the living room. It was my uncle Howell. He gave me a big hug. "Why, you're getting' taller every time I see you," Uncle Howell said with a big smile on his face. He was tan and wore cowboy boots. He had a cap on over his short black hair and was chewing tobacco. He was one of my favorite uncles.

"Where's Danny and Curtis?" I asked. Danny and Curtis were my cousins.

"They're with their mom right now." Uncle Howell had recently been divorced. I had forgotten.

"Everybody, let's eat!" Grandma called out. She began saying grace just the way my mom always did, beginning with "Our dear heavenly father." She was always reading the Bible, circling quotes in it with a red pen. She attended one of those Southern Baptist churches with a tall white steeple. I went with her one summer. The preacher shouted his sermon so loudly that I found him intimidating.

The breakfast was delicious. We had cheesy, buttery grits, bacon, ham, and homemade biscuits that I loaded up with honey. It felt warm and welcoming sitting around the table listening to my relatives talk with their deep Southern accents, sharing laughter and their jovial outlooks on life.

After breakfast, my mom drove into town to pick up a few groceries while Uncle Howell left for work. So I started the day doing what I liked best: playing. I took my Barbie dolls outside with me to the screened-in front porch. When I grew bored with that, I decided to take a stroll around the place. I walked down the long white-sand driveway that lead up to the quiet highway. I looked both ways before crossing and headed to the brown wooden house with a tin roof where Uncle Howell lived there now. My mom had grown up in that house with her siblings Buford, Nora, Jack, Howell, Beth, and Colin. Paula was the oldest, but she had drowned. My grandfather worked as sheriff for a while before becoming a train conductor. I only have two memories of my grandfather. He died from emphysema when I was four. I remember him sitting in a chair in his living room holding his cane. My other memory of him was holding a breathing machine up to his face, desperately inhaling oxygen.

As I started wandering around the house, I noticed the windows seemed dark and kind of spooky. The front porch was rickety, with a swing hanging by chains from the roof of the porch. I wondered if the swing was safe to use. The old house was surrounded by banana trees, pine trees, and a pair of magnolia trees with big white blooms that smelled of perfume. There were lots of palmettos and yucca plants around too. Spanish moss hung from other trees around back. I found a water pump and a chicken coop. The chickens looked silly. They walked around, eyeing me closely, making funny clucking sounds. I continued to explore after crossing the highway back to Grandma's house. On her back porch, which was screened in as well, I found her washing machine and dryer out there—how curious. I sat on top of the washer to look out past the large vegetable garden into the trees. I noticed an old abandoned car that had vines growing around it. It was just sitting there rusting. "Whose car was that?" I thought out loud. The humidity was making me sweat profusely, so I went in to cool off.

"I saw you exploring out there, Junie." My grandma poured a glass of lemonade and handed it to me.

"Thanks," I said.

"You're welcome, honey. Now, anytime you want to eat or drink something, just help yourself, okay?"

"Okay."

"Honey, please don't cross that highway without telling us because sometimes those *big* trucks go by *really* fast."

"I know, I did look both ways. I just wanted to look around."

My grandma pulled out a galvanized tub from under the sink. "Do you want to help me in the garden? I'm gonna pick some zucchini, tomatoes, and cucumbers to have with dinner tonight."

"Sure," I said. This should be interesting. I had never picked from a garden before. As we walked out in between the rows of vegetable plants, I thought it was awesome to see the abundance of huge, bright-red tomatoes! Some of the tomatoes were as big as softballs, but with funny shapes. They weren't perfectly round like the produce in the grocery stores. On the other side of the garden there were zucchini, yellow squash, eggplant, and okra.

"See?" Grandma Lily bent down like a pro and grabbed a tomato, turning it while pulling it off the vine at the same time. She showed me how to pick. It was fun finding vegetables that were ready to pick and putting them in the galvanized tub. The sun beat down on my back and I felt like it was cooking me. Sweat poured from my forehead, but I didn't want to stop finding vegetables. It was like that never-ending search for the perfect seashell at the beach. As we picked, I could hear cows mooing. The cows swatted flies with their tails in a pasture nearby. I could hear large dragonflies buzzing around. They sounded like miniature helicopters.

"Okay, I think we have more than plenty for dinner tonight."

"Who all is coming?" I asked, hoping other aunts and uncles would show up.

"Let's see. Your Uncle Jack and Aunt Freda Nelle, Aunt Beth, and Aunt Nora."

"Yay!" I said excitedly. "Will Uncle Howell come too?"

"Oh sure he will. He comes over *each* evening for dinner."

I held one end of the tub and my grandma held the other end, and we carried the vegetables inside to be rinsed. She dumped them in a large colander in the sink.

"Can I help clean them?" I asked.

64

"Oh, why sure you can, darlin'. Aren't you such a *good* little helper?"

Grandma Lily put a stepping stool under the sink so I could reach better. I began carefully rinsing each tomato.

"Grandma?"

"Yes dear?"

"Whose car is that out in the field? Did someone wreck it?"

"It's been out there *so* long, honey. I can't really remember. It might have been one of your grandpa's."

I was going to ask why they didn't sell the old thing when my mom came in with some groceries. I was proud and wanted her to see the vegetables we had picked.

"Those are beautiful," Mom said, picking up a tomato. "We grew up raising a garden like that. We even had cornfields and cotton fields that we would work hard in before and after school. Talk about hard work! Our hands would *bleed* from it all."

I couldn't understand how someone could cut their fingers on cotton. When I was done rinsing the vegetables, I went outside on the front porch and sat in the rocking chair. I listened to the wind blow through the tops of the pine trees as bugs buzzed around. Every so often, like my grandma had warned me, a large truck would go screaming by.

I noticed a galvanized tub in a corner of the house. It was larger than the one we used to put vegetables in. I thought I could fill it with water and sit in it to cool off.

"Mom, can I swim in that tub outside?"

"Tub?" My mom looked muddled.

"Oh, she's talking about the large galvanized tub out front," my grandma said. "*Sure* you can, honey. We're not using it right now."

"Well, put on your bathing suit," my mom said.

I went into the little bedroom and changed. I grabbed my baby dolls and a towel, and then headed outside. My mom had the garden hose in the tub, filling it up. I cooled off in the water before bringing my dolls into the water. Mom came out with a glass of sweet iced tea and watched me from the porch. She sat in the rocking chair and let out a big sigh.

"How come the clouds here are fluffier and the sky seems bluer?" I asked, looking up.

"Well, I don't know. Maybe because the air is cleaner out here in the country." The air did smell fresher, especially with green plants, green grass, and tall pines all around. It smelled sweet.

Later my aunts and uncles showed up for dinner. They all gave me a hug and said the same thing. "You *sure* are gettin' *taller*." After dinner, when I went to bed, I laid there listening to them talk. I loved their Southern drawls. My mom, grandma, Aunt Beth, and Aunt Nora were sitting around the midsized galvanized tub that was placed in the middle of the floor, snapping snow peas, tossing them in. They had arranged chairs in a circle around the tub facing each other, and were talking about when they were little and old friends and places I wasn't familiar with.

The next few days passed quickly. My dad would call each evening to see how we were doing. I mostly played with my dolls outside. One afternoon, we all piled in two cars to drive over to Uncle Colin and Aunt Carolyn's double-wide trailer. It sat right next to a lake. The lake was fresh water and so brackish that it looked like black olive juice. There was a dock that went out on the lake. When I let my feet dangle in the water, I thought it was strange how dark the water was. I looked down trying to see my feet in the water. I couldn't.

That night, when we returned to my grandma's, I looked down at the white sand of the driveway. It seemed to glow under the moonlight. There were so many frogs croaking and crickets chirping, I felt like I was in the jungle. I imagined giraffes and elephants wandering around. I was in awe when I noticed how many lightning bugs there were! There were thousands. Some seemed to have a greenish glow, and there were the usual oranges and yellows. I ran down the driveway, enthralled by them. I just wanted to run through them.

"Come back! The mosquitoes will bite you to pieces!" my grandma called.

I turned around and went inside. It was a good thing I went in when I did, because I was already covered in mosquito bites. Grandma came in once I was settled in bed and put calamine lotion all over me.

The next morning, we got up and packed to head out to Louisiana. First we drove by the family cemetery. We followed my grandma in her little red car. I saw the grave of my mom's eldest sister. My grandma put flowers on Grandpa Lonnie's grave. It was hot walking around the sandy family cemetery. I started getting impatient, kicking the sand as I walked.

"Honey, don't kick the sand. There are fire ants out here and they will sting the *fire* out of you."

As soon as Grandma warned me, I felt fire spreading all over my feet and ankles. I started screaming as my mom and Grandma came running over. Grandma Lily started swatting them off me.

"That's why I *warned* you," she said as she brushed them off as fast as she could. I could tell it upset her that I got stung. When we left Florida, I thought about how she must know an awful lot about the land and how she was a true Floridian.

Louisiana

We got on the highway again. I didn't know which road we were on. Uncle Howell had gone over a map with my mom the night before we left. For the most part, it was a pretty drive.

My brother was the manager of some apartments, my mom told me. "He gets his place *rent-free*. He also doesn't rent out the apartment that's over his, so guest can stay there."

Finally, after a long drive, we pulled up in front of Tim's apartments. His wife Sheila met us on the sidewalk. She looked the same as the last time I saw her when I was four: tall and thin, with short black hair and long red nails. We all hugged and she welcomed us to their home. We followed her down the sidewalk to where they were living. Their apartment was on the first floor, surrounded by a courtyard that had a grassy lawn and playground equipment.

"You got here in time for our nice weather. For a while there, we had tornado warnings and people had to bring in their plants and things off their porches. We're in the clear now though," Sheila said in her long Southern drawl. I almost couldn't understand her. She pronounced plants as "play-unts" and tornado as "toor-nay-do." Once we were inside their apartment, I noticed Tim and Sheila still called each other "Momma" and "Daddy" as they had at our last visit. But it made more sense to me this time, as they now had a baby boy. Christopher was his name. He was a cute baby with blond hair and blue eyes, taking after my brother. He was sleeping as we looked down on him in his bassinet. I hoped I would be a nice aunt to him.

My mom had always told me that Tim never misbehaved. "You better behave when you're around Tim or else!" she would say. I often didn't understand exactly how I was misbehaving, or why she thought I was going to. I was always trying to act like a proper, well-mannered girl. I did get spankings for not finishing my dinner sometimes, and would especially be in trouble if I said "I can't finish eating." One evening I got into trouble because I couldn't keep down bluefish, as always. It was served once a week when we lived in Norfolk. I would really try to eat it, but it was so disgusting to me I couldn't help but to throw it up. I really got yelled at for that. Did Tim like bluefish? Could he keep it down? I suppose so.

Tim showed me the upstairs apartment where my mom and I would be sleeping. He reminded me of my uncles: real laidback and friendly. He didn't talk down to me; he treated me like any other person. After we were settled in, they ordered pizza for dinner. I felt kind of bored sitting there at the kitchen table with nothing to do. I didn't feel like playing with my dolls and I couldn't ride my bike. Their apartment was small and bland with a small black-and-white TV.

"Junie, why don't you go out on the playground? The kids around here are pretty nice, and I think it will be more fun for you." Tim suggested.

"Okay."

"I'll walk you over."

We only had to go out the front door and across the lawn to reach the playground. A couple of kids about my age were going down the slide, a girl and a boy.

"Hey, y'all come here a minute," Tim said. They knew he was the manager of the complex.

"Yes sir?"

"This is Junie, my little sister visiting from Virginia."

"Hi, I'm Becky," the girl said. She had long blond hair and a deep dark tan. She had the same accent as Sheila.

"I'm Toby," the boy said. He had black hair with a deep dark tan as well. "You can play with us."

"Junie, I'll be right inside the apartment if you need me."

"Okay, thanks," I said. I was thankful. We went down the slide several times and then got on the swings. "So are you going to move here?"

"No, I'm just visiting."

"How old are you?"

"I'm seven."

"Oh, I'm eight," Becky said. We swung until it grew dark out and the mosquitoes started biting. Some lady called from the second balcony for Becky and Toby to come in.

"Bye," Becky said. "We'll see you tomorrow."

"Okay," I said, happy to have someone to play with. I missed my friends back in George Town.

Sure enough, the next morning Becky and Toby were knocking on the door looking for me. We played on the playground for a while before I was called in.

"Mom and Sheila are going to take Chris and do some boring shopping. You don't want to do that, do you?" Tim asked.

"Not really," I answered. I hated waiting by the shopping cart while my mom spent what seemed like a lifetime staring at clothes.

"Good. Why don't we go see a movie instead?"

"That sounds good." I was thrilled. Tim drove us in his yellow Corvette down to the local theater. We saw *The Apple Dumpling Gang*, which was a comedy. I accidently spilled my popcorn all over during a funny scene. I worried that I would get in trouble. Tim just laughed and asked if I wanted another popcorn.

"No, thank you." I was relieved he wasn't mad at me. He even seemed to enjoy my company. When we had to leave the next day for our journey back home, my heart sank a little. When would I see Tim again?"

Home at Last

Our drive back home seemed endless. My mom panicked at one point when we were surrounded by a convoy of trucks. We had to cross a narrow bridge with huge trucks ahead of us, behind us, and on the left.

"Look at all these damn trucks!" my mom yelled. I sat up in the back seat and saw an eighteen-wheeler in front of us, its tires spraying misty water and making it hard to see. It had been raining all morning. My mom had on the windshield wipers at top speed. "All these *damn* trucks."

I was tickled at my mom's comical overreaction to the trucks on the road. I broke out in hysterical laughter. Every time my mom yelled about the *damn trucks,* one would go screaming by, which made me laugh even harder.

"Why don't you sit up here and help me instead of acting like a retard!" she yelled.

"I can't help it. They're just trucks," I answered back. "What do you want me to do?"

"Well … you can get up here and try to help me look out for them, for one thing." That sounded silly. I climbed into the front seat. Seeing my moms face, I realized how truly frightened she was.

"Just concentrate on the road, Mom. These guys know what they're doing, so don't worry about them."

"See all of them?" my mom said, still almost hysterical.

"Just pay attention and you'll be okay." The truck in front of us eventually turned on his blinker and exited the highway. The road pretty much cleared after that. Some sunlight started breaking through the storm clouds.

After my mom calmed down and we had been driving for quite some time, I played with my baby dolls in the back seat for a while. When I became bored with that, I just stared out the window. We had been driving through the country for quite some time. For miles, I had been looking at a rustic wooden fence.

"Who could have built that fence? It's *so* long."

"Oh, I think Daniel Boone built that."

I tried picturing Daniel Boone with his animal-skin jacket and foxtail cap. He must have spent a long time making that fence.

The sun started getting low in the sky. My mom was growing tired from driving. We found a little motel on the side of the road that had a swimming pool out front.

"Let's stay there!" I said, perking up with the thought of swimming in the pool.

We got checked in and made a short drive down to the local Kentucky Fried Chicken. We brought our food back to the motel and then got ready to take a dip in the pool. The round globes of the lights surrounding the pool were starting to give off a soft glow. I loved swimming in a pool at night. Another lady and her daughter who looked to be about ten years old were swimming already when we arrived. I dove in and swam across the pool. The lights were now completely on. A shadowy glow fell on the sidewalk and hedge that lined the pool. The lady sitting on the pool's edge lit up a cigarette, and handed it to the little girl. They started smoking before getting their towels and leaving.

"Did you *see* that?" my mom asked, astonished.

"See what?"

"That lady let her little girl smoke! She couldn't have been much older than you. Don't you *ever* put one of those things in your mouth. You'll never be able to quit!" Smoking was something I never considered. My parents both smoked and it made me cough or gag at times. My dad's pipes and cigars didn't bother me as much as cigarette smoke, which I thought was nasty.

A good swim at the end of a long day of traveling sure did help me sleep soundly. We woke early the next morning and were on the road again. Finally, after hours of driving, I was glad to finally see that familiar "Welcome to Virginia" sign! It was blue with a red cardinal on it. We were almost home, almost back to George Town.

"Home at last," my mom said as we pulled onto our street. There was a pretty orange sunset underway as we pulled into the driveway. My mom tooted the horn to let my dad know we were home. The air felt a little cooler than in Louisiana. My dad came out of the house to greet us.

"Welcome home."

Samantha was rolling around on her back on the sidewalk. I was happy to see her, and reached down to pet her. I could hear crickets chirping and sprinklers watering neighbor's lawns. I didn't see anyone out, but could hear the sound of distant children's laughter.

Yeah, nothing changed, I told myself. The neighborhood looked like it had just been through a typical George Town day. Yards had been mowed, dinners had been eaten, and people were getting ready to settle down after a long summer's day. My dad helped my mom carry in the suitcases. I loved the familiar feel of our central air conditioning as I walked into the house. By the time I took my dolls out of their special little suitcase and placed them in with the other dolls in their crib, it was dark out. I heard the faucet come on in the bathroom. My mom was running bath water for me. Later, as I sat in the warm sudsy water, I thought about how nice it was to get back to the norm. We had only been gone two weeks, but it seemed like two months. I couldn't wait to play with my friends and ride my bike around.

I woke up to the sound of hammering and men's voices. It was coming from my backyard. I looked out my bedroom window and saw three men carrying parts of our new fence in and stacking them on the back lawn. I also noticed that the little dirt mound in our neighbor's backyard was gone. Their pool had been put in! There were two different hoses hanging over the edge of the pool, and water was pouring in. The pool was huge. There was a diving board on the deep end, and the pretty blue slide had been installed at the opposite end. I missed the dirt mound though. No more playing king-of-the-hill. It was Saturday, so my dad was already awake, doing his usual routine, sitting at the kitchen table, reading the newspaper, drinking his cup of coffee. Mom was cooking grits, eggs, and bacon.

"We're getting our new fence put up today," my dad said when I walked into the kitchen. I could tell he was excited about it. My mom set a glass of orange juice down on the table for me.

"I know, I saw them carrying in the parts," I said, trying to sound somewhat enthusiastic for my dad's benefit. I knew how much the fence meant to him, even if I was worried about it interfering with our hide-and-seek games. My mom had me set the table for breakfast. She made delicious grits, just like Grandma. I loved stirring my over-easy eggs into my grits before crumbling bacon on top. After we were done eating, my dad went outside to observe the fence being put up. My mom put the dishes in the sink, pouring liquid Dove soap on them as water gushed out of the faucet. I went for an early-morning bike ride around the block to see who was out. Dew was still covering lawns, and I could feel the humidity rising. There was a new house being built on a nearby street. As I rode by, I could hear power saws and hammering. I could smell the new wood, a scent I liked. Some people were out mowing their lawns or pruning their hedges. I saw two different families packing coolers and beach bags into their cars, getting ready for a day at the beach. After riding around the block, I went home with plans to get a cold drink before heading over to a friend's house. As I drank down some cold sweet iced tea, the doorbell rang. It was Joanie, Janie, and Krissy. They were all glad that I was home. I squealed with excitement as we all shared a big group hug.

"How was Florida?" Janie asked.

"Oh, it was okay, but I missed you guys so much."

"Guess what?" Joanie asked as we walked into my front lawn.

"What?"

"We've been playing—"

"Oh yeah, we've been playing," Krissy interrupted because she was impatient to tell me new news. They both started talking at once.

"Okay, okay," Janie said. "Let me tell her."

"No, I started first," Joanie said.

"All right, tell her," Janie said.

"We have come up with a new game to play. Charlie's Angels. We even bought some plastic police badges and guns."

"That sounds like fun, but aren't there only *three* detectives?"

"We've decided to make up a fourth one."

We all headed over to Janie's backyard picnic table to discuss our new game. This was how our summers would start. We would decide on a game, and then we would get into character and play for weeks until we came across something else. It felt so good to be back with my friends again.

"I think it's nice that you're getting a fence put up, Junie. You're so lucky," Janie said, much to my surprise.

"Really? I'm not sure I'll like it being closed off."

"Why not?" Joanie asked.

"Because it might get in the way of our hide-and-seek games. And I'll have to go through the gate every time to get out."

"No, think of the privacy you'll have. No one can stare into your yard at you when you want to be alone."

I appreciated Janie telling me that. I felt a little better about the fence going up.

"We can have *camp-outs*!" Krissy added.

"That's a *great* idea." I said.

"We can get flashlights, sleeping bags, and a cooler full of sodas." Krissy said with wide eyes.

"When will the fence be finished?" Janie asked.

"I'm not sure I'll have to ask my dad." The new fence wasn't so bad after all.

I was riding on a bicycle, but my feet weren't pedaling, they were resting across the handle bars. My vision was blurry. I saw James go by on his bike, staring at me funny.

"What happened?" he asked.

"Oh, she just had a little bicycle accident," I heard my dad's voice say from behind me. *Why was he behind me?* I realized I was leaning against him. *He* was pedaling the bike. *Why?* I wondered. He told James I had a bicycle accident. *No I hadn't. Had I?* I felt dizzy. Everything was in slow motion. I woke up to see my mom and dad standing over me. My mom was fussing at my dad about something. They were trying to put my shoes on my feet. Was I expected to walk somewhere? *I don't think I can. I really feel sleepy, I can't hold my eyes open. Please don't make me walk.* I tried opening my eyes again. *How did I get in the back seat of my parent's car? Was I dreaming?* I was lying down, that was for sure.

I could feel the cold vinyl on my back through my shirt. I heard sirens and could feel the car swerve as my dad pulled over to the side of the road. I could see a traffic light out the windshield over my dad's head. A police officer's face appeared through my dad's window. The officer had a blue hat and a chubby face. He seemed older than my dad. My dad rolled down his window.

"My daughter needs to go to the hospital. I don't have time for this, I need a lead!" The policeman looked at me and went pale.

I woke up again, this time looking up at white lights. There was a lady there, as well as two men dressed in white. I closed my eyes and heard the lady say "I've seen fat lips before, but *not one like that.*"

"What hapfund?" I asked, not sure if I was awake or not.

"You fell over the handlebars on your bike," I heard my dad's voice say.

I wondered how I managed to fall over my handlebars before the sleep took over again.

I opened my eyes again, feeling the cold vinyl on my back. I was back in the car. As my dad was about to close my door, I noticed a gray cat in the parking lot heading off into the bushes.

"Get the cat, Dad, he's stwanded."

"No," my dad said in a matter-of-fact tone before shutting the door.

I woke up the next morning and felt the bandages around my head. There was a patch over my left eye. I sat up, but the room started to spin. *What's wrong with me?* I slowly managed to sit up right on the edge of my bed. I could smell dried blood.

"Mmum?" I tried calling, but my upper lip was making it hard for me to speak. I got up slowly, making it over to my dresser. I leaned against it with my palms and looked into the mirror. I couldn't believe my eyes.

"What hapfund?" I questioned out loud, astonished. Before me stood a girl I didn't recognize! My upper lip *was* the fattest lip ever! I remembered the lady from the night before. She must have been a nurse. My upper lip was so swollen it was touching my nose! White bandages were wrapped around my head. *Why did I have an eye patch on? Was I hit by a car?* The rest of me was still intact. No cast. I poked at my unnatural-looking, enormous lip. It felt rubbery and numb. I laughed out loud at my reflection. My mom walked in, looking concerned.

"How are you feeling this morning?"

"What hapfund?"

"You don't remember anything?"

"No, I dun't." I was trying to remember, but only could recall James's face as he rode by staring at me on his bike. I remember the nurse's voice at the hospital saying I had the fattest lip ever, and I remember a gray cat. "Did we bwing the cat hume, mumm?" It was so difficult to talk with a deranged face.

"Honey, I think you should lie back down and take it easy. Do you hurt?"

"No, I dun't fweel anyfing. Did I get hit b-by a car too?" I sat on my bed with my back against my pillow. My mom walked around sitting on the foot of my bed. "Your dad said that while you two were out bike riding you all of a sudden took off pedaling really fast, saying something about the Six Million Dollar Man. When you turned to look back at Dad, you turned the handlebars with you, flipping the entire bike over. You flew several feet before skidding face-first along the street. Are you sure you don't remember?"

I couldn't recall any of it. "No." I told my mom about the nurse and the cat. "I remember the nurse and her trying to keep everyone at ease by joking a little, but I don't remember seeing a cat. Let me bring you some lunch."

"Mmum ... mmawm?" I tried enunciating the word correctly. My mom looked at me from the bedroom doorway. "Will my lip always b-be like this?"

She chuckled a little and then grew serious. "Oh no, the doctor said the swelling will go down a little each day. Just don't touch it. He also said for you to not lie down too long during the day. Just try to sit up in bed and take things slow. I'll bring you some Jell-O," she said before walking down the hall toward the kitchen.

Over the course of the next two days, I had visitors come to see how I was and to keep me company. Mrs. Ceaver brought over her rich upside-down pineapple cake and gently kissed me on the forehead. Mick and James visited a while, making me laugh by pretending to play with my dolls, imitating little girls. To my surprise, both Mr. and Mrs. Ainsworth came to see me, setting a beautiful bouquet of flowers on my dresser.

"Joanie and Morris would really like to visit you later," Mrs. Ainsworth told me as they started to leave.

"Okay," I said wanting to see my friends. I was soon able to sit at the kitchen table when it was time for lunch. My lip was still gigantic, making it hard to get my food in my mouth. My dad had told me my left eyebrow was completely rubbed off. I had such bad road rash that the whole left side of my face was like one big scab. My left eye was swollen shut, which made me clumsy; I had to walk slowly. What was odd about the whole ordeal was I never felt any pain. I didn't even need stitches, but I did suffer a minor concussion. As I was making my way back to my bedroom, the doorbell rang. I was pleased to see Joanie when I answered.

"Hi, come in," I said. She just stood there staring at me through the screen door. All of a sudden she burst out in laughter.

"I'm sorry," she managed to say in between laughs. She opened the storm door, came in, and gave me a hug. "I'm sorry but I've never, ha ha, I've never seen—"

"I know. *A lip so fat.*" I finished the sentence for her. Now she was crying and giving me another hug. Joanie walked with me back to my room and sat on the foot of my bed. I explained what had happened according to what my dad had told me. I had no memory of any of it. After chatting for quite some time I started getting sleepy.

"You look tired, Junie. I'll come back later. Get some rest, okay?"

"Okay, see ya."

Not long after Joanie left, I dozed off. After an hour or so, I woke up. My eyes were still shut but I sensed someone in my room. I opened my right eye and saw Morris standing there looking at me, his eyes wide.

"I-I'm s-s-sorry, I didn't know y-you were sleeping." He turned to go. My mom must have let him in. "No, wait. Please stay, I'm awake now."

"A-a-are you sure it's okay to v-v-v-visit awhile?"

"Yeah, have a seat." He pulled out my desk chair and placed it at the foot of my bed, straddling it backward and facing me. "Damn, girl! That must have r-r-r-really hurt."

"Not weally, I can't remember anyfing. Listen to me, don't I sound funny?" I was still having problems pronouncing my words.

"Y-y-you almost sound a-a-as funny as I do," Morris said.

Janie, Joanie, and Krissy all came back after dinner, bringing me a shoebox that had different pictures from magazines glued all over it like a collage.

"Thanks guys." I could tell that they spent quite some time making this for me, putting a lot of thought into it. On the lid it read *Get better soon!* The girls had all signed it, and drawn smiley faces and flowers.

"See?" Joanie pointed to the magazine pictures. "Some of the pictures are all the things we like to do together, and other pictures are things that remind us of you." There were magazine pictures of little girls jumping rope, playing dolls, or dressing up. One picture was a little girl looking in the mirror putting on lipstick. Other pictures showed kids riding bikes and swinging on swing sets. There were photos of the beach, Barbie dolls, and roller skates.

"Wow. Thanks, y'all. I love this!"

"Open it up!" Joanie said. I opened it to find a sock puppet made, bubble gum, a miniature vase with plastic flowers, and a stuffed *tiger*— my favorite animal. "I think this is the nicest gift anyone has ever given me."

Later in the evening when everyone was gone, I took my crayons and folded different colored pieces of construction paper in half to make everyone a thank-you card.

As the days passed, my lip got back to normal, the bandages came off, and my eye healed. My dad would tease me sometimes, saying I made a hole in the pavement with my head. It was nice when my face was back to normal.

My parents had bought a new gas grill that was mustard-gold colored and had a window in the lid so we could see our food cooking. The one person who could cook better than my grandma was my dad. It was just part of his personality to do things *perfectly*. My dad would sit and ponder over something until he had the answer to whatever the problem was. His navy co-workers came to him with all sorts of questions that nobody else could figure out. My dad told me once that he could fall asleep thinking about a problem and the solution would come to him in his dreams. When he woke up, he had the answer. He could fix anything that was broken, not just around the house but on the aircraft carrier too. Some called him a genius. He was anti-social, though. He was always overly logical about things. My dad, whose looks reminded me of Desi Arnaz or Dick Van Dyke from TV, certainly had a strong personality. He once spent an entire week painting the trim of our house. I remember seeing him carefully painting around the edges with a small brush. When he was done, we had a flat gold colored trim and dark red drain pipes to match the bricks. I thought it was an ugly color scheme, but didn't say anything.

In our backyard, along the new fence, my parents tilled the dirt and planted tomatoes and cucumbers. My mom knew everything about plants and could make them grow like no one else. Between her and my dad, we had the greenest lawn and best hedges on the block. Unsurprisingly, their vegetable garden was *great*. We had big red tomatoes like my grandma had in her garden, and some of the oddest-looking but best-tasting cucumbers. Some were in the shape of horseshoes! I liked going out into the hot, humid air on a summer morning to see if any new tomatoes had grown. One of my favorite summer lunches was a tomato sandwich with mayonnaise, salt, and pepper on plain white bread.

My parents and I spent many afternoons riding our bikes around the neighborhood. Once we rode up to the high school. There were some tennis courts that were open to use. "We'll have to get some tennis rackets and tennis balls and come up some time," my dad had said. We stood watching as a couple played tennis. They were pretty good. Tennis was something I was never able to master when Joanie and I tried playing. Directly behind the tennis courts was Indian River Lake. It was manmade. Joanie told me once that a crane was stuck in the bottom of it. The high school's football field was on the left of the tennis courts, and a paved trail ran in between the fields, leading over to the middle school.

When we got home and put the bikes back in the garage, I noticed all the neighborhood kids were in the street playing. Some were riding bikes and others skateboarding. I went over to Katie, Kelly, and Krissy, who were teaching Joanie how to play Chinese jump rope. The rope was a large elastic band.

"Okay, first you start with it around your ankles," Katie instructed Joanie and Krissy. "Then you step on it with your left foot and then the right." The levels became harder as we went along pulling the large band further and further up our legs. The challenge of the game was what made it fun.

"All right, Junie, it's your turn," Katie said when Joanie's foot missed and her end of the rope went loose. I surprised myself by being pretty good at it.

I looked up and saw Janie and Ruth wearing their bathing suits, carrying towels heading around the side of their house.

"Hey" I yelled across the street. I thought they might come over to chat a minute. I was curious as to where they were going swimming. They just waved back and continued walking.

"Hey, come here a minute!" Joanie yelled.

"We can't," Janie yelled back. "We're heading over to the neighbor's house to go swimming. I'll see you all later!"

Just as I suspected! The neighbors that lived behind me had invited them over. Ruth was friends with Donna who lived there, and was invited over all the time. I thought it was unfair that they never invited me over, especially because my dad let them borrow his pickup truck to haul their rocks for the pool. I decided to ask them if I could swim one time when it was sweltering out. I had asked from my backyard, peering through the cracks in the fence. Their answer was no.

"Junie?"

I looked up from our game of Chinese jump rope to see my mom calling from the porch. It was probably getting close to dinnertime, so I told everyone I'd see them later after dinner. I approached my mom, hoping she would say dinner wasn't for another hour, which would give me more time to play.

"I need you to help set the tables out back. We've invited the Ceavers over for a cookout."

"Okay," I said. I liked the idea of having people over for a change. "Are Mick and James coming too?"

"I think they said just Mick." *Oh goody good,* I thought. A friend I could have dinner with before going out to play. I set out all of the plates and silverware. I put ice in the glasses and set them in the fridge to chill. My dad was barbecuing chicken on his new grill. The hickory, smoky smell will always remind me of summer. I was pleased to see Mr. and Mrs. Ceaver as they approached from around the side of our house. They were such a nice couple. Mrs. Ceaver had flawless skin with auburn hair cut short and permed in curls. She was pear-shaped with small shoulders and broad hips, maybe even a little too heavy in the hips.

"Where shall I set this down, honey?" she asked, referring to the baked beans and pineapple upside-down cake she was carrying in Tupperware containers.

"Oh just right over there on the table will be fine." I took them from her and set them on the side table that matched our patio tables. My dad came back out with tongs.

"Hey there, Den!" Mr. Ceaver said, holding his hand out to shake my dad's. I thought Mr. Ceaver was one of the nicest men I had ever met. He never yelled or seemed to get upset. I liked how he always had a smile on his face. He was tall, thin, and had large ears, reminding me of the Howdy Doody puppet from an old 1950's show I had seen once. Mick came shortly after and helped me carry the other side dishes and condiments out.

As we ate, we could hear Donna, Ruth, and Janie going off the diving board and splashing into the pool. I told Mick how my dad lent them his pickup truck to haul their rocks in for the pool and they wouldn't even let us swim.

"That's pretty unfair there," Mick said, shaking his head. Mick and I sat at a separate table from our parents, which was nice, giving us the privacy for our own conversations. "Let's get everyone together for a game of kickball when we're done eating."

"Sounds good to me, Junie."

When we were done eating, after finishing our dinners as fast as we could in order to not miss out on precious playtime, we gathered our plates. I filled the sink with soapy dishwater before we ran out to gather everybody for a game. Being the tomboy I was, I dressed like one of the guys with my blue jean cutoff shorts and white knee-high socks with two stripes at the top. Our first stop was Morris and Joanie's house. Morris answered the door saying he would be out later after dinner.

Janie's family wasn't home. Mick and I jogged down to Keith's, and then the three of us gathered Michael and Jack.

While the five of us sat on my front porch steps waiting for Morris and Joanie to come over, a girl named Dana went pedaling slowly by on her bike. Every time she rode by on her bike, the song "Spiders and Snakes" by Jim Stafford would pop into my head. She had thick brown hair cut shoulder-length with what were called Farah Fawcett wings. She was smiling, showing off her pearly whites. She was wearing a sleeveless pink T-shirt with extremely short shorts, a large comb stuck in the back pocket. I thought it was strange how she always went barefoot on Sundays. I was told it had something to do with her religion, which I thought was strange. Dana lived a couple of streets down but would occasionally ride her bike down our street. All the boys would flirt with her. Joanie told me it was because she had big boobs for a thirteen-year-old.

"Nobody loves me," she said as she pedaled by, staring at my friends.

"I do!" Mick said, staring back.

"I do!" Keith said as well. How stupid. *Why do they love her? How can she just ride by and say something silly like that and they actually respond to it?* She wasn't all that pretty, just average looking. Dana wasn't cool either; she never wanted to play dodgeball or kickball like I did. I was glad that she didn't. I hated how the boys gawked at her. Dana didn't stop to speak. She just kept riding down the street, reminding me of a cat slinking off. I had noticed her toenails were painted bright red.

"Who could love *her*?" I asked, perturbed.

"She just has *it*," Keith answered.

"Has *what* exactly?"

"Junie ... youre so ... " Keith said, shaking his head condescendingly at me.

I felt awkward knowing that they were attracted to her, and also a little jealous. Later Paul told me that she was easy and would do things bad boys liked. I had only a vague idea of what he meant. I just didn't like her.

Morris and Joanie finally showed up, and the kickball game was on. It became even more exciting when Janie and her little brother Tommy came home and joined our game. We all shouted "go, go, go!"

to our teammates as they ran the bases in Janie's front yard. Of course we couldn't get through a game without Morris and Keith arguing over about someone being safe or not. The sun seemed to sink quickly, and before we knew it, night was upon us. Once it was too dark outside for kickball, we started our intense hide-and-seek game. We would tackle one another just to make someone "it." Whoever became "it" would have to count to ten without peeking while we sprinted off to hide. If they peeked, they would have to remain "it" again. We didn't just hide behind bushes. We climbed up pine trees, scaled rooftops, and even hid under parked cars. We took it easy on Joanie who could only jog because of her wooden leg. After getting hot and sweaty from running around in the humid night air, I excused myself for a minute and ducked inside my air-conditioned house to cool down a minute. I went into the kitchen for a cold drink. I could see out my kitchen window looking onto the back patio. My parents and the Ceavers were laughing and chatting. They had cocktails in their hands, most likely rum-and-Cokes or mint juleps. I pulled a bottle of Sprite from the refrigerator and opened it with a bottle opener that was held on the side of the fridge by a magnet. As I started guzzling the soda down, Mick approached my mom out back. She said something, and then he turned, coming in through our utility room door.

"C'mon, we're waitin' on ya."

"Want a drink?" I asked, holding up what was left of the Sprite.

"Yeah, thanks." He grabbed it and guzzled the rest. "Okay, let's go" he said, setting the bottle down on the counter.

After everyone else had to go in for the night, Mick and I went inside my house to watch TV. The show *Name That Tune* was on. During the commercial break Mick got up and ran out the front door. I started wondering what he was doing and if he was coming back over. He quickly returned.

"Look at this!" he said, holding up a fake ice cube that had a plastic Black Widow spider inside. I started giggling as I followed him out back where our parents were, knowing what he had in mind. We sat outside on the back steps listening to our parents talk. When Mrs. Ceaver's glass started getting low, Mick asked if she needed a refill. She handed him her glass, telling him "Put this much rum in the Coke, please," holding her fingers to show the measurement. We headed into the kitchen. I watched as he put the fake ice cube in the bottom before making the drink.

We sat watching as she sipped. Sure enough her eyes went wide as she spotted the Black Widow in the bottom of her glass.

"Mick!" she yelled. "You know I hate it when you do that!" She started laughing. "Okay, very funny. Now get me another drink, hold the spiders."

Mick showed everyone the cube and everyone laughed, merrily full of mixed drinks. I started hoping we hadn't scared her too much.

"I do that sort of thing all the time," Mick reassured me.

Third Grade: A Setback

For my birthday celebration, my mom rented a cabana at the Officer's Beach. I invited all of my friends: Joanie, Morris, Janie, Krissy, Mick, James and Michael. Keith didn't come. His mom said he "didn't need to attend a little girl's birthday party." Keith's mom seemed to think that he was better than everybody else; so did Keith. Paul was always off doing his own thing, mostly hanging out with his own circle of friends from another street in George Town. Neana was too young to be hanging out with us.

It was fun riding the waves, building sandcastles, and just strolling along the shore collecting shells. After we had cake and ice cream, the wind started kicking up, blowing sand around. The clouds over the ocean became ominous, turning dark gray before rain came down in sheets. We were stuck under the cabana. As soon as the thunderstorm died down, we packed up and left.

Krissy's birthday was the day after mine, and because of the typical August rainstorms, we just stayed in her house for a traditional little girl's birthday party. Her cake was a pink-and-white dress made of white vanilla cake and frosting wrapped around an actual Barbie doll. Katie and Kelly had made it for her.

One week later, all of us kids gathered in the street after the mailman came. We were all anxious to see who our teachers would be for the upcoming school year. I opened my yellow envelope. The usual school supply list was enclosed. I couldn't quite locate my teacher's name on the funny-looking computer paper. There were several names listed. Morris looked at my assignment, showing me where the teacher's name was typed at the bottom.

"You g-g-got Mrs. Pierce. She's an old battle axe. I feel bad for y-y-you."

"Why do you say that?"

"I had her three years ago. She's really mean."

"Oh great," I said, feeling uneasy. Once again Michael Clark and I got different teachers. His teacher was a male teacher, whom we heard was a nice guy. Krissy's class would be right down the hall from mine. Everyone else would be going to middle school. I felt disappointed knowing I wouldn't see them as much. I thought about Randy and wished he was around.

It was hard getting up that first morning and putting on the school clothes my mom had laid out for me the night before. The familiar routine, rigid. I sleepily dragged myself to the kitchen table and stared at my bland bowl of oatmeal.

"Are you sure you don't want me to drive you to school on your first day?" my mom asked.

"No, I'll be fine. Krissy, Michael, and I are walking together."

Krissy and Michael stopped by my house and we headed down Crown Crescent, book bags and lunchboxes in tow.

As I passed by Mrs. Brown's classroom on the way to my new class, I could hear her telling the new students to sit wherever they like. I had memorized my new room number and found my class right away. I claimed a seat and plopped down. The teacher hadn't arrived yet. When Mrs. Pierce finally showed up, she closed the door behind her without smiling or speaking. She picked up a piece of chalk, writing her name across the blackboard and underlining it. She had short, curly gray hair and wore gold-colored horn-rimmed glasses over her cold gray eyes. *Steel eyes*, I thought. "Listen people! Put your school supplies in your desk except for *one* sheet of loose-leaf paper *and* a pencil. I hope you all followed directions and brought in the *number two* pencils I asked for on your list."

I did as I was instructed, determined to not have the problems I had had the previous year.

By the end of the first week of school, I was feeling a bit optimistic. We were going to learn *cursive* handwriting. Krissy and I had practiced writing cursive during the rainy August weeks. We had sat on the floor around her coffee table with Katie and Kelly helping us. They had an instruction manual on cursive handwriting that illustrated how to start at the top and swoop down with the letters. The capital D was my biggest challenge. Krissy and I got pretty good at it, and so I felt cursive would be an easy A for me.

Mrs. Pierce's assistant teacher, Ms. Terwilliger, who was a very friendly, pretty woman with long blond hair, announced "This year we're going to *travel the world*" one afternoon when we had returned from lunch. All of us kids looked at each other with big eyes, trying to picture such a radical field trip, even though we knew it wasn't literal. "Open up your minds and let your imagination carry you to discovering foreign places. Let your brains open up to lots of learning." She had our attention. "Monday, when we return to school, we will be going to England. But today we will make our passports, because you can't travel abroad without one."

Mrs. Pierce and Ms. Terwilliger started passing down black construction paper along the rows of desks. I had never heard of a passport, but figured it must be something like my mom's military ID card that she needed whenever we were on the naval base.

"Okay! Listen up people!" Mrs. Pierce said holding up a black piece of construction paper. "*Take* your paper and *fold* it this way *in half* and then again *this way*." She folded hers slowly for us to follow along, as if we were in kindergarten. At the end of the day, after our passports bore our names and had several white pieces of paper stapled inside them like a little book, Ms. Terwilliger went around collecting them from everybody.

Mrs. Pierce spoke over the bell that meant the school day had ended. "Don't forget your cursive handwriting practice papers for homework!"

Everybody was scurrying around gathering their book bags and lunchboxes to head out. I looked in my desk and found two different work sheets. I wasn't sure which one was the homework assignment. Most of the kids were already gone, along with Ms. Terwilliger who had bus duty.

"Mrs. Pierce?"

"Yes?"

"I can't remember which one of these was the one for homework." I held them up, showing her.

"Young lady, if you had paid attention, you would know the answer to that, now wouldn't you?"

I felt embarrassed. "I'm sorry."

"Now stand there and think about it."

I stood with my face burning red looking at the two identical papers.

"*Well?*" She asked.

"They look alike, it's confusing."

"One paper has a '1' at the top!" she snapped, snatching it out of my hand and pointing to it. "The '1' means classroom only! *What's the '2' for?*" she asked rhetorically.

"Homework," I said.

She handed me the "1" paper so I could put it back in my desk. I quickly left the room humiliated. *I sure did make her mad*, I thought. *I'll never ask her anything again so help me God.*

After finishing my "2" homework practice sheet of writing upper case As, Bs and Cs, I went over to Krissy's house.

"She's on her way to piano lessons, Junie" Katie told me.

Joanie and Morris weren't home, and neither were Janie or Michael. I headed home to play with my dolls in my room. I heard my dad come in through the front door and set his keys on the front table before heading into his bedroom room to change out of his uniform. It was the same routine Monday through Friday. He went into the den and put on the news. I decided to go into the den and sit in the lounge chair to watch the news with him. My mom would be starting dinner soon.

"President Ford had an attempt made on his life today by one of the disturbed disciples of Charles Manson," the newscaster announced. They showed men in suits running with worried looks across their faces trying to surround President Ford. "Lynette 'Squeaky' Fromme had a loaded gun, but it didn't shoot."

"Why was she going to shoot the president, Dad?"

"Shh, listen and you might find out something!"

I didn't really understand what they were saying on TV. Their vocabulary was bigger than mine. I didn't understand why some lady would try to shoot the president. *I don't think I like watching the news very much*, I thought to myself. *Always something bad.* I went back into my peaceful room to play in a better world. I pretended my queen doll was like Wonder Woman and no one could bring harm to her or my Barbies, whom she ruled over benevolently.

Autumn came, the leaves changing into their brilliant colors in the cool, crisp, smoky air. School was going okay, but I wasn't happy. I didn't really bond with any of the kids in class, except one girl named Robyn, who was hardly ever there. She was always out sick due to stomach flu or head colds. Morris was right; my teacher was an old battle axe. Ms. Terwilliger wasn't around on a daily basis, which was a letdown.

I did enjoy studying about foreign countries. During the first month of school, we studied England. We saw slides of England on the classroom's film projector. We had a guest speaker tell us about living in England. I liked her English accent, thinking it was pretty and wishing I could speak like that. Mrs. Smith told us about how England has a queen who lives in Buckingham Palace. I imagined bowing before the queen if I lived there, and how polite I would be. England was intriguing to me. I wondered why the English named their giant clock "Big Ben," imagining it being something like in the movie *Alice in Wonderland*, speaking to people passing by on the street in a loud booming voice.

After school, when I had finished my homework, I would pretend I lived in England, walking around in thick fog and speaking with an English accent. On one particular morning, it was unseasonably cold out. When my mom let the car run a while to warm up, I walked through the exhaust pouring from the back tail pipe pretending it was fog.

During dinner, I told my dad all about England. He had been there, among many other countries. One day he brought home English coins he had kept aboard ship. "These are called pence," he explained. "These are called pounds." He handed me a couple of their dollars that didn't look like dollars. "Why are they called pounds? They don't even weigh a pound!"

"That's just what the English call them."

I received extra credit on the final test about England. Ms. Terwilliger passed my coins and pounds around to show everybody in class. She stamped our passports after checking to make sure we had the correct information in them.

During the month of October, we studied Scotland. I wore the red-and-green plaid kilt my dad had brought home from his naval tour over there. The kilt was made of a scratchy material and made me itch. I was glad to get out of it at the end of the day. I did however wear it again for Halloween, dressing up as a Scottish girl.

My parents were proud of me when I got my first report card, which was straight A's. During the Christmas holidays, while we were out of school, I spent a lot of time at Janie's house. Krissy's family and Joanie's family were both out of town visiting relatives. Janie's formal living room was empty except for a piano. Their den had a simple couch and chair along with floor-to-ceiling book shelves. There was a small black-and-white TV in the corner. Janie's mom had been a full-time school teacher before switching to substituting, which gave her more time for her four children. Janie loved reading and forever had her nose in a book. I sat with her at her kitchen table one afternoon looking through books, both library books and books from their shelves. There were pictures of all kinds of arts and crafts and instructions on how to make them. Another book had cookie recipes for kids.

"Okay, I'm going to make these. Do you want to help?" Janie showed me a recipe for "stained glass cookies."

"Oh, that's cool," I said, wondering how to make the stained glass.

"We need to get different flavored Life Saver candies and break them up with a hammer," she explained as she dug through the kitchen pantry. "My mom said she was going to get me some at the store the other day. Here they are!"

Janie held up a plastic bag filled with individually wrapped Life Savers. She set them on the table. "Read the rest of the ingredients off to me." I started reading. Janie found each ingredient as I named it and set it on the table. I was proud of myself to be helping her make cookies. I was learning something I had never known how to do before, namely, to cook. Janie mixed the flour, sugar, and eggs with the electric mixer while I hammered the red Life Savers. We formed the dough into squares and put them on a cookie sheet covered with aluminum foil. We filled the middle of the squares with the Life Savers.

Ruth walked through the kitchen, grabbing dough to eat. Janie became frustrated when Ruth came in again to grab more dough out of the bowl.

"Stop, Ruth! You're wasting it!"

"I only got a little bit!" Ruth shouted back.

Ruth was older than Janie but was a bit immature. The sisters had only a slight resemblance, but did have the same straight black hair, pointy noses, and thin lips. Janie's hair wasn't long like Ruth's. They had opposite personalities. Ruth was interested in Tie-Dye, lava lamps, and Sonny and Cher. Janie was the practical one.

"Enough in there, you two!" We heard Mrs. Deen say from the other room.

Janie pulled the first tray of cookies out to cool and picked up the second batch. Jimmy and Tommy went racing through the kitchen, almost knocking the cookie sheet out of her hand.

"Mom!"

"Stop running through the house, boys," Mrs. Deen's voice came from the other room again. She still sounded calm and composed. I don't ever recall Mrs. Deen not being cool, calm, and composed.

"See Junie? Be glad you don't have brothers or sisters to worry about. You're so lucky. *I wish I were you.*"

I had never had someone tell me that before. What Janie didn't realize was that my home wasn't perfect. I wish I had brothers or sisters around to console me on bad days. I wasn't allowed to try to cook like Janie. I was scared of getting burned anyway. My mom sometimes asked me if I wanted to help her bake a cake or cookies, but she would expect me to already know how and get frustrated when I asked a question. *What do you mean where's the softened butter? You have to get it soft first! Do you want me to get Neana down here to show you how to do something so simple?* I would not only be discouraged but upset. *I hate cooking!* My dad would start yelling at me for back-talking, and then everything would become a fiasco. I would always end up getting a spanking when everything had started out normal. I lost interest and avoided the kitchen at my house. Janie's house was an easy place to be myself, without all of the attention being focused on me and what I couldn't do. Her home was casual with everyday furniture that we could set our feet on. We didn't have to take off our shoes or wear clean socks when I was at Janie's house like I had to at my house. The Deens' living room was a place to sprawl out on the floor to play board games or make crafts. My living room was a nice, elegant formal living room. But I did enjoy having pretend tea parties with my friends in it.

The next day, I went back to Janie's after she invited me over to help decorate their tree. All of us sat on the floor with a needle and string to put cranberries on. We made a string of popcorn as well. Mrs. Deen played Christmas music on the piano while we strung up the cranberry and popcorn garland. I felt like a part of their family.

As the New Year approached, the winter months grew dreary, and so did I. I hated this time of year, when my friends were busy with school or wrapped up in after-school activities. No one was ever home when I ran out my front door looking for someone to hang out with. Krissy was either at ballet or piano lessons, not getting home until well after dinner time, leaving us only the weekends to hang out. Michael Clark had Boy Scouts, so he stayed pretty active after school. Janie was taking acting classes, which was very time-consuming. With the cold, windy, gray days and Mrs. Pierce's ruthless ways, I began to lose all motivation. Mrs. Pierce showed no mercy. She was quick to insult us after assigning a week's worth of homework in one night. I felt isolated in class with Robyn constantly out sick and the other students not wanting me in their cliques. Mick and Morris played football, and when that season was over, they dove headfirst into baseball. Joanie was a cheerleader and played the clarinet in the middle school's band. I didn't want to be a Brownie again because it was so boring. I decided to hang out with Neana, playing with her dolls and stuffed animals. We watched *Sesame Street* on the dark green shag carpet in front of the TV while eating her mom's delicious homemade sugar cookies. Neana's face always lit up whenever I showed up at her house.

After another long, tedious day at school and a lonely walk home in the cold, I got home and took off my coat, hat, and boots before heading into the kitchen as usual to grab an afternoon snack. My mom came into the kitchen, telling me she had bad news.

"What?" I asked.

"Your daddy had a lung collapse today and had to go to the hospital."

I just stared at my mom, not fully understanding. I didn't want to ask if he was dead, so I asked if we could visit him instead.

"Yeah, as soon as you're done with your snack, we'll head over to the Portsmouth Hospital."

"What's a lung claps?" I asked my mom on the drive over.

"I'm not sure. He sounded fine on the phone though." I was relieved to hear my mom had talked to him already. I was beginning to picture him in a hospital bed, incoherent.

We found a parking spot right up front at the hospital. The naval hospital was huge—it was fifteen or sixteen stories high overlooking the Elizabeth River. Civilians who didn't know that it was a hospital often assumed it was a high-rise condo building. I followed my mom down a long corridor to the elevator. We got off on a much higher floor. The windows had a view of all the city lights as far as the eye could see now that the sun had gone down. I looked below while waiting for the nurse to bring my dad out to see us. I saw lights reflecting off the river below. Many tugboats and pilot boats were going by on the river, busy with their own missions.

When the nurse brought my dad out, he didn't look like I expected. He wasn't in a wheel chair. He was walking but pushing a machine that rolled along beside him. I noticed a tube going from the machine *into* his side.

"Can I have a hug?" he asked. I was unable to take my eyes off the tube in his side. *What would happen if it was pulled out?* I wondered. I was careful when I hugged him.

When we all sat down to talk, I asked him, "What is a lung clasp?"

He chuckled. "You mean a lung collapse."

"What's that?"

"My lungs just closed up and I couldn't breathe," he said matter-of-factly.

"Why?"

"I don't know. They're doing tests to find out what caused it."

"Will you have to live with that machine?"

"No. They'll take it out by the end of the week. It's just helping me get air right now."

I felt better knowing he was up walking and coherent. He didn't return home until a week later. When he had painted a table with Flecto trying to restore it for a new coffee table a couple of weeks back, the fumes had coated his lungs. My dad quit smoking after that.

My grades were declining. I was back to lying my way out of as many homework assignments as possible. The doldrums of winter were taking a toll on my spirit. I started getting more and more behind in class due to not studying at home. After another day of not bringing in a homework assignment, Mrs. Pierce stood by my desk and asked what my excuse was this time. All eyes were focused on me. I felt my face burning with embarrassment. I just hung my head and shrugged my shoulders. I felt helpless. I just didn't have it in me to do homework every day.

"What's your excuse?" Mrs. Pierce insisted.

"I don't know," I answered honestly.

"Get up!" Mrs. Pierce commanded, pulling me by my arm in front of the class. Some of the kids were snickering. "Now pick up the chalk and write fifty times '*I will do my homework.*'"

I turned and did as instructed. I was nervous and could feel the students' stares burning through me.

"This is an example of stupidity," Mrs. Pierce said with her sharp voice. The class became even quieter; they were intimidated too. I was relieved when the day ended. I purposely left my homework behind just to have the last word. As I walked home with Krissy, a couple of boys from class ran by us calling me "stupid girl," looking right at me.

"Why did they call you that?" Krissy asked.

I told her what happened in class.

"If my teacher treated me like that, I would tell my parents!"

"No, Krissy, I can't tell my parents. They will just say everything is my fault and I'll get into trouble."

"Why?"

"I don't know. They'll get mad at me."

Spring finally arrived which made walking to and from school a little more pleasant. My mom was combing my hair in the bathroom one morning before school. She was hurting my scalp, tugging, pulling, and scratching as if she wanted to yank my hair out. I had a chronic problem of getting knots and tangles in my fine, thin hair.

"Ouch!" I whined "Stop that hurts!"

My mom, ignoring my tears, picked up the pink ribbon that sat on the bathroom counter and tied my hair in a ponytail. My hair was too thin to hold the ribbon and it fell loose. Mom snatched the ribbon the rest of the way out along with some of my hair.

"Just forget it!"

I wasn't going to argue with that. "Why are you being so *mean*?" I asked feeling hurt and not just because of my scalp. I figured maybe she had had another fight with my dad, because she usually took it out on me afterward when they fought.

"Go to school!" she yelled, shoving me out of the bathroom.

No problem, I thought. *I'd rather be around Mrs. Pierce!*

"Oh by the way, your grandma *died* last night."

I picked up my book bag and lunch box with tears welling up in my eyes. *Should I stay home and take care of my mom? Should I be doing something?* I wondered.

"I'm sorry," I said through tears as I headed out the front door. I cried all the way to school as the realization sunk in about my grandma. The students were nicer to me than usual when they saw my red eyes. They could tell I had been crying and their sensitivity toward me made the day go by easier. Mrs. Pierce ignored me, of course.

I prayed that night that Grandma would look in on me from time to time. "I hope you'll have a nice garden up there, Grandma," I said, looking out my window at the night sky and seeing tiny stars shimmering. "Say hi to Randy for me." I felt better knowing I could talk to her any time I wanted now. I had to stay behind when my mom flew down for the funeral. I was glad that my mom had her brothers and sisters to console her. After school I stayed over at Krissy's house until my dad got home from work. Before school, my dad would get me up extra early so I could go to Krissy's and he could get to work.

My parents were upset when Mrs. Pierce told them only two weeks before school let out that she wasn't going to pass me into fourth grade. My dad became angry, asking why she never gave him any warning. I don't remember what her answer was, but I do remember my dad staying furious with her for many years afterward. When Krissy found out I wasn't going to pass, she looked at me with tears in her eyes.

Morris said "Damn, girl! I told you that teacher w-w-w-was an old battle axe." I didn't really care that I was going to be held back. I just wanted out of school.

When summer was finally upon us, I tried forgetting all about school, Mrs. Pierce, and overwhelming homework. I was thrilled to get back into long summer days of kickball, sleepovers, hide-and-seek games, and catching lightning bugs.

One afternoon while playing hide-and-seek; Michael Clark was chasing me, and was right at my heels. I ran toward my fence, springing up and catching the top of it. I threw my left leg up over the side and climbed over.

"Wow! You just jumped a six foot fence!" Michael said, standing on the other side. "How did you do that?"

"I don't know you just have to get a good running start."

Michael tried but never could make it over. He was a little too heavy. I was in good shape. I was always doing cartwheels, handsprings, or walking around on my hands. I remember climbing up the fence and holding onto the drain pipe that ran down the side of our house to pull myself up on the roof. The roof was an escape for me sometimes when my parents were arguing. I could ignore everything when I was on the roof.

As we woke early one morning to prepare for our summer trip down to Florida, I thought about Michael Clark and how he had said he was moving. The family would be moving out while we were on our vacation.

"Where are you moving to?" I had asked.

"I don't know exactly. I can't remember the name of the neighborhood. My mom said our new house will be a lot more affordable to live in."

"I hope you can come back and visit."

"I will."

"See ya," I said throwing up my hand and hurrying away before my sadness showed.

"See ya," he said, doing the same.

My dad drove while I rode in the back seat and my mom in the front seat of our Pontiac. It wasn't fun when my dad drove on long trips. He didn't like stopping at all. If I had to go to the bathroom, I had to hold it for a long time until *he* was ready to stop. He would become irritated when I announced I had to go to the bathroom.

"You're going to have to hold it until we need gas," he'd say.

When we finally arrived in Lake City, I felt excitement as we passed by palm trees, tropical plants, and flowers. We pulled up into the steep driveway of Aunt Nora and Uncle Rex's house. I loved their house because it was unique. The front yard had three steep rolling hills. I would get grass stains on my clothes from rolling down those hills, laughing until I reached the bottom. I would run back up and roll down again until I was dizzy.

The guest bedroom where my parents would be staying was in the back of the house. It was a large room with French doors leading onto a tropical patio surrounded by banana trees and fig trees. Aunt Nora used to make the best fig jam right from those trees. There was also a manmade waterfall leading down into a small creek made of concrete, the bottom of which was covered in moss. I loved playing in that creek with my Barbies. I'll never forget the feel of that green mossy bottom. I would run my hand over it, feeling how smooth it was. The water was icy cold. The bathroom was in the middle of the house, with a frosted window in the shower that looked through into another hallway. I stayed in the second guest bedroom, which faced the front yard and had a view of the lake. The large lake across the street from Aunt Nora's house was infested with alligators. I was told to stay away from it, but I didn't. While my parents played cards and drank rum and Cokes with my aunt and uncle, I ventured out in the hope of getting a glimpse of a gator. The dark green lake was lined all the way around by Spanish moss-covered trees. There was a neighborhood street that wrapped all the way around the lake, lined with beautiful Spanish colonial style homes. I stood as close to the edge as I could, staring into the water and looking for a gator. They looked so cute on TV, as if they were smiling. Mick told me once to run in a zig-zag pattern if one ever chased me. I was a fast runner, so I wasn't afraid. I saw several turtles, their heads popping up every now and then. Tall white cranes slowly walked along the water's edge looking for tiny fish. If an alligator wouldn't bother a crane, they wouldn't bother me. I took off my sandals and stepped into the water. The bottom felt mushy, not smooth and sandy like the beach.

Yuck. I stepped back out and put my sandals back on before crossing the street to my aunt's house. I felt disappointed.

Aunt Nora and Uncle Rex belonged to a golf resort club that had a nice swimming pool on the property. When everyone spent the afternoon golfing, I swam in the pool. There was a lifeguard on duty the whole time. At night we went to the resort's nightclub. It was picturesque, a white Spanish-style building next to a lake with a large fountain in the middle. At night, the fountain was illuminated with an array of colored lights. I drank Shirley Temples and played songs on the jukebox while my parents and aunt and uncle visited with friends of theirs in the lounge and drank cocktails. I played pinball in an arcade room next to the lounge with some other kids.

Florida was a nice getaway, helping me forget the disappointment of failing third grade and Michael moving. We didn't go by where my grandma had lived, so I didn't think about her too much except when I was outside. I remembered to wear sandals or shoes to avoid the fire ants that she had warned me about. I pictured her in Heaven, tending an amazing vegetable garden.

I would always remember Florida as the place for eating catfish, swamp cabbage, bright red garden tomatoes, and the juiciest oranges. Florida had the most brilliantly colored sunsets—pink, orange, and red–of any place I'd been. It had the liveliest night sounds of locust, frogs, and crickets. I loved how the evenings were hot and humid. The air smelled of sweet grass and tropical flowers. Floridians were the friendliest people, always smiling, laughing, and welcoming. I thought it was true what I had always heard: there's nothing like Southern hospitality. There was also no place like George Town East, no place like home.

We left after only a week's stay. Usually we would stay longer, visiting other relatives to go fishing in the Gulf of Mexico or boating through the Homosassa Springs. But my dad was anxious to get back because he had paid some neighbors to mow our lawn and feed Samantha. We needed to get back within the timeframe he had told them.

Humidity, Crickets, and Lightning Bugs

It was another hot evening in George Town. We had just finished a good game of kickball, and everybody had gone inside for the evening. As the lightning bugs started to appear, I decided to go for a ride around the block on my bike. It was just too nice of an evening to go inside. The crickets seemed to be singing a happy tune. The wind on my face felt refreshing as I pedaled all the way around onto another street. I passed by a home on a corner lot with a six-foot cedar fence like mine. I could see shadows dancing against the house from the lights in the pool. Whoever lived there was having a pool party. I wished I could join them. The sound of the diving board echoing followed by someone splashing especially made me envious. I wished I had a pool of my own. *How fun would that be? To have an in-ground pool, how terrific!* I thought as I stopped along the curb, watching the pool lights dancing on the brick house and surrounding pine trees. *I could invite everyone over to my very own pool parties. I could lay out all day and get a dark tan the way I've always wanted, if I only had a pool of my own.* The streetlights were on and had *been on*, which typically meant for me to head straight home. During the summer months my parents were a little more lenient about my curfew after getting to know the neighborhood and seeing it was a safe place. I did however have to be in my yard no later than 9:30. I slowly started circling around on my bike, enjoying the pool party sounds. Their radio was blasting out "Jackie Blue" by a band called Ozark Mountain. I started heading home, not sure of the time. As I turned the corner onto Crown Crescent, Mick turned the corner coming from the opposite direction. He was on his bike as well.

"Whatcha doin' out here riding your bike in the dark all by yourself?" he asked, surprised to see me.

"I'm ridin' around being bored."

"Being bored, huh? I *heard* that," he said, pulling up his handle bars and doing a wheelie. I tried doing the same. As we reached the front of our houses; I put my bike in my garage as Mick rode his across his lawn into his garage. I went inside to let my parents know I was home. To my surprise, I found Mick's parents at the kitchen table playing poker with mine. I smelled the familiar smell of rum and Coke and my mom's cigarette smoke filling the kitchen. Mr. Ceaver smoked Marlboros, and my mom smoked Salems at forty-eight cents a pack. My mom usually made special trips to the base to buy them because they were cheaper. I went out the front door and sat on the steps. Mick crossed the street into my yard.

"Are my parents over there?"

"Yeah, they're playing poker."

"Oh." He sat next to me. "I hate sitting around with nothing to do on such a nice night," he said.

"I know. It seems like everybody's out doin' somethin'." I heard splashing and laughter coming from out back. "C'mon Mick."

I jumped up and ran around back. Mick followed. I went over to the corner of my yard by my bedroom window and started climbing up the fence. I put my foot up on the drainpipe and pulled myself up on the roof.

"Damn, girl! Get down from there before you fall and break a leg or something!"

"C'mon. There's a great view from up here. I do this all the time," I said in a loud whisper so the people that were gathering around my neighbor's pool wouldn't take notice.

"Really?" Mick asked.

He jumped up on the slats of the fence and climbed up the drain pipe like I had done. We carefully walked up to the peak of the roof, which was easier to sit on than the slanted part.

"Wow, what a view! This is bad," Mick said. We had a panoramic view of my neighbor's backyard. Their pool was lit up with tables set all around. Some tables had red tablecloths, some were yellow, and all had plates of food and drinks. There were streamers taped along the edge of their roof and balloons were floating in the pool. It was lovely as well as festive. All the teenage girls were in bikinis—they all seemed to have long hair and nice tans. *I hope I look like they do when I'm a teenager,* I thought. The teenage boys were handsome, some in shorts and T-shirts, others in bathing suits. They were showing off by diving headfirst off the diving board. One guy went headfirst down the slide, trying to be silly.

"I always wanted to go down that slide." I said.

"Would be fun." Mick replied.

Some of the teens were standing around in groups, holding drinks and smoking. Every now and then they would burst out in laughter. Their radio was blasting out "Island Girl" by Elton John.

"Damn," Mick said, shaking his head. "Must be nice."

"Yeah," I agreed. Mick leaned back, crossing one leg over the other, and lit up a cigarette.

"Where did you get *that*?" I asked.

"My dad leaves them lying around all the time."

"That's gross," I said wondering how a ten-year-old boy could stand it. "Good. And if I ever catch you with one, I'll whip your ass," Mick said, pointing to me with the same hand he was holding the cigarette in.

I never understood why people who smoked would lecture me on not smoking. Morris did the same thing.

"Mick?" I heard a familiar voice calling from out front. It was James. We both turned looking down at him. He was standing in his driveway calling out for Mick.

"I'm up here!" Mick shouted down. James looked around bewildered.

"Up on my roof!" I shouted.

James looked up, and then walked over into my front yard. "How the hell did y'all get up there?"

"We climbed," I said in a matter-of-fact tone.

"Well, Mom called and said for you to come home," James told Mick.

"All right in a minute."

James turned to go back inside. It was getting late; the breeze was turning cooler. We climbed back down and went inside my house.

"Mick, where have you been?" Mrs. Ceaver asked.

"Just sitting outside."

"Well, it's getting late, so go on home."

I walked Mick to the front door.

"Hey, thanks for giving me a not-so-boring evening," Mick said.

"See ya."

"See ya," he said, nodding his head at me.

"Be careful up on that roof or I'll have to whip your ass," I heard him say as he went down the steps. I went to bed with my window open to listen to the festive pool party sounds.

I'll never forget Mrs. McNeil. On the first day of school, she made a special announcement to the class that I would make a good helper if any of the other students needed help with their class work. She knew it was my second time around in third grade. Her compassion put me back on track. I felt motivated to do well again.

She once pulled me aside and said, "Junie; every time you bring in a homework assignment *completed*, I will give you a certificate. By the end of the week, if you hand in all of your certificates; you'll be allowed to skip a homework assignment the following week, okay?"

"Okay," I agreed.

Mrs. McNeil was very sweet and soft-spoken. She had a warm, friendly smile, soft blue eyes, and short blond hair. I was never afraid to ask questions in her class. I never missed a homework assignment. She organized field trips for us, instead of making us sit in the classroom all the time. I loved our trip to the planetarium and took an interest in astronomy. We also took a charter bus north to Jamestown and Colonial Williamsburg. We walked through all the old huts in the Jamestown colony, which was the first English settlement in North America. We saw how glass was made back then. The Jamestown staff was dressed in the style of the early settlers, and spoke with English accents. When we went aboard a replica of the Mayflower, I couldn't believe such a tiny ship made it across the Atlantic! I had seen sailboats bigger than that! I wasn't afraid of the ocean waves, but the thought of being on that tiny ship getting tossed by massive swells was daunting. In the tourist shop, I bought a little rabbit skin with the money my mom had given me. *This will look good in my Barbies' living room*, I thought. I also bought rabbit's-feet key chains for Joanie, Janie, Krissy, Mick, and Morris. The imitation rabbit's feet were supposed to bring good luck.

During the long winter months, Mrs. McNeil made sure we stayed active in class. We read out loud from plays out of our textbooks. Some were funny and some were scary. Mrs. McNeil let us take off our shoes and stand on our desks while we read our lines. We spent other afternoons making costumes for the plays, and we borrowed tambourines and bells from the music class. There were days when the school bell rang that I didn't really want to go home. We had *fun* in class. Mrs. McNeil always brought in hot chocolate on cold mornings, and on Fridays, she let us pick out a piece of candy from a basket she held as she stood in the doorway while we exited the classroom.

When the weather grew milder, we made a trip to the Norfolk Zoo. Our homework assignment was to write a paper on our favorite animal. If all the spelling was correct, we would receive a Hershey's bar. My favorite animal was a tiger, but the one animal the zoo didn't have was a tiger. So I decided on the spider monkeys. They were absolutely hilarious, swinging by their tails and making a funny laughing sound.

The school year seemed to pass quickly, and before I knew it spring was upon us. I helped my mom dye Easter eggs the night before Easter. In the morning, I went with mom and the Ainsworths to church. When we returned, we had an Easter egg hunt in my backyard where my dad had hidden all the eggs. Morris, Joanie, and I searched competitively, running from one egg to another as we spotted them. When we grew bored of that, we sat on the back patio chairs exchanging jelly beans. We gave Joanie all the black licorice ones, and I got all the pink ones.

The air was still cool, but the sun felt warm. Daffodils and tulips were starting to bloom—they smelled amazing. Later in the day, Joanie and I went to Krissy's when she returned from church. Krissy's family attended the Mormon church. My family attended a Southern Baptist church. We played in Krissy's room, wearing long dresses that Katie and Kelly no longer wore. We put on lipstick, along with Krissy's mom's old high heels and wide-brimmed hats. Nothing was more fun than pretending to be grown-up rich women—Southern belles or English princesses. We danced clumsily to Shaun Cassidy's "Da Doo Ron Ron" in our heels. We laughed and giggled as we toppled into one another. When it was time to go, I helped Krissy pick up her room before heading out.

When I got home, I went into my room and sat at my desk. I started writing a one-page story, an extra credit homework assignment, about what we did over the Easter holiday. I wrote everything about the egg hunt and playing dress-up, but only could come up with a paragraph. So I put my pen down and decided to go watch TV. Simon, the Siamese kitten that we kept when Samantha had her last litter, was now a big, clumsy, silly cat. I would giggle whenever Samantha chased him down the hallway, because he wasn't agile enough to make the sharp turn at the end. "Bam!" I could hear his head smack into the wall. He never learned, silly old Simon. I'll never figure out how he managed to take hold of the toilet paper and string it all throughout the house. He had drug it all the way down the hall and around the corner into the living room. "Goofy old cat," we'd call him. He was either mischievous or stupid, or both. I decided during our Easter ham dinner that I would write the rest of my paper mostly about silly Simon and Samantha. The cats were entertainment for our family.

Mrs. McNeil liked my story and had me read it out loud in front of the class. The kids laughed along with my story, finding the cats entertaining as well.

On the last day of school, I was confident about the report card that would be coming in the mail a week later.

"Junie, have a wonderful summer and enjoy fourth grade; you'll do just fine," Mrs. McNeil told me with a wink as I headed out of the class.

"Have a nice summer," I told her. I couldn't have meant it more.

As Krissy and I walked home, I noticed she didn't seem very happy, considering it was the last day of school.

"Is everything all right?" I knew she had passed her grade; she was a straight-A student.

"Junie, I just found out last night that my dad is getting transferred. We're moving in only two weeks."

I felt shock and instant sadness. "No Krissy! Do you have to?"

"Yeah, we're moving to Oregon. My mom says it will be better than living here because we have lots of relatives there and the schools are supposed to be better."

I tried picturing the neighborhood without my first and best George Town friend, and couldn't do it. *I'm going to be so lost without Krissy.* "Will you promise to visit?" I asked, picturing her staying with me over the summer or during holidays.

"Yeah, I'll visit and we can become pen pals," Krissy said with a smile, which made me feel better too.

Krissy and I spent as much time together as possible over her last two weeks. I would spend the night over her house, or she would spend the night at mine. We would stay up half the night playing Barbies while talking. My mom brought Krissy, Joanie, Janie and I to the indoor pool on base one day, and to the beach on another day. Joanie, Janie, and I put together a shoebox with pictures we cut out of magazines, pictures of girls that reminded us of Krissy. We pasted them all over the shoebox like they had for me when I had my bicycle accident. We filled the box with Mad Lib notepads and a Wooly Willy toy to make faces on with the magnetic pen during the long drive across country. We put in pretty pink floral stationary with matching envelopes so she could write us. We added bubble gum and a small stuffed animal that looked like Samantha. Krissy always loved my cats. For her last day in George Town, I invited her over for dinner and a sleepover. She gave my mom a ceramic squirrel to hang on a tree or to set in the garden, and she gave me two of her Barbies that had long been among my favorites. She had to get up at 5:00 AM to get ready to head out. My mom woke her up.

I sat up, still half-asleep. "Good-bye, Krissy."

"Good-bye, Junie." We gave each other a hug. With tears in her eyes, she turned and walked out. I fell back to sleep knowing that when I awoke again; George Town would be short a good friend.

The latest craze in 1977 was the movie *Star Wars*. I loved space movies and other science fiction movies, but for some reason, the previews of *Star Wars* on TV didn't interest me. I loved *King Kong* but was sad in the end when King Kong was gunned down and fell off the Empire State Building to his death. My dad took me to see *The Black Hole*. We liked it enough to go back and see it a second time. Joanie and Morris went along with us. The big red evil robot was really scary, especially when he killed one of the space crew. I had to get up and leave during that scene. I waited in the bathroom until I thought it was over. When I finally did see *Star Wars* with Joanie and Morris, I ended up becoming quite the fan.

Mom enrolled me in Girl Scouts, which I enjoyed more than Brownies. We had weekly meetings in a small church like in Brownies, but we did a lot more. We put on costumes and staged the play *The Bremen Town Musicians*. We camped out in our troop leader's backyard, putting up tents and learning how to cook hot cakes on top of coffee cans after they were warmed over a campfire. We told ghost stories when night came, all of us sitting on our sleeping bags inside the biggest tent. We giggled while holding flashlights to make shadow puppets on the tent walls. Another weekend was spent with my mom driving me around to several neighborhoods to sell Girl Scout cookies. I ended up selling 220 boxes. When it came time to deliver them, my dad organized a specific time to pick them up at our house one Saturday morning. We had our big garage door open and set up tables for the boxes of cookies. My dad helped me hand the right amount of cookie boxes to each customer. I received an award for selling the most cookies, along with a badge. I didn't earn all of the Girl Scout badges, but did get quite a few. I memorized the Girl Scout pledge, and held up my right hand when I recited it.

Later that summer, I received my first letter from Krissy. I went out to check the mail early one morning. It was only 9:00 AM, but as I stood flipping through the envelopes by my mailbox, I could already feel the sun burning on my back. I was starting to sweat from the high humidity and went inside to read the letter from Krissy. My life had changed after Krissy left. Girl Scouts helped to keep my mind off the loss of my friend. Even though I never felt alone because I had the rest of the gang to hang out with, there was still a void. I felt kind of sorry for my mom, who lost two of her friends, Mrs. Coddle and Mrs. Donaldson, who had also moved away.

I sat down on my bed and opened Krissy's letter.

Dear Junie,

How is your summer going? We moved into our new house and it has an upstairs where my bedroom is. Dean lives close by and is married now. Katie will be starting college. We have pretty lakes here to swim in but they are really cold. I miss going to the beach with you. Say hi to everybody for me and write back!

Love,

Krissy

I wrote Krissy, back telling her about Girl Scouts. I told her about Joanie, Morris, and I watching the latest movies and that the Donaldsons moved back to Louisiana. I mentioned how I was hanging out with Neana, enjoying her company and teaching her how to play Jacks and how to draw using a Spirograph. I would visit with Neana for about an hour or so, playing with the Lite-Brite's glowing pegs or playing Operation, an electric board game. The buzzing sound, along with the man's red nose lighting up, would make Neana jump when we accidentally hit the sides with the tweezers. Pulling out the wishbone was always the hardest challenge. Paul was never home, always hanging around Sharon, a girl who lived in another cul-de-sac in George Town. I got used to not looking for him.

Joanie, Janie, and I continued playing our imaginary games inspired by TV shows. We were cowgirls for several days, right out of *Bonanza* or *Gunsmoke*. We decided not to play *Charlie's Angels* any more after Krissy left. We moved on to being bionic, imitating Jamie from *The Bionic Woman*, a spinoff of *The Six Million Dollar Man*. I imagined being able to run sixty miles per hour or lift cars above my head. It occurred to me why I had decided to take off real fast on my bike on that day I flipped over the handlebars: I was trying to go *sixty miles an hour*! I told my dad about my realization while I was stacking condiments, paper plates and napkins on a tray to carry over to the Ainsworth's house for a barbecue.

"I remember that. You mentioned something about it, and then all of a sudden started pedaling real fast," my dad told me. "What made you flip over the handlebars was when you looked back to see if I was watching. You turned the bars with you."

I still couldn't recall any of the accident.

Mr. Ainsworth had his charcoal grill ready for hamburgers and hot dogs. I never could decide which I liked better. I loved ketchup, mustard, onions, and relish on my hot dog with the bun toasted, and yet I loved a good old grilled hamburger with mayo, lettuce, and tomato. My stomach wasn't big enough to eat both, so I did the *eeny-meeny-miny-mo* thing in my head, pointing back and forth at a hamburger patty and a hot dog. My finger landed on the hamburger.

"You dork," Morris teased after watching me decide. "W-w-why don't y-you just eat b-both?"

"No way, José. I cant eat that much."

"Wimp."

"Wuss."

"Settle down, you two," our dads said at the same time. Morris and I could get into a brutal wrestling match easily, and they knew it. We never *really* fought, but we could give a good show of it, which made our moms nervous. I think Morris liked that I could roughhouse with him without crying or getting hurt. We had potato salad, baked beans, and potato chips as well. I was always taken aback as to how Morris; as skinny as he was, could gulp down two whole Cokes along with both a hamburger and a hotdog.

The evening ended as usual, with all of us playing kickball. Hide-and-seek was next on the agenda after the sun went down. After the guys left, Janie, Joanie, and I sat on my front porch.

"Let's have a campout," Janie suggested.

"Okay, I'll ask my mom," I said, hopping up. They followed me into the den, where my mom and dad were watching *The Lawrence Welk Show.*

"Well, I don't know," Mom said when I asked.

"Oh why not? They'll be okay," my dad told mom.

"Yeah, we have sleeping bags and we're fenced in," I said reassuringly.

"You have to check with Joanie's and Janie's mom," Mom said.

"We will," we all said as we headed out the door. Their moms approved after hearing that my parents did as well. We gathered sleeping bags and pillows and put them under the cluster of pine trees in the corner of my backyard. I brought my radio outside, and we twirled our batons, making up routines in hopes of putting on a show for our moms.

We had been taking baton lessons down at the local recreation center on Tuesday afternoons. We would walk home together, cutting through the junior high's field before crossing Providence Road in the same spot where Randy was killed. It was a somewhat long walk across the lawns of the George Town East homes that lined Providence Road.

As the night grew darker, we lay on our sleeping bags and looked up at the stars.

"There's the Big Dipper" I said, pointing up.

"Can you find the little one?" Janie asked.

We were looking for the Little Dipper when the pool lights came on, shining through the cracks of my fence. We heard someone jump off the diving board, making a loud splash.

"How's the water?" I heard a girl's voice ask.

"Not bad, it's pretty warm actually," came the response. I was jealous. How unfair to never invite us over. Not even once, not even on a sweltering day. There had been so many hot summer days spent in our backyard running through the sprinkler to cool off while they did laps in their pool. My dad refused to put a pool in. "No, it's too much damn work to keep up and much nicer having a green lawn," he would always say when my mom and I brought it up.

I got up off my sleeping bag to look through the cracks in our fence. Joanie and Janie quietly walked over to do the same.

"Shh," I whispered, holding my finger to my lips. I let out a slight giggle as I flung a rock over the fence. *Ker-plunk.*

"Hey, did you hear that?" one of the girls asked the other.

Joanie picked up a rock and threw it over. We were trying to muffle our laughs with our hands when Janie tossed a third rock. One of the girls got out of the pool, staring out into the dark, not knowing where the rocks were coming from.

"Hey! Whoever is doing that needs to stop!" she shouted. She was one of the pretty teenagers I had seen the night Mick and I sat on the roof. She was tall, thin, and tan, with long blond hair just like a Barbie. I wanted to throw a rock at her for it. I hated her for being pretty, because I wasn't. I flung another rock much bigger than the last one; it even made a splashing sound.

"Try to see where it's coming from," one of the teens said.

"I can't."

Joanie threw a large rock. *Splash.*

"Come on, let's just get out." They quickly got out of the pool and went back inside, turning off the pool lights behind them. We laughed so hard I almost couldn't catch my breath. We collapsed on our sleeping bags, hysterical with laughter. Later, when we heard nothing but the sound of crickets and were comfortably settled in our sleeping bags, we tried reciting the McDonald's Big Mac jingle.

"Two all-beef patties, special sauce with pickles ..."

"No, no, no. That's not it. Let's try again."

"Okay."

"Two all-beef patties, special sauce, lettuce, cheese, pickles, onions on a sesame seed bun!"

"Yaaay!" we shouted. "We got it right."

Joanie was the first one to fall asleep, as usual, followed by Janie. I stared up at the pine trees blowing in the breeze before finally dozing off.

We lived near two big amusement parks. One was about a forty-five minute drive north; the other was about a two-hour drive away. Even though Busch Gardens was closer, I chose Kings Dominion for my birthday. Kings Dominion was larger and had a lot more roller coasters. There were many, many rides to choose from *and* live shows. I was scared of roller coasters at the time, so I would only ride the small ones and then only if my friends went on with me. The big roller coaster called Rebel Yell was Morris' favorite. He was such a daredevil, always looking for the biggest, tallest, fastest, and scariest roller coaster to ride. He would ride it over and over. I was in awe when he rode the King Cobra, a coaster that went upside down.

Mr. Ainsworth drove us in their red station wagon.

"Since it's your tenth birthday Junie we will give you a small gift every ten miles," Mrs. Ainsworth said as we pulled onto the highway.

"Oh thanks." *That was really nice of them*, I thought. I couldn't imagine not having these people in my life. My mom, Morris, and I rode in the back seat, with Joanie and Janie in the far back. We were getting excited. We chatted about which ride we would get on first, and which ones were our favorites. I always tried to savor every moment when spending the day in fun places like Kings Dominion. It felt like being in another world, one full of magic.

"Is it okay if we all see the dolphin show first?" I asked, knowing everyone would probably agree, seeing as it was my birthday.

"When we get there, we'll get a program to see the showtime listings. That way, we can decide on how to see all of the shows throughout the day," Mrs. Ainsworth said. "Okay! We've hit our first ten-mile mark!" She brushed her long black bangs out of her eyes as she looked back at

Morris, giving him a go-ahead nod. Morris reached into a paper bag he had placed on the floor of the car that I hadn't noticed until now.

"Let me see," Mrs. Ainsworth said as Morris held up a gift. "Yeah, that's the right one."

Morris handed the present to me. I un-wrapped the tiny box.

"This is from all of us, Junie," Mrs. Ainsworth told me.

Mr. Ainsworth gave me a small smile as he glanced back at me briefly. He was the quietest man I had ever met, tall and very thin, unlike Mrs. Ainsworth who was of average height but overweight. I opened the little ring box. What I saw inside delighted me. It was a braided sterling silver ring with blue colors painted on top.

"Wow, thank you, guys!"

"Does it fit?" Morris asked.

"Yeah. See?" I said, holding my hand up to show everybody.

"It fits perfectly," my mom said, holding my hand to see.

"Let *us* see?" Joanie said. I turned ,reaching my hand in the back so they could get a look at it as well. Mrs. Ainsworth got together with Janie and me when it was Joanie's birthday, and we gave her the same kind of ring except it was painted pink on top. When we picked out one for Janie's birthday, we chose green on top.

"We picked it out because blue is your favorite color," Janie told me.

"It's very pretty," I told them, feeling special that they had put time and effort into picking out my ring. *I will always cherish it*, I thought.

My next gift was a stuffed tiger. "That's from me," Morris said proudly. "I know it's your favorite animal."

"It's from *me*, too!" Joanie argued.

"It's from *all* of us," Janie reminded them.

"Turn on the radio," Morris told his dad.

"Yeah, let's have some music," Mrs. Ainsworth said cheerfully.

Elevator music was playing, so Morris reached over the seat and changed it to a rock 'n' roll station. "Best of My Love" was playing by a band called the Emotions. Joanie, Janie, and I started singing along while dancing in our seats and snapping our fingers. "Oh-woo-oh, you've got the best of my love," we sang. My mom seemed to be enjoying herself, sitting there with a smile. My next gift was a homemade coupon that read "Good for one kite."

"Whenever you give it to us, we'll get you one." Mrs. Ainsworth said. I pictured spring arriving and all of us flying the kite out in the elementary school's field. I started remembering how my dad and Teddy's dad had bought kites when we lived in Norfolk. I couldn't believe how high they flew!

"Oh turn it up, Mom, I love this song," Joanie asked. "Play That Funky Music" by Wild Cherry was on. We started singing again. Throughout the rest of our journey to Kings Dominion, I received little coupons saying "Good for one Slurpee from the 7-Eleven" or "This coupon is good for a McDonald's cheeseburger." My mom tucked them inside her purse so I wouldn't lose them.

"Turn that song up again for me, I *love* that song!" Joanie said. "I'm In You" by Peter Frampton was playing.

"Look!" Janie said, pointing out the window.

We all spotted the Eiffel Tower, which meant we were getting closer. Kings Dominion had a mock Eiffel Tower that was really tall, though not as tall as the original in France, of course. After parking, we stretched our legs before heading in. Mrs. Ainsworth had us all gather around at the entrance.

"Now listen, I want us all to meet at the Eiffel Tower no later than 1:00 PM for lunch." She was good at organizing; she was a high-school English teacher. Morris headed off to do his own thing as usual. He would probably ride the Rebel Yell twenty times in a row. My mom and Mrs. Ainsworth walked around, looking in shops and seeing the shows.

As we each paid our admissions fee of $13 dollars to enter, I grabbed a brochure that opened up into a map of the whole park. We went over the showtime listings.

"Look, the dolphin show is listed at 10:00 AM, again at 1:00 PM, and 3:00 PM," Janie read out loud.

There were other shows too. One in particular called "The Age of Aquarius" was one of our favorites. It was a musical showing different times throughout history, ending in the future, which was my favorite part. They had psychedelic creatures walking around glowing under black lights. It was so cool.

Kings Dominion was beautifully landscaped. There was a garden with all kinds of flowers that featured a giant clock made of flowers. Each hour was a different blossom, and the hands in the middle kept accurate time. There was a long reflection pool with water fountains running down the middle. The reflection pool was at the foot of the Eiffel Tower. European-style shops lined the streets throughout Kings Dominion. First we all climbed the Eiffel Tower, standing on the observation deck looking out at the entire park and the trees beyond. Later we rode all kinds of rides that spun around. We drove 1920s-style cars that ran along a track. We laughed as we got splashed by the dolphins at the dolphin show. We became dizzy walking through the Scooby Doo house, which had slanted floors and dark, cave-like walls. There were scary sound effects of stormy winds blowing that came from speakers hidden in the walls. We met up with Mrs. Ainsworth and my mom at 1:00 PM, getting our hands stamped at the exit area so we wouldn't be charged again for re-entering the park. It was too expensive for all of us to eat at one of the park's restaurants, so we had made a picnic lunch. We saved our money for drinks and tourist trinkets. As usual, Mr. Ainsworth was asleep in the station wagon, which he had parked under a tree for shade. He would always drive us on any outing, but because he worked night shift as a manager in the local grocery store, he would spend his days sleeping. We sat under a nearby tree at a picnic table. We loaded our paper plates with cold fried chicken, baked beans, potato salad, and chips, and drank Coca-Colas. When we were ready to go back into the park, we decided to go to the safari section. Joanie's favorite animal was the elephant and Kings Dominion had an elephant ride. A real live elephant! They had camels too. It was odd getting up on the large basket-like seat to ride the elephant. The animal stood next to a platform, so we only had to step onto its back. An attendant dressed like a tribal African helped us board.

The amusement park took on a whole new life when night came. Multicolored lights appeared in the water fountains. Workers in the park walked around selling green glow-in-the-dark necklaces. We each bought one. We had never seen such a thing before. I sat watching the fountain lights change colors, listening to their cooling sound and waiting for Joanie and Janie. They were standing in line to buy ice cream. I didn't feel like eating anything. I just sat watching families walking around enjoying themselves. When Joanie and Janie had finished their ice cream cones, we decided to go look for Morris. It was getting on toward closing time, and we were supposed to regroup by 9:00 PM. As we hurriedly walked through the safari area, now lit by tiki torches, I could hear the sound of tribal drums being played. It made me feel wild and free. Morris was right where I knew I'd find him, on the latest attraction, the King Cobra, different from other coasters because it went *upside down*. Morris was on the ride. I watched him on the exciting loop through the ride.

When he got off, he asked me to come with him. "C'mon, ride it!"

"No way!"

"C'mon, wimp." He picked me up and carried me.

I tried to squirm away.

"C'mon. It's *fun*, I swear. It's not scary at all, I promise. I'll ride it with you."

"It's so scary."

"Just close your eyes when it goes upside down and you won't even realize it. Then the ride is over just like that."

"Just like that?"

"Y-y-yeah." He put me down.

"Okay but just this once. I'll kill you if I die on this thing."

Joanie and Janie stood back watching with wide eyes. Morris sat next to me. It took off really fast. I closed my eyes when we started heading toward the loop. *No turning back now*, I thought as I gritted my teeth. Morris was right; going upside-down was no big deal with my eyes closed . But going *backward upside-down* sure was different. It spooked me. I made it, though. I didn't die.

"S-s-see, that wasn't so scary, was it?"

"No." I wasn't sure if I could ride it again, though.

On our way out of the park, Morris exchanged a knowing look with Joanie and Janie. "Oh yeah, we forgot! We didn't spank the birthday girl."

He put me in a headlock and swatted me, with Joanie and Janie swatting as well and counting to ten. As we met up with our moms, I noticed some girls walking out with large paper flowers.

"Can we get one, Mom?" I asked.

"Yeah, can we get one?" Joanie asked Mrs. Ainsworth.

"Well, let's see how much they cost."

"The single-colored ones are $5 and the multi-colored ones are $10," the sales girl told us. I chose a blue one, Joanie chose a pink one, and Janie chose a green one.

On the drive home, I was tired from such a full day of fun. I closed my eyes and leaned on Morris' shoulder, while he leaned against the window. The radio announcer was saying something about Elvis Presley's death. I didn't know Elvis had died. I liked his version of "Shake, Rattle and Roll" and played it over and over on my little 45 player. They called him the "King of Rock 'n' Roll." I pictured having a doll of him to go with my queen doll. What an odd pairing that would be: the king of rock 'n' roll and the queen of my Barbies.

The next day I was appalled when my dad said "Good, the creep's dead." My dad hated rock 'n' roll music. He hated all music for that matter, except what was on Lawrence Welk's show.

My dad was a very opinionated person and was right most of the time about a vast majority of things. He was a genius; having phenomenal math skills. He probably could do calculus in his head without the need of pencil and paper. My dad could answer any question anybody had about anything. Lots of people turned to my dad with their questions. He wasn't very sociable though, in part because of his intelligence. He always had to have the final say in every conversation, which made him argumentative. But he was an honest person who never went back on his word. Friends and co-workers held him in high esteem.

During the Carter years, our den was an unpleasant place during the 5:00 PM news. My dad would scream and shout out all kinds of profanity at the TV, complaining about everything Carter said and did. I don't think I'll ever hear the phrase "son of a bitch" used as much as I did when Carter was president. I can still hear my dad now. He would say the president's name "Jimmy Car-ter" with disgust and sarcasm, emphasizing the "t." I didn't really care who was president when I was ten. The only thing I counted on was that the sun still set and rose in George Town and I had my friends, whom I considered brothers and sisters.

The J-Birds

The doorbell rang one afternoon while I was sitting at my desk, carefully holding my hand steady as I painted a clown on the paint-by-numbers set I received for my birthday. I got up after setting my small paintbrush in a glass of water I was using to rinse off the brush when changing colors.

"Hi, Joanie."

"Can you come out?"

"Sure."

"New neighbors moved into Krissy's old house today. I met the mom and she seems really nice. She has two daughters. One is only two and the other is only seven."

"Does the older girl seem nice?"

"I don't know yet. Her mom told me her name is Amy and she's over at the elementary school's summer camp right now if we want to walk down to meet her. Her mom said she has short, flaxen blond hair. We can't miss her."

"Sounds good. Let's go." I saw Joanie's light blue ten-speed bike parked in my driveway, so I went around back to grab my purple Schwinn. As we rode our bikes out of my driveway, I noticed the moving van parked in front of Krissy's old house. My heart sank a little. *What would we be doing today if she still lived there?* I wondered.

Down at the elementary school, there were a handful of kids sitting in the cafeteria playing board games. Amy's mom was right: Amy's bright flaxen blond hair stood out.

"Hi, Amy," we said as we sat next to her.

Amy looked up from her Etch A Sketch. She didn't say anything.

117

She just sat staring at the two of us, waiting for an explanation of who we were.

"I met your mom, Mrs. Barton, and she told me it was okay to come down to meet you. You're our new neighbor. I'm Joanie."

Amy still didn't say anything. She turned her head to look at me.

"I'm your neighbor too. I'm Junie."

"Hi," she said, quickly going back to her Etch A Sketch. Joanie could see that Amy was shy and still uncomfortable.

"We'll see you later, Amy."

"It was nice meeting you," I said.

"Bye," she said waving with her right hand before quickly looking back at her Etch A Sketch.

"She seemed even shyer than me," I told Joanie on the way back home.

"She'll talk more once she gets to know us and the others in the neighborhood."

"I should introduce her to Neana, they're the same age."

"Neana is seven now?"

"Yeah."

New neighbors were moving in everywhere. Not long after Amy moved in, new neighbors moved into the Donaldsons' old house as well as Michael Clark's. The Phelps moved into the Donaldsons'. Their son had black hair unlike his little sisters Katherine and Susan who had blond hair. They didn't resemble each other at all. Katherine was Neana and Amy's age, and they all befriended one another, usually playing with their dolls out back on the old swing set the Donaldson's left behind. Where there used to be Matchbox cars scattered on the lawn there were now baby dolls. The Phelps were quiet, staying to themselves a lot. They were very religious and judgmental as well. They ended their friendship with Neana after finding out she was Jewish. I had Neana come down to my house to play every so often. I didn't want my little friend feeling left out.

My mom always considered herself a Christian, but I'll never forget her saying though "At least I'm not a fanatic like *they* are," referring to the Phelps. My dad would drink his wine on the front porch on occasion just to annoy them. Amy's parents were a nice couple but didn't fit in because they were a generation or two younger than everybody else's parents. They were only in their twenties, leaving a lot of parents wondering what Mr. Barton did for a living to afford a George Town home. He wasn't a doctor or a teacher, and he wasn't in the military or a store owner. Mr. Barton was a handsome man who seemed friendly, but was also mysterious. He was hardly ever home, leaving Mrs. Barton alone to raise Amy and Jenny while being pregnant again. One day while we were sitting on her front porch playing with her paper dolls, I asked Amy what her daddy did for a living.

"He works in a small airport."

I never even knew that small airport existed until I rode with Amy and her mom one day to visit him for lunch.

When the elderly man that lived next door to us died, his wife moved out, quickly selling their house to another couple. The new couple was older but not quite retirement age. Mr. Shirrel became a favorite among the neighborhood kids. He was very friendly, always offering us a Coke or a Pepsi, or a ride around the block on his motorcycle. He was a motorcycle cop on the naval base and his wife held a high-ranking government job. Mr. Shirrel grew a vegetable garden in his backyard that rivaled my mom's. He was forever filling plastic bags full of huge bright red tomatoes and cucumbers for us. My most vivid memory of Mr. Shirrel was how he loved washing his red pickup truck on hot summer days. He would take his time, blissfully hosing it down while listening to country music on the little radio he had in his garage. His garage was his favorite hangout. He always had the garage doors open with a couple of lawn chairs set out and a fan blowing in the corner. He had a refrigerator stocked full of beer and sodas. It always took me by surprise when I would see him washing his truck not once but twice in one day. Any excuse to be outside.

George Town's first black family moved into Michael Clark's old house. They had two daughters, Pernell and Shirnell. The girls used to love brushing and putting barrettes or ribbons in our hair. Joanie, Janie, and I would sit on my front porch with Pernell and Shirnell sitting behind us pretending to be beauticians. I had my hair cut short into the Dorothy Hamill wedge, but they still enjoyed brushing it, which was nice. They made my stringy, fine hair pretty and shiny. My mom would politely ask them to head home and bring me inside. Being friends with black kids was an issue with most parents in the '70s.

While Neana, Pernell, and I were playing hopscotch in the cul-de-sac one day, we started discussing school. Summer was getting boring as it neared an end. We were ready for school, cooler weather and the new sitcoms that would be coming out.

"What grade will you be in?" Pernell asked.

"Fourth," I said, hopping on one foot then two on the hopscotch squares.

"Me too."

"Maybe we'll be in class together," I said. "Let me know when you get your school notice in the mail."

At the end of the week, when we all stood in the street going over who our teachers would be, I was disappointed to see Pernell and I had different teachers.

I liked my fourth grade teacher. She was young and kind of cool. She didn't put up with any attitude, although she did have a good sense of humor. Once when she left the class for a couple of minutes, she returned finding us out of our seats and chatting loudly. "Sit down now!" she screamed at us, her face turning red. Ms. Beagle was also really nice and caring. She would call us "Baby" if we did a good job on a class assignment or were well behaved, like remaining in our seats quietly when she left the room. Her left hand was deformed, so when she wrote on the chalkboard, she would have to swing her left arm up and hold it with her right arm.

"My hand developed this way when I was a little girl because I had polio. They didn't have polio shots when I was little," she explained. We enjoyed sitting at the lunch table with her, listening to her chat. One of the students asked her if she was married. When she said no, they asked her why.

"I don't want to get married, because my favorite dog is a beagle, just like my last name. I don't want to change my last name by getting married."

I wasn't sure if she was teasing or not, but there were other days she would talk about her two little dogs, both beagles.

At Halloween, my mom brought Janie, Joanie, and I to the Haunted Forest. I saw Ms. Beagle standing in the long line, laughing with ladies her age. It struck me odd to see a teacher having a life outside of school.

The Haunted Forest was something new to our area. Lots of volunteers set up various scary spots off the trails that wound through a thick forest. It was close by George Town, right off Military Highway. We had a guide take us through in groups of ten to fifteen. It was frightening hearing screams in the dark woods. At the first spot, a group of witches stood cackling while stirring what they called "Witches Brew" in a black cauldron. There was a spotlight shining down that had been wired up on a tree. Joanie clung to my mom and Janie and I clung to one another as we passed the six witches, all dressed in black robes with tall, pointy black hats. They cackled and pointed at us. "We'll get you, my pretty," One of them said, looking at me.

After visiting ghosts, goblins, vampires and mummies, we came to the end of the trail, where we saw one of my mom's biggest fears. There stood a six-foot-tall person dressed as the Grim Reaper. He was holding a sickle and not saying anything. We couldn't see his face because of the hooded robe he was wearing. My mom let out a loud scream, which scared Joanie so much she took off running. She ran straight out of the forest, not even looking back once. I had never seen her run that fast in my whole life.

Joanie, Janie, and I laughed about our Haunted Forest experience the next day while sitting on Janie's back patio. Amy listened intently as we explained it to her. It was a chilly autumn day. Amy and I decided to climb on the monkey bars. Janie called the set a "Jungle Gym."

"Watch this," I said. Standing at one end, I jumped out into the middle and grabbed the fifth bar down.

"That's cool," Amy said. She tried the same thing. But when she flew across, she missed the fifth bar and landed flat on her stomach, which knocked the wind out of her. We were surprised, and knew it must have hurt quite a bit. When Amy got up, she was bawling and holding her stomach.

"Let's walk her home," Janie said, holding Amy's arm. We all walked her home, explaining to her startled mom what had happened. We felt so bad as we headed back over to Janie's house. We sat on the floor in Janie's living room warming from the afternoon chill.

"Let's put together a get-well box," I suggested.

"*Great idea* Junie." Janie pulled out her arts-and-crafts box from the closet. We took an old but clean sock, some cardboard, and two buttons to make Amy a puppet. We folded construction paper in half, taking turns writing our best wishes on the card. When we brought it over to Amy, she was sitting up in bed, already feeling better.

"Hey," she said with a wide smile. "How come all three of your names begin with J?"

We all looked at one another.

"I had never really thought about that before." I said.

"Yeah, Amy, me either," Janie said.

"The three of you remind me of a special group of girls. They ought to call you the Dynamic Trio or something, or the three Nancy Drews."

How sweet of Amy to think of us as being special like that.

"Thanks, Amy." I said.

"We'll see you later. Get to feeling better so we can play again." Janie told her as we started heading out.

"Thanks," she said, still smiling.

On Saturday night, I invited Joanie and Janie over for dinner. My parents didn't mind their company; they were both well-behaved. We ate in our formal dining room, as it would fit all five of us, unlike the kitchen table. My dad talked about being transferred onto a new aircraft carrier called the *John F. Kennedy*. He spoke highly of Captain Tuttle. Tuttle is a name that will always remain in my memory. My dad said that there are future plans for the J.F.K. to be leaving for a seven-month deployment in the Mediterranean. I couldn't imagine going that long without my dad. *I would have to take care of my mom*, I thought.

It was nice having Joanie and Janie helping me clear the dinner table and wash the dishes. Everything got done a lot faster with the three of us pitching in together. After staying up late to watch *The Love Boat* followed by *Fantasy Island*, we went to my room, leaving the TV to my mom. My dad had already gone to bed. I turned on the radio. "The Hustle" was playing, one of our favorites. We took turns painting our nails candy-apple red. After our nails dried, we took turns putting on a baton-twirling show for each other to the song "That's the Way (I Like It)" by KC and the Sunshine Band. We danced "the bump" before switching to John Travolta dance moves when a Bee Gees song came on. The radio station played lots of Bee Gee songs in the '70s, with disco being all the craze. I hadn't met a girl who didn't think John Travolta was a hunk. There were lots of heartthrobs: Leif Garrett, David Cassidy, Shaun Cassidy, and my personal favorite, Donny Osmond. During the summer months we would practice disco dancing in Janie's backyard with Mick and Morris, who were both terrific dancers.

My mom came in to tell us to call it a night. It was getting late. I was getting sleepy. We turned off the radio and somehow managed to all fit in my double bed.

"We are a unique bunch, aren't we?" Janie said.

"Like sisters," Joanie said.

"Remember what Amy said about our names beginning with J?" I asked.

"Yeah, we should come up with a name for the three of us." Janie replied.

We tried coming up with different names.

"The Three Jays?" Joanie suggested.

"No. How about the Dynamic Jay-Os?" Janie added.

"The J-Birds," I said.

"I like that, Junie. What do you think, Joanie?"

"Yeah, that's good."

So it was official: we were now the J-Birds.

"We can make J-Bird membership cards." said Janie.

"I think we should come up with a J-Bird saying too, like the Girl Scouts have."

We fell asleep, first, Joanie, and then Janie, and then I. All of us had J-Bird Club ideas going through our silly little-girls-with-a-big-imagination heads.

Happy New Year 1978

My parents threw the best New Year's Eve parties. As usual, all of the neighbors were invited including some navy friends of my dad's from around Tidewater. Tidewater is what all the surrounding cities were called: Virginia Beach, Chesapeake, Norfolk, Portsmouth, and Newport News.

Our dining room table during the holidays was something I'll never forget. It was spread with hors d'oeuvres. My mom used her finest china to put out caviar and black and green olives. There were all sorts of cheeses arranged on a round glass platter along with Ritz, Town House and Champagne crackers. Janie, Joanie, and I helped my mom make shrimp dip with sour cream and a sprinkle of chives on top, along with an array of other creamy dips. We put them in white china bowls with silver scalloped spoons set next to them. In the living room and den, we J-Birds set out bowls filled with pretzels and a spicy cousin to Chex Mix called Doo Dads. We placed bowls of mixed nuts and pistachios on the foyer table along with mints.

My dad and I had gone to the package store on base the previous day to buy all the drinks needed for the party. I loved the smell of that store: fragrant fruits, wines, and whiskey. Shopping with my dad during the holidays will always be a special memory for me. My dad let me push the miniature shopping cart designed for bottles. He set in different varieties of rum, vodka, champagne, merlot, and white wine. He had to get a second cart for the beer and sodas. I picked out ginger ale, my favorite, along with other sodas.

"Don't eat all of those now," he teased as he put a couple of bottles of red and green maraschino cherries in the cart. I had gotten sick one year after eating an entire bottle of cherries. After loading the car, we walked down to the hot dog stand and got a couple of hot dogs, loaded with everything but sauerkraut. We stood eating under the awning as rain came down. When we were done, we dumped the wrappers in the trash can and headed home. I was glad to get back in the warm car on a cold, dismal, and gray day, however joyous New Year's would be.

We J-Birds hung a banner across the mantle reading *"Happy New Year 1978!"* Our excitement grew as we hung streamers and balloons throughout the house. We all were dressed in nice slacks with silk blouses. My dad wore a button-up shirt. As guests started to arrive, Joanie, Janie, and I greeted them at the door and took their coats to place on the guest room bed, just like my mom had instructed. If the guests brought a dish with them, we were to place it on the dining-room table with the hors d'oeuvres. By 10:30, the house was packed with guests. Joanie, Janie, and I enjoyed listening in on the adult conversations. They seemed to get livelier as we brought them more rum and Cokes in festive plastic cups. We made our own drinks: ginger ale with orange wedges and maraschino cherries. At the stroke of midnight, everyone shouted "Happy New Year!" and held up their champagne flutes to toast one another. My dad let us J-Birds have a glass of champagne. Smiles were on everyone's faces and laughter was in the air. I wondered why grown-ups got so excited over such a holiday. We didn't receive presents and only had the next day off from school, instead of a whole week. *Oh well, if everybody's happy, then I'm happy. Happiness does rub off,* I thought.

After the holidays, we started learning division at school. My dad made me a credit-card-sized times table chart, going up through the multiples of twelve. I could never remember all of them, which made it more difficult for me to understand division. "Keep that card with you and just try to memorize some of it. Then it will start to stick in your memory," My dad told me. He worked with me each day, giving me ten division problems. He would scream and holler at me, breaking my pencils before throwing them across my room in frustration because I just wasn't grasping it.

"How many times does four go into twenty-four?" he would ask, standing over me while I sat at my desk, loathing math.

"I don't know," I would reply. *As many times as it wants,* I thought.

Finally it clicked one afternoon, when he changed the way he worded the question. "What times what equals twenty four but cannot go over that number?"

"Oh. Why didn't you just say that before?" I asked, grasping the whole concept.

"That's what I've been trying to tell you!" he said, frustrated and relieved at the same time. I became so good at division after that, that Ms. Beagle had me help my classmates who were struggling with it. The weeks passed quickly, but the gloomy, drizzly weather was giving everybody the blues.

I woke one morning to get ready for school and sucked in my breath when I saw the snowflakes gently falling down outside. I watched in wonderment, looking at the blanket of snow on my back lawn. It sat in perfect little pieces on each pointed edge of our fence. *Snow is perfect, snow is pure*, I thought. There was well over a foot on the ground, which only meant one thing: no school! As I turned to go tell my mom, she came in, excitedly asking me if I'd seen the snow yet.

"Will there be any school today?"

"No. The radio already made the announcement that it would be closed today."

I quickly got dressed, putting on three pairs of socks, a T-shirt, and then a heavy sweater. I put on gloves, knee-high boots, and a red knitted cap. I tore out the front door and ran across my new lawn of snow. I stopped to look up at the white, feathery flakes. *Wow, it's so quiet*, I thought. Later Joanie, Janie, and I made a snowman. My mom snapped pictures of us trying to capture every minute of the rare Chesapeake snowfall. Mick, James, Morris, and Keith built a couple of walls in their front yard, using a cooler for a mold to make bricks. They hid behind the walls throwing hard-packed snowballs at one another. Their antics were amusing to watch, especially when Keith got pegged in the nose hard enough to cause a nosebleed.

My dad returned home from work at 5:30 as usual, complaining all throughout dinner about how east coast drivers couldn't drive in the snow. "Snow was normal where I grew up. We would get many, many feet every winter, and you had to learn how to drive in it." He had grown up in Washington State.

When night fell, I went back outside and walked down my street alone. I was in awe at how quiet George Town was with the muffling snow everywhere. Everything was bright out. I didn't need a flashlight or the streetlights to see, even though they were on. I could see flakes falling all around the streetlights. It was like being in another world.

We only had three snow days, and then the temperatures rose into the fifties again, melting everything and making the roads slushy and muddy. The days turned gray again, leaving Morris, Joanie, Janie, and I desperate to get out of the neighborhood and do something. We spent weekends walking around the mall or going to movies. Sometimes Morris and I would pair off in the mall, looking in record stores and buying little 45 records of the latest songs. Joanie and Janie were starting to become interested in wearing makeup. They bought blush, eye shadow, and lipstick. Makeup was something I couldn't fathom at the age of ten, but Joanie was thirteen now and Janie twelve.

My mom and I went to see the movie *Logan's Run*. I was enthralled by how futuristic the movie was. Farrah Fawcett starred in it. In the movie, everyone lived inside large domes. When they reached the age of thirty, they were exterminated. Logan and his girlfriend escaped, setting everyone free in the end after learning the world outside the domes was safe again. After seeing the movie, whenever I saw something modern-looking, I would say "Cool ... future!" This drove Joanie up a wall.

One afternoon, while Joanie and I were walking to the house of a friend of her's, she told me not to say ignorant things.

"Like what?" I asked, feeling a little perturbed.

"Like 'cool ... future,'" she said, imitating me.

I hadn't realized I had made such a habit of saying that.

We were going to Dana's house. I secretly called Dana "the slinky cat." Dana was actually very friendly.

She greeted us with a big smile, saying "Hey, y'all. Come on in now." Dana had a big family, three sisters and two brothers. They all seemed happy. The radio was blasting, as two sisters danced in the living room with some friends of theirs. Another sister, Donna, had some of her friends with her in the kitchen. They were baking cookies using chocolate chips and M&M's. I thought about Janie. She would like that recipe. I would have to tell her about it when she got home from acting class. The two brothers were with some of their friends out back swimming in the large in-ground pool, which was covered by a huge plastic dome to keep heat in. A couple of the guys were doing cannonballs off the diving board. I was envious of them. I wish I had a pool with a cover so I could swim in the wintertime. Their parents weren't home, and some of the girls were smoking pot. I hated the smell of pot. It was worse than the smell of cigarette smoke. I wondered what it would be like to have a big family like this, with friends over all the time, hanging out without parents. No one paid attention to the fact I was in their house and they'd never seen me before. Their den was completely modern, with a white sofa, an all-white shag carpet, glass tables, lava lamps, and a round Plexiglass hanging swing.

"Cool—" I started to say. But Joanie's glare reminded me not to embarrass her. There was the smell of incense in the air as well. Some of the teenage girls that were dancing and playing records in the living room invited me in. The living room didn't have any furniture; just a stereo with a black velvet painting of a bull on the wall. We danced to the song "Car Wash." I was relieved that I knew how to do the hand-clap part of the song. I think Joanie was relieved that I was fitting in and not embarrassing her by acting like a space geek.

Soon spring arrived, and the weather warmed up. It had become a tradition for Morris and Joanie and their parents to join my mom and I at church before heading back to our house for the Easter egg hunt.

On the last day of school in June, when it was hitting eighty-five degrees by 11:00 AM, we were happily anticipating summer vacation. Ms. Beagle, along with some of the other fourth-grade teachers, arranged for our classes to spend the day outside. The day began with relay races. I won a couple of the ribbons Ms. Beagle had made up for us for being the fastest runner. Later, we sat under the pine trees in the field to cool ourselves. The pine trees lined a clear, sandy-bottomed stream. We drank Kool-Aid from Dixie cups. After our break, our teachers had us gather in a circle to form kickball teams.

"Oh no," Ms. Beagle said, gazing across the field. We all looked and saw three rough-looking teenage boys lurking under the pine trees. I realized what the problem was. The teachers had left their purses under the pine trees.

"Hey, you! Stay away from there!" one of the other teachers yelled, pointing at the guys. One of them smiled real wide at her before grabbing a wallet from a purse. He ran off with his buddies following close behind. It was odd how all of us kids suddenly darted across the field to chase them. There must have been eighty fourth-graders chasing the three thieves. We screamed as we ran after them. The wallet was dropped as they jumped over the creek. The teens hopped a chain-link fence and disappeared behind a house.

"Get back here *now*!" we heard Ms. Beagle shout. No one could ignore that shout. We stopped running and waited for the teachers to catch up to us.

"Did they get your money?" a girl named Cindy asked.

"It's not the money I'm worried about, it's my credit cards. Nope, they didn't get anything, thank God!" The other teacher said while digging through her purse.

We were all scolded for chasing the boys.

"What would you have done when you caught up to one of them and they held a knife up to your throat?" Ms. Beagle asked, making us think. What *would* we have done?

I received all A's on my report card, which was a nice way to start off summer vacation.

"See, I knew you could do it," Joanie and Janie both told me when I showed them my report card.

Morris tickled my side when I showed him. "Oh, you're a l-l-little Miss Smarty Pants now, huh?"

That summer, Aunt Nora came to visit us in Virginia with her new husband, Elvin. My mom and I picked them up at the airport one hot, sticky summer afternoon. My dad was out to sea somewhere, perhaps down off the coast of Florida. He was only scheduled to be gone for a couple of weeks. The *JFK*'s plans for deployment to the Mediterranean hadn't been permanently made yet.

Uncle Elvin was one of the nicest, most easy-going gentle-man I had ever met. I didn't ask my Aunt Nora why she divorced her first husband. I didn't feel comfortable doing so. My mom told me later that they just stopped getting along.

We took them to the Fort Munroe historical museum right on the Chesapeake Bay. The fort contained an old prison. Edgar Allen Poe was held captive there at one time. People must have been really short back then, because we had to bend over to walk through the old stone corridors without bumping our heads. It reminded me of the time we went with the Ainsworths to Washington DC, where one of the museums displayed some of the dresses of First Ladies from history. *Martha Washington's inaugural ball gown was tiny enough to fit a small ten-year-old girl*, I thought.

Before Aunt Nora and Uncle Elvin boarded their plane to leave, she told me to go see the latest movie, called *Grease*. "I went to see it and it was the cutest movie. I know you and your friends will enjoy it," she said. I hated to see her go.

I cheered up when Mrs. Ainsworth invited my mom and I to go strawberry picking with them. Mrs. Ainsworth drove us in the red station wagon, the back filled with stacks of pails. Before we left, Joanie and I insisted that Janie come along with us.

"Mom, please bring all the J-Birds," Joanie had said.

"Okay, the J-Birds go strawberry picking. Sounds good to me," Mrs. Ainsworth agreed.

Joanie, Janie, and I each put on red floral shirts with blue jean cutoffs, trying to match our outfits. We spent several hours searching for the biggest strawberries we could find. Our faces and the back of our necks were getting sunburned. Our fingertips were turning pink from the strawberry juices. Once our pails were overflowing, we brought them up to be weighed on an old rickety table that the farmer and his wife had set up. There was an old-fashioned cashier's box next to the scales. Our moms paid the farmer as we washed our hands in a water spigot.

When we returned home, we washed the strawberries in the sink and my mom and Mrs. Ainsworth trimmed off the stems. We divided them equally. Later Janie called.

"Let's have a J-Bird sleepover tonight," I said.

"That sounds great. Have you called Joanie yet?"

"No, but I will."

"Whose house shall we stay at?"

"How about mine? We can camp out," I suggested. I was the only one with a fence around my backyard.

Later, before the sun had gone all the way down, we sat on my bedroom floor and cut little squares out of pink construction paper for J-Bird membership cards while my mom made us virgin strawberry daiquiris. We could hear the blender as we anticipated drinking icy-cold daiquiris.

It turned out to be a hot and humid night with stars shining and a bright moon. Later we sat Indian-style on our sleeping bags, sipping our daiquiris.

"Hey, did you know they're not home this week? They went out of town on vacation," Janie said, referring to my neighbors with the pool. We thought about going over and jumping in.

"I dare you," Joanie said to Janie.

"I will! I'm not scared," Janie answered back.

I got up. "Watch this." I climbed over the fence, walked over to the deep end of the pool, and dove in headfirst. The water was nice and cool, not too cold. I swam to the edge.

"I can't believe you just did that," Janie said laughing. I hadn't realized she had climbed over. "I can't climb the fence," Joanie said.

"Go around," I told her. Janie jumped in feet first, holding her nose.

"It's not *too* cold," she said when she surfaced.

As we swam around, Joanie made her way over to join us. She had to cut through the back yard of the neighbors that had apple trees all over their backyard before reaching the pool neighbor's yard. Sometimes we would pick the tiny green apples to eat during our campout sleepovers. We never saw anybody outside. It was always a mystery as to who lived there. We just called them the apple tree neighbors. Joanie sat on the edge of the pool with her good leg dangling into the water. She didn't want to take off her false leg in case someone came home and we had to run. Janie and I got out of the pool, dripping wet and completely cooled off. We walked the long way around back to my backyard.

"I don't want to stay in these wet clothes. Let's go in and change," Janie suggested.

When we woke up, the sun was beating down on us. It was going to be a hot day. We gathered up our sleeping bags, along with the soda bottles and empty bags of chips. The air-conditioned house felt refreshing. We were sunburned from the previous day's strawberry picking.

"Let's go see that new movie," I suggested.

"*Grease?*" Janie asked.

"Yeah."

"Okay, sounds good. But first I got to go home and get some things done."

After Joanie and Janie left, I helped my mom edge and sweep the grass after she was finished mowing. When I was done helping her, I got in the shower. For some reason, the song from the children's show *Zoom* kept playing in my head. It was annoying and wouldn't go away. "Come on and zoom-a-zoom-a-zoom." Neana and I would watch that show sometimes, along with *Sesame Street*, another show that annoyed me. Neana liked them, so I would watch them with her.

When I was done showering, I pulled out the large Fred Flintstone coloring book Aunt Nora had bought me when she was visiting. I pulled out a black crayon to sharpen in the back of the box. The phone rang and I jumped up to answer. I ran into my parent's bedroom and picked up the receiver.

"Hello?"

"Tell your momma we are all going to the 3:00 PM showing for *Grease*." Joanie told me.

"Okay. Did you ask Janie too?"

"Of course. Call me back if you can go."

"All right. Bye." I hung up and asked my mom if we could go, peeking my head in through the bathroom door as she was in the shower now.

"I don't care. Sounds good to me," she said. When my dad wasn't home, it was much easier to just get up and go without making rigid plans. I called Joanie back.

"Okay, we're going. Let's wear our matching pink T-shirts and jeans."

"Why jeans? It's hot out."

"Not in the theater. They keep it freezing in there."

"Oh yeah, that's right. Okay, see ya."

"See ya."

Grease was a pleasant surprise to all of us. We even went back and saw it a second time. Joanie, Janie, and I each bought the soundtrack album and memorized every song. I pictured my high school graduation being just like in the movie, with everyone singing and dancing at a carnival on Indian River's football field.

We were all obsessed with the movie's characters. Joanie told me "I think I'll be a goody-goody just like Sandy" one evening while we were waiting for Janie to come join us for a sleepover at Joanie's.

When Janie arrived, we put on the album in the den and elected Morris as the judge for our singing and dancing contest. I didn't like it when he laughed at me, saying I was the worst dancer he had ever seen. I jumped on him and wrestled him to the floor, not an uncommon occurrence. We would often punch each other in the arms or pinch each other, leaving real bruises. He would always win, pinning me on the ground and sitting on me, which left me unable to breathe. I would pinch him to get him off. We would go tumbling, sometimes knocking over a table or a lamp. It always ended up with us getting yelled at. Mrs. Ainsworth would always yell at Morris not to hurt me. We would tackle each other later out in the yard when nobody was looking. It was just fun for us, as harsh as it may have appeared.

The J-Birds were inseparable. We would have one of our moms take pictures at every opportunity, posing with our arms outstretched as if we were on a magazine cover. We made up little skits to act out, using our moms as an audience. We even handed them our homemade programs for *Starring the J-Birds*. They seemed amused. Our audience sat in lawn chairs in my backyard, and we used the patio as our stage. Other times we made up baton-twirling routines for a show. When my mom signed me up for gymnastics, my dad bought a piece of wood that was the size of an actual balance beam. I would show Joanie and Janie what I had learned in gym class, so we could have competitions in my backyard.

St. Matthew's

I kept hearing rumors about the middle school I was about to attend, how it was rough, full of students fighting all the time. Janie's brother Tommy, who was my age, didn't want to go to Sparrow Road Middle School because of what he had heard, which raised my skepticism.

"There are lots of fights there. The kids are pretty rough," Joanie had told me. Joanie was pretty tough herself. "The bus ride is loud with lots of fighting too."

One day Mrs. Deen invited my mom over for coffee. Mrs. Deen told my mom about a nice private school she was going to enroll Tommy in.

"It's a Catholic school, but it's not required to be Catholic to attend. The students wear uniforms, and are expected to take their Catholic religion class," Mrs. Deen explained as we sat around her kitchen table. Ruth and Janie were away at acting class. The boys were outside playing. I could hear them shouting as they kicked the soccer ball around. My mom was a Baptist, and that's how she had brought me up. As a result, she wasn't sure if St. Matthew's was right for me. I found other cultures and religions interesting, though. Even at the age of ten, I felt I had a mind of my own when it came to choosing beliefs. I thought about the time I had attended the Sunday service with Krissy at her Mormon church. I also went with Neana once to temple.

"We can take turns carpooling," Mrs. Deen mentioned. "I know two other ladies in George Town who would be willing to carpool as well. Their daughters go to St. Matthew's."

St. Matthew's. I wonder if it's a difficult school. I wonder if it's overly strict.

"I'll speak with Dennis about it and get back to you, Sylvia," my mom told Mrs. Deen.

We talked about it over dinner. My dad simply said "Go to the school and check it out. It may end up being a better way for Junie to get an education."

Mrs. Deen set up an appointment for the four of us to visit with the principal, Sister Christine. The school was only a twenty-minute drive from George Town. I liked the look of school when we pulled up. It had large windows in every classroom and a nice-sized playground. There were swings, unlike George Town Elementary. I was nervous about how strict the nuns would be, and so was Tommy. The school was small, having only two corridors. There was only one class of each grade from kindergarten up through eighth grade. There wasn't a gym, so physical education class was held in the cafeteria or outside in the field. They had a music class, but no band. Sister Christine was very stern, but nice enough. She didn't wear the black-and-white uniform nuns usually wore on TV. She had very short black hair and wore a plain pink dress that covered her arms and chest.

"If you're not a member of the Church, we do charge a monthly fee from the parents," Sister Christine informed us. "When classes attend Wednesday Mass, *all* of the students are expected to go."

"That's fine," my mom said. I was becoming more interested in going to the school after seeing how small it was. I liked Sister Christine's cool, calm demeanor. One of the corridors was really long and led down to the church. I thought the church was beautiful with its red carpeting and gold trimmings. All of the classrooms seemed like regular classrooms, except for the floor to ceiling windows that gave a view of a large grassy field and pine trees. I could see the nun's convent, a small, white building at the end of the field.

When we got home, we explained what we'd seen to my dad over dinner.

"They have an infirmary that I can volunteer to work in once a month. They have bingo nights once a month that we can attend," my mom explained.

"How much is the monthly fee?" my dad asked.

"It's $250 a month."

"Well, if it seems like Junie will get a better education, I think it's worth it."

So I would be going to a private school, sporting a white blouse and plaid skirt. We were to wear knee-high socks as well.

The end of summer vacation was upon us. I had a pleasant eleventh birthday party. There was no rain, and everyone invited showed up. All the girls wore pastel sun dresses, looking very pretty and festive. Everyone arrived was holding a gift wrapped in pink or yellow paper. Mick, Morris, and even Teddy came over, which made it even more fun. I hadn't seen Teddy Jeffries in over a year. We would get together for a movie or bowling every now and then. Teddy organized a croquet game in my backyard. Whenever someone hit my ball, he would walk over, pick up theirs, and toss it across the yard. He lit all the candles on my birthday cake, and everybody gathered around to sing "Happy Birthday." My mom had a blue Princess Anne phone installed in my bedroom. It seemed like all the other girls were getting phones installed in their rooms, which made it easier for me to talk my mom into letting me have one. She even painted my bedroom baby blue.

I felt sort of odd putting on my plaid skirt, knee-high socks, and white button-up blouse for school. I was glad I didn't have to walk to school anymore. Mrs. Deen volunteered to drive the carpool the first week. My mom would drive the second week. Tommy had on a button-up light blue shirt with dark blue slacks. The boys' uniform wasn't as dorky as the girls', I thought. We picked up Kim, who lived on Whitehaven, two streets down from ours. Kim walked out of her house wearing the same uniform as I. I tried picturing every girl in the whole school dressed exactly alike. Kim was very friendly and easy to talk to. She had black straight hair that came down to her shoulders. She wore black-rimmed glasses over her pale, freckled face and had blue eyes. Our next stop was in George Town Point. We picked up Tori, a seventh-grader.

"St. Matthew's is a nice school, Junie," she told me when I mentioned being a little nervous about attending a private school.

To my relief, my teacher was a super nice lady and not a nun. Her name was Mrs. Eubanks.

She instructed us all to stand up as Sister Christine's voice came over the loudspeaker. "Welcome, students, to a new year. We will start with the Pledge of Allegiance then the Our Father prayer." At the end of the prayer, everyone made the sign of the cross, starting with their hand on their forehead, and said "In the name of the father, son and holy spirit. Amen." That was new to me but I didn't mind. To my surprise, I enjoyed religion class. I found it sort of therapeutic. We would start class by standing in a circle around a table that had a candle. We lit the candle at the beginning of class and then blew it out at the end after saying the Our Father prayer.

Sister Alexenia, one of my all-time favorite teachers, told us "If you stare into the flame, it will make you feel warm and peaceful inside."

We had a spelling work book. We were to learn twenty-five words each week. Whenever a homework assignment wasn't handed in. We had to stay after school until it was done after calling our parents telling them they would have to pick us up late. It took some getting used to, but overall I was satisfied with St. Matthew's.

With Easter on the way, my mom had to make a lamb for a ceremony at school. Not a real lamb, just something edible that looked like a lamb. She ended up calling the school to see what exactly that entailed.

"Just a cake or Jell-O would do, just so as it's in the shape of a lamb," Sister Christine told her.

One of the nuns let my mom borrow a molding pan shaped like a lamb.

My mom came up with the idea of filling the mold with Rice Krispies treats. Mom and Mrs. Deen were our room mothers. Neither of them was Catholic, ironically. On Good Friday, the cafeteria was decorated with lavender streamers. The color had something to do with the holiday. The tables were covered with white tablecloths and a lamb centerpiece sitting on a platter. There were two lavender candles on each side of the centerpiece. The oldest girl in each class had to stand up, light the candles, and then read out loud a verse from the Bible that had been printed on a card. I was the oldest in my class, so I had to do this. I became nervous with all eyes on me. I lit the match and then the candles. I blew out the match but accidentally blew out the candles too, which meant I had to start all over again.

Unlike public schools we went to Wednesday Mass, and then were released from school at noon. I found myself enjoying Mass. I listened to Father Jim and knelt on the cushioned bench to pray. After Mass and religion class, I felt enlightened. Sister Alexenia had a great way of teaching us to behave maturely and take responsibility for our actions. She always praised us and pointed out when we behaved properly. When she brought in rosaries and sold them for a quarter, I decided to buy one. I bought a white one, reminding me of purity and peace like the snow. She taught us how to pray, holding one bead at a time while reciting the Hail Mary. "If you ever are having a bad day, carry the rosary in your pocket so you can grab hold of it. It will give you peace of mind, reminding you that Jesus is near."

Each night I held my rosary and said the Hail Mary and Our Father before falling asleep soundly.

I passed fifth grade, acing my final exam. I had memorized all fifty states and their capitals.

We got sad news: Janie's family would be moving. Her dad was getting transferred all the way to Germany. We held a special J-Bird going-away sleepover for Janie at my house. Joanie, Morris, Mick, and I sat out on my front porch with Janie. Periodically, one of us girls would start crying. Morris and Mick put their arms around us to console us. They were disappointed too.

"The neighborhood won't be the same without you silly J-Birds walking around, twirling your batons and dancing out in the front yard," Mick said.

Joanie, Janie, and I burst into tears again.

Janie's house stood empty and silent. Joanie and I felt like a part of us was gone. We tried keeping things the same by having sleepovers, going to the beach, and riding bikes, but it wasn't the same without all three of us. We wrote dozens of letters back and forth, always signing *Love from J-Bird Junie* or *J-Bird Joanie*. I began inviting Neana for sleepovers more often. I taught her how to ride a two-wheel bike and to twirl a baton. Neana was a happy-go-lucky girl, laughing at almost anything. She had a different view of the world which enlightened me. She would get me to laugh at the little things. I enjoyed sitting with her in her kitchen when the temperatures were soaring outside. We would drink cherry Kool-Aid and eat potato chips, laughing hysterically until Kool-Aid came out of our noses, causing us to laugh even harder. Now that she could ride a two-wheel bike, she would ride up to the elementary school playground with me. We would sit on top of the monkey bars drinking the grape Shasta sodas we stole from her mom's pantry. Neana was only eight when I was eleven. She viewed me as an older sister, asking me questions as a younger sister would. Every time I would explain something, she would ask me "Why?" No matter what it was I said, she would ask "Why?"

"I'm tired today."

"Why?"

"I just didn't sleep well last night."

"Why?"

"I don't know why!"

"Why?"

"Shut up!"

"Why?"

Eventually I would end up laughing at her, and then she would start laughing just because I was, which would make me laugh even harder, making her laugh even harder. It was nice not being the youngest in the bunch for a change, having someone look up to me. I started going to sleepovers at her house, which was fun because we would get the den and the TV to ourselves. We would pull out the sofa bed and stay up late watching *Saturday Night Live*, which we weren't supposed to watch. Her mom felt it was an inappropriate show, but we watched it anyway. I would chuckle in the morning when I woke up and Neana was exercising in front of the TV to *The Richard Simmons Show*. Paul would stand in the doorway laughing at us as we danced along to *American Bandstand*. Saturday mornings weren't complete without Dick Clark. We would watch *Soul Train* before heading outside to play. Everyone listened to Casey Kasem's syndicated radio show. With neighbors out washing their cars and doing yard work on Saturday afternoons, Casey Kasem's voice echoed throughout George Town from radios in every other garage, it seemed. I always found his voice soothing. He read letters from listeners with such sincerity.

I hugged my dad good-bye at Pier Twelve as he boarded ship.

"I'll send postcards from each port," he told me before he hugged my mom. After that, he headed up the gangway.

Even though my mom had lots of help from the neighbors, I felt

I needed to look after her. I was proud of her when we got snow later, as she actually chopped firewood, swinging an axe over her head and splitting a log. She made a roaring fire in our fireplace that we toasted marshmallows over. After saving money from previous garage sales she'd held, she had a brand-new white carpet professionally installed in the master bedroom along, with new curtains and a bedspread. One day, while I was at school, she had a beautiful blue carpet installed in my room. If I ran my hand over the blue carpet, it would briefly appear to have a silver tone. I really appreciated my mom having carpet put in my room, along with the heavy blue velvet drapes. Mom also bought an expensive dark blue velvet bedspread for my bed, which transformed my room, making me take pride in it for the first time. I always tried to keep it clean and tidy. She would okay things with my dad on the phone before doing anything to the house. Eventually, she talked him into letting her have the rest of the house re-carpeted. She had the ugly, worn-down Dutch blue carpet put in the room over the garage. Every other week my dad sent me a postcard from a different country. My favorite one was from Spain. It had a Spanish dancer on it, with actual material glued on as her skirt. On every postcard he wrote "Make Mama quit smoking." Eventually she did. She quit cold turkey, another reason to be proud of her.

The Normans

The Normans moved in. Their arrival changed everyone's lives. It took away a little of our innocence.

I woke up one morning and rolled over in bed, looking up out my window at the white fluffy clouds flowing slowly across the light blue sky. The tree on the side of our house was blowing in the wind, its light green leaves dancing. My mom had rearranged my room again, putting the head of my bed against the back wall. If I lay on my left side, I could see down the hall if my door wasn't shut. I mostly kept it shut, for privacy and to drown out noises from the rest of the house.

I noticed some movement going on in Janie's old backyard. I could see through the white sheers hanging from my window. I sat on the edge of my bed and pulled the curtain a bit to the side to see who was moving around. *Wouldn't it be nice if Janie's family moved back in?* I thought, knowing that wasn't possible. As I peered out, I saw a girl about my age with lots of frizzy blond hair blowing in the wind. She walked up the back steps and went inside. There was an older girl sitting on the wooden picnic table that the Deens had left behind. Two blond-haired boys were sitting across from her. Their hair was kind of long, and I could see how skinny they were. They were wearing only cutoff blue jean shorts. They were eating Popsicles. One of the boys finished his and threw the white wrapper along with the stick in the yard. He then started licking it off his fingers where the Popsicle had dripped. *Disgusting*, I thought. I quickly moved away from the curtain, hoping they didn't see me.

I picked up my phone and called Joanie.

"Hello," She answered. I could tell I had woke her up.

"Joanie, I'm looking at our new neighbors."

"Huh?"

"Yeah, they're sitting on Janie's old picnic table."

"What do they look like?"

"It looks like there's a girl about your age with long brown hair, a girl my age, and two younger boys."

"Maybe we should go over and meet them later."

"Okay," I said. "Come over after you get up."

"I will." She hung up and probably fell back asleep.

I went into the kitchen and poured some Captain Crunch into a bowl and added milk. My mom was still sleeping. With my dad gone, she would sleep in pretty late sometimes. I liked having the house to myself. I took my bowl of cereal and sat on the floor in front of the TV. *Match Game* was on, a game show I wasn't always good at playing. But I enjoyed watching the celebrities laughing and joking around. They must have had so much fun. After pouring another bowl of cereal, I changed the channel to watch *Land of the Lost*. We only had three different channels: NBC, ABC, and CBS. The Sleestak monster on that show always spooked me, so I was glad when I heard my mom coming down the hall.

"Good morning," she said. I was happy to see she was in a good mood.

"I saw the new neighbors this morning" I told her as she went into the kitchen to make coffee. "Joanie and I are going to go over to meet them later."

"Let them get settled in first. We don't want to bother them while they're moving in." My mom usually brought over a plant with a welcome card when someone moved in. I pictured us doing that in a day or so after they were settled.

"Let's go to the beach today, Mom. It's sunny out," I suggested.

"That sounds good, but first let me put on a load of laundry."

"Can Joanie come?"

"I don't care." I jumped up to call Joanie.

"Hello?" she answered. I could tell I had woke her up again.

"Let's go to the beach. My mom is taking us!"

"Okay. I thought you said we had new neighbors?"

"We do, but my mom wants to let them settle in before we go over to meet them."

"Oh, okay." I could tell she was more awake now.

"Ask your mom if you can go with us, okay?" I said.

"I will. Just let me get up."

"See ya."

"See ya."

On the way to the beach, the radio announcer spoke about Jimmy Carter inheriting an economic mess that he couldn't clean up because of ever-rising oil prices.

"That's why we have to spend so long waiting in line at the gas station," my mom said.

I hated waiting, stuck in the pick-up truck sweating because it didn't have an air conditioner. Seeing the long line of cars ahead of us only made it worse. There was a Burger King next to the gas station that we would go to before getting gas. My mom bought us the latest-cartoon character glass filled with Pepsi. The Pepsi was cooling while waiting in the gas line. Joanie and I sipped on our straws looking at the new Pepé Le Pew cartoon skunks on our new glasses.

"I want to get the Bugs Bunny one next," I said while my mom was pumping gas.

"Me too. And the Tweety Bird," Joanie said while sipping through her straw. My mom preferred driving the pick-up to the beach, so as to avoid getting sand all over the inside of our gold Pontiac.

On the route we normally took to Fort Story Beach, there was traffic piled up for miles ahead of us due to a car wreck. We decided to take the nearest exit and head to Virginia Beach instead. A storm had passed through a couple of days before, making the waves much larger than usual. Joanie and I jumped up trying to ride the waves, but they were too big.

"You'll have to dive under them!" I shouted to Joanie as a wall of a wave came toward us. I dove through it, feeling the water get colder as I passed through. On the other side of the wave, I found myself in mid-air, falling to the base of the next wave, which tossed me like a rag doll. I couldn't believe how strong the water was! I tried swimming to the top, but another wave crashed down on me, tossing me all around. I was a little scared not knowing which way was up or down. I had to get up, I had to get air! I had been underwater for quite some time and was running out of oxygen. I started to panic, feeling weak. I kicked and moved my hands and arms to paddle up. Dog-paddling was how I first learned to keep myself above water in the deep end of the pool when I was a small girl. Somehow this baby step in swimming helped me reach the surface. As soon as I reached the surface, I gasped for air. I felt so tiny in the midst of it all. Right as I breathed in, another enormous wave crashed down on me, tossing me like a sock in the drum of a dryer. *This is it*, I thought. *I'm going to drown.* I let myself go limp as a wave sucked me out. I felt relaxed after I quit fighting the waves. *It's only water, Junie, think!* I felt the bottom. The sand was cool. I put my feet on the floor of the ocean and pushed off with all my might. I hoped I wouldn't gasp for air before reaching the surface. My body forced me to blow out some air which helped a little. I looked up toward the surface of the water. I could see the sun and the silhouette of a surfer sitting on his surfboard. I made it to the surface and breathed in hard. Air had never been so welcome to my lungs. I put my hands on the surfboard.

"Take me in, I can't make it!"

The guy looked shocked to see me. He helped me up on the board after he rolled off into the water.

"Hold on!" he said, pulling the board with me on it. "When the waves start getting rough, just keep paddling with your hands. The wave will take you to shore!"

I did as he instructed. I ended up right on shore with rough white water rushing madly all around me. As the water receded and pulled me back, I abandoned the board, crawling on all fours to the dry sand. Joanie sat up on shore and stared at me.

"Where did you get the board?" She saw the surfer. He picked up his board and jogged over to us.

"Hey, are you okay?"

"Yeah, *thanks*. You saved my life out there," I said, out of breath.

"You shouldn't be out there with the water this rough. Stay on shore!" He ordered before turning with his surfboard and running back out into the waves.

"After that first wave, I crawled up on shore and wasn't able to see you," Joanie said, sounding worried.

"I know." I was still trying to catch my breath as I plopped down next to Joanie in the sand. "The waves kept pounding me down." I swallowed hard. "I would have drowned if it wasn't for him."

Joanie was looking at me with concern. "Are you all right?"

"Yeah, I'm fine now. I just wanna learn to surf."

As we trudged back toward my mom; Joanie held my arm and hopped along by my side. She had to take off her wooden leg before going into the water. My mom was sunbathing, oblivious to everything that had happened. Obviously the lifeguards hadn't noticed either, which gave me an uneasy feeling. I didn't want to tell my mom, and asked Joanie not to say anything either. My mom would only panic.

When we got home, I checked the mail after Joanie headed back to her house. I had two postcards from my dad, one from Valencia and one from Barcelona. Sometimes I would receive two or three post cards at the same time. They all had interesting pictures on them. I liked the one with the bull fighter and the one with the Spanish dancer the most. I received several postcards with pictures of pretty ostentatious-looking cathedrals. I couldn't imagine going to church in such a building.

"Did you see the trash moving in next door?" my mom asked when I was finished with my shower.

"What do you mean?" I asked, guessing she had seen something. The kids I saw this morning weren't very clean looking, and they didn't seem to have the best manners in the world either.

"Look out your bedroom window," Mom said. She followed me down the hall. There was an old beat-up pickup truck parked in Janie's old driveway. The truck's rear was filled with pee-stained mattresses and old, worn-out tables and chairs. I saw a man with an afro and a shaggy beard. He was somewhat muscular and wearing nothing but cutoff blue jean shorts. He was carrying in a worn-out-looking couch with an older fat man, also shirtless, helping him.

"Maybe they're really nice, Mom," I said, feeling kind of sorry for them because they looked dirty and poor.

"I hope they are. We didn't save all our money to move into a nice neighborhood to live next door to hillbilly trash."

The phone rang and my mom answered. I could tell from her conversation she was talking with Mrs. Ainsworth. When she got off the phone, she told me to not go over to the new neighbors until her and Mrs. Ainsworth had gone to meet them first.

The next morning I woke up and headed to the kitchen still in my pajamas. I poured myself a bowl of cereal before sitting in front of the

TV. As I pressed my Captain Crunch to the roof of my mouth, trying to suck the milk out of it, I watched *The Pink Panther* and then *Looney Tunes*, featuring Sylvester the cat trying to outwit Tweety Bird. Joanie and I had already collected the Sylvester Pepsi glass. I remembered her saying she wanted the Tweety Bird one. My mom was still asleep, and I didn't feel like waiting for her to get up. When I finished with breakfast and my morning cartoon shows, I decided to go ahead and get dressed.

Soon I was getting my feet wet from the early morning dew of the yard. I pulled my bike out from the green tin shed my dad had put up some time ago. I unlocked the gate and headed out onto the street. As I passed by the so-called hillbilly neighbors' house, I noticed their garage door was up.

"Shut up, you fuckin' pussy!" I heard before I even saw the youngest blond-haired boy crossing the garage. I turned my head back toward the road ahead of me, hoping he didn't see me looking. I wondered what he was so mad about. *Who was he cursing at? Would he get into trouble?*

I continued riding around the neighborhood, breathing in the sweet smell of freshly mowed lawns. It was going to be another great day for the beach, but after getting tossed in the waves, I didn't feel like going back to the beach yet. I thought it would be awesome though if I could learn to surf, but until then I was going to stay on land, at least for a while.

When I got back to my house after my ride around the block, I put my bike back in the shed and went inside to pour a glass of tea. My mom was up and dressed. I was pleased when she asked me if I would like to go with her and Mrs. Ainsworth to meet the new neighbors. She had bought an aloe Vera plant and a small greeting card as welcome gifts. As we crossed our lawn, I saw Mrs. Ainsworth and Joanie crossing their lawn as well. Mrs. Ainsworth was carrying a plate full of brownies. We walked up the steps together and I rang the doorbell. A large lady opened the door. She had big blue eyes and short, thick blond hair. She was clearly pregnant.

"Hi," she said.

"I'm Mrs. Ainsworth and this is my daughter Joanie, my friend Audie, and her daughter Junie."

"Hi" I said. She didn't invite us in, instead just standing in the doorway smiling. I don't recall what she said her first name was, but I caught the last name *Norman*. Her oldest daughter appeared from behind her, smiling.

"Tanya, go get everybody."

So Tanya was her name. Her mom pronounced it "Tann-ya." The other three siblings that I had seen the other day came to the door, crowding out onto the porch with us.

"This here's my oldest chile, Tanya Sue, and that's Johnny Ray, that's Marsha Lyn, and the baby there is Benny." Mrs. Norman pointed to each one as she introduced them. They all had wide eyes and seemed absolutely thrilled to be meeting us.

"Well, we don't want to keep you from anything. It was nice to have met you. Here is a welcome-to-our-neighborhood plant for you and your family," my mom said, handing her the plant with the card tucked into it. Mrs. Ainsworth handed her the plate of brownies.

"Much obliged," Mrs. Norman said. I thought it was odd how she never mentioned her husband.

Over the next few weeks, the Norman kids were eager to get to know us. Every morning they would come over, ringing the doorbell until someone answered. My mom had to tell them more than once to please only ring the bell once, and that we would get to the door if we were home. I didn't understand at first how a family with four children and one on the way didn't have any bicycles, soccer balls, skates, or tennis rackets. It didn't take me long to figure out they were indeed dirt poor, and the state was paying for their housing. The neighbors didn't like them, but tolerated them.

Marsha Lyn liked to be called Marsh. Marsh was my age, which was nice. I was so used to my friends being three years older than me or three years younger. Marsh was very friendly, but overly compliant. She would do whatever I wanted without ever making suggestions of her own. When I let her borrow my mom's bike so we could ride around the neighborhood together, one would have thought I gave her a million bucks. She had her long, frizzy hair cut short after seeing that I had my hair cut short. Marsh appeared impressed about everything I had in my room, as well as my bikes and clothes. It helped me appreciate everything I had after seeing the inside of the Normans' house. They had lawn chairs for furniture in the den, along with an old couch with tears and holes in it. In each of their bedrooms they had a mattress on the floor for a bed. Mrs. Norman always sat in her rocking chair in front of a fan like she was dying from heat. *Why didn't they just turn on their air conditioner?* I wondered. Marsh was completely delighted when I gave her my old pair of roller skates. I had dozens of jump ropes and let her keep a few of them, along with an extra kickball I had in the garage. Marsh loved my bedroom and much preferred to play at my house. My mom suggested I give her some of the clothes I no longer wore after seeing Marsh in the same outfit every other day. Marsh thanked me profusely with tears in her eyes.

Tanya was Joanie's age, and they quickly became friends. Tanya wasn't anything like Marsh. She was boisterous and tacky, saying whatever was on her mind. She couldn't finish a sentence without using the word "shit." Johnny Ray was only a year older than me. He smoked constantly, always smelling of cigarettes, worse than when my parents smoked. Johnny's profanity was almost as bad as Benny's, who was only eight. Benny also smoked, to my surprise.

Mr. Norman came and went, always on the move looking for work. I later found out he was illiterate.

"When we lived in Ohio, my dad was a trapper," Marsh once told me. I wasn't sure what a trapper was. I pictured Mr. Norman trapping animals and probably skinning them for their fur, and thought of the rabbit fur from the Jamestown tourist shop.

Marsh would avoid hanging out at her house whenever possible. My dad had bought me a rust-colored three-speed bike awhile back, so I let Marsh borrow my purple Schwinn, even letting her keep it at her house. I wasn't allowed to give it to her.

I was surprised when Marsh told me she had never ridden a roller coaster, or any carnival ride for that matter. She was completely enthralled when my mom brought her, Joanie, Tanya, and I to Busch Gardens for a day. My mom bought all of us giant papier-mâché flowers, just like the ones we had bought at Kings Dominion. Marsh had the time of her life. She treasured her red papier-mâché flower as if it was gold. Tanya, on the other hand, couldn't have cared less.

I was a bit surprised when my mom let me go to the beach with the Norman family one morning. Marsh had come over to invite me with her eyes wide with excitement. I think Mom allowed me to go because Joanie was going along as well. We kids rode in the back of the Normans' pickup truck along with surfboards, a portable radio, and coolers full of grape Shasta. I wondered where the Normans had gotten their used-looking surfboards from. I couldn't wait to try surfing. I remember "Hot Child in the City" playing on the radio when Johnny Ray whispered in my ear, singing "Running wild, playing with her titty." I laughed, but was shocked at the same time by his vulgar way of thinking.

Johnny Ray had a crush on me. He always smiled when he saw me, giving me a big "Hello, Junes," while waving and generally acting completely surprised to see me every time. I was flattered to have a boy think I was pretty and flirt with me, but I still thought he was a toad and not a prince, and a rather doltish toad at that.

We hit the beach. Mr. Norman and Johnny Ray grabbed the surfboards right away, running straight out into the ocean to try surfing. Marsh, Tanya, Joanie, and I spread out our towels on the sand. Mr. Norman and Johnny Ray eventually were able to get up on the board and ride the surf, which was impressive, as it was their first time.

"Can I try?" I asked Johnny Ray, knowing he would let me.

"Sure," he said, pushing the board in my direction.

I had watched surfers my whole life, so I had an idea of what to do. When the right wave came, I paddled furiously, trying to keep up with the wave. I managed to push myself up and stand, knees bent, arms out to help me balance. *I was on top of the world! I was surfing!* After the wave passed, I let myself fall off the board and laughed in elation.

"I surfed, I surfed!" I yelled, jumping up and down.

"Great job, Junes!" Johnny Ray said, cheering me on.

When it was Johnny's turn to use the board, we traded. I gave him back the surfboard and he gave me a boogie board. Another amazing thing happened while I was boogie-boarding, something I had never expected. As I was riding along, boarding on a perfect wave, the water *curled* around me. I heard air being sucked in. The wave had encircled me. I was in its barrel! *So this is heaven*, I marveled as I passed through. I touched the wall of water briefly, the boogie board carrying me through a magical world. I was alone; this was *my* experience only, no one was with me inside the water tunnel. *Wow.* I rode all the way up onto shore and stood up, grabbing my boogie board, too stunned to speak. I turned running out into the ocean spending the rest of the afternoon trying to catch another wave hoping to end up in its barrel. I never was able to experience that again, but I'll never forget it. Riding waves was a little taste of heaven.

The Norman kids didn't really fit in with the George Town kids. Even though the Normans were friendly, my mom was right: they *were* hillbilly trash. Tanya's behavior was the worst. She was no lady. Most of the George Town boys lost their virginity to Tanya. It concerned me how Joanie and Tanya became such good friends. Joanie started picking up on their language, and so did I. I found myself saying "aw, shit" a lot. Mick started smoking pot, thanks to Tanya, his supplier. Mrs. Norman wanted her kids out of the house, and she was never concerned about where the kids were or what they were doing. Mr. Norman was never home, always out supposedly looking for work.

One day, Mick was sitting on his front porch, his hair slicked back, still wet from a shower. I hated when he did that and showed his white forehead. On this particular day, his parents weren't home from work yet. He was smoking a joint on the porch. His stereo speakers were propped on his bedroom window ledge, blasting the song "Cocaine" by Eric Clapton. The music was blaring through the neighborhood. I couldn't believe Mick had the audacity to just sit there and look around, not giving a damn. My mom sent me next door to Mr. Shirrel's to pick up some garden vegetables he had picked for us. I waved at Mick as I headed over. Mick just nodded his head back. Mr. Shirrel opened up his big garage door as I approached his driveway. When he waved to Mick, Mick went inside and turned off his stereo.

"Would you like a Coca-Cola?"

"Oh, no thanks."

"Go ahead, grab yourself one," Mr. Shirrel said as he opened up one of the refrigerators he had in his garage. Mr. Shirrel's garage was his place to get away from his wife. They bickered a lot. Once I heard Mrs. Shirrel yelling "Shut up, old boy, or I'll cut your head off!" The chilled bottles of Coca-Cola looked inviting, so I grabbed one.

"Anytime you want one, just help yourself," he said. "Oh, wait here." Mr. Shirrel headed out his side garage door.

He was wearing a white T-shirt, beige shorts, and sandals. He was a burly man, with tan skin, thinning gray hair and glasses. His wife was quite plump, with black hair and fair skin. Her black horn-rim glasses made her skin appear even whiter. She stayed inside most of the time, no matter how nice it was outside, watching soap operas while baking pies.

Mr. Shirrel returned seconds later with a plastic bag full of large red tomatoes, cucumbers, and yellow squash.

"Make sure your mom gets these," he said as he handed them to me.

"I will. Thanks."

My mom's eyes brightened when she saw the delectable vegetables. She made us our favorite, tomato sandwiches, for lunch.

That evening, Joanie, Tanya, Marsh, and I spread out our sleeping bags on my back lawn for a campout. Morris, Johnny Ray, Benny, and Keith set up tents in the Normans' backyard. When night fell, we lay in our sleeping bags and looked up at the stars. All of a sudden, something hard hit me right in the stomach. I picked it up, trying to examine it in the dark. There was a stem on it. It was an apple. Suddenly we were being pelted by small green apples from the other side of the fence. I could hear Benny laughing. Another apple went flying over the fence, hitting Marsh on the head, and then another, and another.

"This means war!" I yelled.

Joanie burst out laughing at what I had said. I picked up some of the apples and threw them back into the Normans' yard, hoping to hit the boys. Marsh was the first to help me, and then Tanya and Joanie joined in. But the apples kept flying back over the fence at us, one hitting me in the head.

"C'mon," I whispered. "Let's sneak inside."

We picked up our sleeping bags and quietly ran inside, headed for the room over the garage. *They'll wonder what happened to us,* I thought, laughing while running up the stairs.

"I'm gonna whip their stinky asses tomorrow," Tanya said as we spread out the sleeping bags on the floor.

I didn't like Tanya and her trashy way of talking. She had her own language, substituting words like "butt wiper" for toilet paper. Tanya was disgusting. She would stop anywhere, it didn't matter to her, to reach down inside her shorts and scratch her crotch. "Damn it itches," she would always say. Marsh was mortified by her older sister. Tanya never liked Marsh's seemingly embarrassed response, and bullied her, shoving her or getting in her face and cursing. I would always defend Marsh, shoving Tanya back. Tanya decided she didn't like me, and set out to cause trouble for me. Tanya would lie to Joanie, claiming I said something negative about Joanie when I hadn't. Tanya would go out of her way to cause friction between Joanie and I. When that didn't work, she told Morris I had made fun of his stuttering, which led to Morris and I getting into a shoving match in the middle of the street. I was so hurt and angry when he confronted me. I couldn't believe that he actually; after all our years of friendship, thought I would make fun of his stuttering. He should have known better than to take her word over mine.

"D-did you m-make fun of me?"

"Screw you!" was all I could think to say as he stood there waiting for an answer. *No, of course not, silly,* I thought hoping he would realize what was going on. Morris and I would tease each other, but never in a hurtful way. But we became so angry with each other on that day that we even spit in each other's faces, which brought us back to reality.

We apologized and hugged. The neighborhood kids stared, probably thinking we were nuts. I later learned why Morris's view of me was clouded. Tanya had brainwashed him. I know this because one afternoon when Marsh and I had gone to take down the tents that were left up in her backyard after a camp-over, I got slapped in the face with reality. As I unzipped one tent, I heard heavy breathing. *Is someone hurt?* I thought. It was way too hot to be in a tent under the blazing sun.

There in the tent were Morris and Tanya having sex. I zipped the tent back up.

"C'mon, Marsh. Let's get the tents later."

She followed me out of the backyard without hesitating, knowing how her sister was. I wasn't mad at Morris, but I was disappointed. I was mad at Tanya for tainting my friend. I never told anyone what I saw. I didn't want to embarrass Morris.

On one occasion, my mom told me I could invite a few friends to come to the movies. I asked Marsh and Joanie. Tanya became so jealous when she found out that she wasnt invited. She walked right over to my house, rang the doorbell, and told my mom she had caught me smoking. "Im sorry to have to tell you this, maam, but I thought you should know," the cunning little liar told my mom. My mom was suggestible, even naïve at times. Tanya had picked up on that, and took advantage of it. My mom sent me to my room.

"You'll think twice before smoking next time, won't you!"

"Mom, I never smoked, never!"

She ignored me. I went into my room, slamming the door. I was glad my dad was out to sea, because he would always yell at me if I slammed my door, even if it was accidental. I looked out my bedroom window and saw Tanya walking by with a satisfied smile.

I opened the window, enraged. "You are a bitch!" I spat.

"Why don't you come out here and say it to my face? Oh *that's right*, you're on restrictions," she said with a chuckle, satisfied her little ploy had worked.

That got me really mad. I lifted up the screen in my window and jumped out. I sprinted across the grass that separated our houses and pushed her so hard that she went tumbling to the ground. She quickly got up to shove me back, but I slapped her so hard it made her head turn.

"Hey!" I heard a voice behind me. It was Morris. "G-g-go home," he told me, his big brown eyes wide showing the whites around them.

I knew Morris could take me down if we were to ever get into a real fight. I turned to go.

"Go ahead, Morris. Take the slut's side over mine."

Tanya flew at me, but Morris blocked her. "J-just go, Junie," he said, sounding sincere.

I jumped back in my bedroom window, pulling myself over with my hands and skinning my knee on the bricks. After I was inside, I *slammed* my window shut.

Later, after I had calmed myself by sketching pictures on the large sketching pad my dad had bought me, Joanie and Morris came over to tell my mom that Tanya had lied to get me into trouble, and was even bragging about the stunt she had pulled.

"Junie would never smoke Mrs. Nesby," Joanie said.

"I know," My mom said.

They looked at her quizzically.

"We still have time to go to the movies if you want. But leave those Norman kids behind!" my mom said, frustrated.

The outcome wasn't fair to Marsh, but she understood when I explained later.

Even though Marsh and I remained friends, Joanie and I stayed away from Tanya as much as possible. Joanie developed her own circle of friends that were her age, a group of nice young ladies. Some were cheerleaders and others were band members. The age difference between Joanie and I altered our relationship, leaving me more like a little sister than a friend. I remember Joanie and Morris getting their driver's permits. I knew how to drive already, because my mom would take Joanie and me out on nearby dirt roads to let us practice driving. I had known how to drive since I was ten.

Joanie started wearing makeup and hanging out with her older friends more and more. Morris started dating, usually two girls at a time which left no time for kickball or hide-and-seek.

Morris brought one of his girlfriends along on a trip up to Washington DC. I was relieved to see he had found a nicer class of girls to date. He once took me by surprise when he asked me which of his girlfriends I liked better, as he couldn't decide between them. The two girls didn't know about each other. Stacy came from a family with money, and Tracy didn't, which didn't matter; she was very nice.

"Which one do you have more fun with?" I asked.

"I think Stacy. S-s-she laughs a lot."

"Then you should choose her, Morris." I was flattered that he took my advice. Stacy, a brunette, was who he chose to *go steady* with.

Stacy invited Joanie and I over for a sleepover. Stacy's younger sister, who was my age, was named Athena. What an interesting name. I imagined my name being Athena. Joanie said it was the name of the Greek god of wisdom.

Mrs. Ainsworth dropped us off at Stacy's house late one afternoon. Her house was in a newly developed neighborhood further out from the city of Chesapeake. When Athena answered the door, I was awestruck. Their home was quite lovely. The floor in the entranceway was made of white marble, and the wall directly in front of us was curved and tiled with mirrors. In front of the mirrored wall stood a stone fountain. Its sprinkling sound was welcoming. This was the first time I had been in a home that had a fountain. Stacy and Athena's parents were out of town for the evening, so we were at liberty to walk around and explore the neighborhood, some of the girls getting into mischief. There were twelve girls at the sleepover, all of whom save the hosts Joanie and I had never met before. These new girls thought it would be fun to wreck yards, turning over flower pots and snatching up garden flowers to strew them across driveways. A couple of the girls even put sugar in the gas tanks of some of the cars that were parked on the street. I didn't participate. I thought such pranks were mean. I only followed along. I did enjoy the feeling of independence as we walked the neighborhood streets laughing. It was around midnight and all the adults were sleeping. I noticed how this neighborhood's lots were much larger and the streets wider than George Town East. But this fancy neighborhood seemed empty. It was too quiet, most porch lights off and no one stirring except us. The houses were bigger, prettier, and newer, but there weren't any trees or shrubs, which made the neighborhood feel emptier than George Town.

We became tired and bored from walking around as the night went by. I followed the girls to the neighborhood's playground. We sat on the swings, talking until a pinkish-yellow dawn. Early birds were starting to chirp. We made our way back to Stacy's house and all crashed, falling asleep immediately on top of our sleeping bags on the living room floor. Around noon, Stacy's parents arrived. They drove Joanie and I home in their long white Cadillac. They seemed young to be parents of a sixteen- and twelve-year-old. We never told our moms that it was sleepover without chaperones.

I still spent the night at Joanie's from time to time. When she fell asleep, I stayed up extra late watching scary movies on her little black-and-white TV. Joanie wasn't interested in Barbies or a lot of the things we used to play with together anymore. So I started hanging around Neana more often. My mom absolutely forbade me from going over to the Normans' again after talking with Mrs. Ainsworth on the phone one afternoon. Joanie had found out that the Normans were filming pornography in their house, using Tanya in some of them! When they propositioned Joanie to participate, she ran out of the house, stunned. On occasion, my mom would allow Marsh to come over, until my mom found out Marsh's dad and grandfather were selling drugs from their house. I felt bad for Marsh. She was a nice girl with an unfortunate family. I felt sad when I saw her all alone at the picnic table in her backyard, usually reading. None of the neighborhood kids were allowed to have anything to do with the Normans. Johnny Ray and Benny usually hung out in their garage, smoking pot with the big door up. The parents on our street got together to find out who the Normans rented from, so we could sign a petition to have them evicted. Mr. and Mrs. Simons, the Ceavers, and the Shirrels came over for a luncheon one day at our house. My mom had made coffee and sandwiches. Neana and I played in my room while listening in on their conversation about the Normans.

"My dad is so angry at them. He's ready to start World War III," Neana told me.

"They never mow their lawn, they leave trash and cigarette butts in their yard, and the way they dress! Ah, it's filthy," Mrs. Ceaver said dismayed.

"I've never heard such language before coming from children," Mrs. Simons added.

I just hoped that Marsh would be okay. The whole eviction thing was my dad's idea. My mom had told him about the Normans' behavior over the phone. He'd said "Audie, find out who they're renting from, or call Mr. Gentry; he'll know how to dig up the information." So that's what she did.

Whenever I wrote my dad a letter, I wrote letters to Krissy and Janie as well. I told them about all the changes going on in George Town, along with the saga of the weird, estranged Normans. Janie wrote me right back, telling me how she really missed all the fun we used to have and that she hoped she could visit one day. She was sorry to hear about the strange people living in her old house.

Dad continued to send postcards. They came in from Palma de Mallorca, Pompeii, Naples, Taranto, Capri, and Rome. I used thumbtacks to pin them up on the wall above my desk. I stared at the Leaning Tower of Pisa, wondering what it would be like to walk around inside. Were the floors slanted? I imagined it was like the Scooby-Doo Mystery Cave at Kings Dominion, the floors of which were slanted, making it difficult to walk straight. After my dad left Florence, he traveled down to Trieste on the Adriatic Sea. I wondered if the beaches there were nice. I wondered if l could ride the waves there like in Virginia.

I spent one afternoon sprawled across my bed reading a Trixie Belden book. I heard a knock on my bedroom door.

"Come in."

"How would you like to go camping for the weekend with your old Girl Scout troop?" Mom asked.

"Can I? I dropped out, remember?"

"Well, Ms. Cindy called, saying she would really like for you to go along."

I was feeling bored. I had been sitting inside a lot, watching too much of *The Gong Show*, *Adam-12*, and *Baretta* just to name a few shows, if I wasn't reading. I was uncomfortable riding my bike around with the Norman kids sitting out front calling me awful names. It was embarrassing and made me to want to stay inside all day. Besides, I had always wanted to go camping.

"Okay," I quickly agreed.

My mom helped me put together everything I would need. We packed bug spray, Coppertone suntan lotion, a compass, a flashlight, and a change of clothes. My mom added baby powder and Tickle deodorant (with the big, wide ball applicator).

We ended up pitching our tents in a hot, sandy field near a large river. Laura, one of the girls in the troop, was especially glad to have me along. We decided to share a tent, as we were not supposed to sleep alone. Before bedding down for the night, we went to a firework show, which was fun to watch. But the louder fireworks made me nervous. All of the Girl Scout troops from the area were there. There must have been over a hundred of us. On the second day, we went hiking through a nearby forest. Our troop leader pointed out poison ivy, explaining to us how the plant could give us a rash and make us sick. "Never touch it." I remembered my dad telling me once that when he was little he had come in contact with poison ivy, leaving him terribly ill. He showed me a little black-and-white photo of his rash from the ivy. His mom took pictures of everything that happened, whether it was good or bad. I was alarmed at the huge welts all over his face from the ivy.

The weekend flew by. I'd had more exciting weekends, but camping was better than sitting around the house. When I returned from the campout, I couldn't wait to get into the shower. It was so hot and sandy, and we didn't have access to showers.

When I got out of the shower, my heart jumped when I saw blood on the towel. "Oh no," I said. I knew what was happening. We had learned about getting periods in religion class at school. I remembered Joanie talking about getting hers, but had never thought much about it happening to me. Joanie was fourteen when she first got hers. *I'm only twelve*, I thought. I was embarrassed, and decided to hide it from my mom. I went to my bedroom to lie on my bed, and read a book to take my mind off it. Maybe it would just go away. But my mom found out because she did my laundry.

"Junie, why didn't you tell me you started your period?"

For some reason, I lost control of my emotions and started crying. "I don't know," was all I could think of to say before rolling over to cover my face in my pillow.

"It's okay, it's perfectly normal. I'll simply get you some Maxi-Pads. It's no big deal."

"How can I live like this?"

"What do you mean?"

"How can I ever go swimming again? Will it last forever?"

"Oh no. Only about five or six days tops, once every month, until you get old."

"Only five or six days?" I felt better knowing I would get a break from it. I was still concerned though, because I was supposed to go to Joanie's pool party that night. Mrs. Ainsworth had rented out a public pool, and I had been looking forward to it for quite some time. When I told Joanie I got my period, she was surprised.

"You did? Really?"

"Yeah. Now I can't swim."

"I still want you to come to my party. Why don't you just put on a pad and wear shorts over your bathing suit?"

"Okay," I said skeptically.

The pool was beautiful, all aglow with its night lights. I watched the teenage boys and girls diving in and swimming, enjoying themselves as I sat on the edge of the pool, dangling my legs in, feeling like a leper. I envisioned myself going off the diving board and looking like the shark from *Jaws* had just attacked me. Blood would rise to the surface, spewing everywhere. All of the teens would think I was a freak, like in the movie *Carrie*. They would all scream and swim away from me. When I saw Morris, I became worried he might pick me up to throw me in. I got up and headed into the girls' bathroom. I lost control again and started crying as I was washing my hands. Two of the teenage girls came in, with Joanie following.

"Hey, why aren't you swimming?" one of the girls asked.

"Oh, she's just worried because she got her period," Joanie said like it was no big deal.

"Ohh. I understand. Don't be worried. You can still swim."

"It happens to all of us," the other girl said. She had a short Hamill wedge hair cut like mine. "Once you're in the water it stops."

"Does it really?" I asked, not sure if I believed her or not.

"No, really. Just remember when you get out to change back into a Maxi-Pad."

"Oh okay. Thanks."

"No problem. Us girls have to look out for one another sometimes."

My confidence returned. I went right out and dove off the diving board, enjoying the rest of the evening. When it was time to leave, I had to run and grab a life-saving Maxi-Pad. I thought the torture of adolescence was over, until I had to visit the orthodontist.

I had the worst teeth. They were so crooked, with overlapping canines and a big gap between my two front teeth. I gagged, trying not to puke, as the dental assistant held an impression tray full of goop in my mouth. The top wasn't so hard, but the bottom impressions were sheer torture. The assistant was trying to be very sweet and kind.

"You're doing a great job, Junie. Just hang in there and pant like a little dog," she told me.

My eyes were tearing up. Just when I was about to yank the goopy tray out myself she said "You're all done. You made it." She took out the tray. "The hard part is over. Getting braces on will be a piece of cake." I was glad to hear that. On the following week's visit to the orthodontist, they showed me how they were going to attach the braces, using my impressions as a model. The bonding agent smelled horrible as they applied a little on each tooth before attaching the brackets. My mouth was full of cotton rolls, which was a very uncomfortable feeling. At least this small bit of torture wasn't as bad as having impressions taken. It sure was easier than getting a cavity filled. I had eight cavities filled when I was about five, and I had screamed the entire time, the dentist holding me down with one arm while drilling with the other.

I felt like a robot as the orthodontist wrapped wire ligatures around my brackets. They got tighter and tighter. When the orthodontist was all through, the assistant gave me a packet of wax. "Put this over your braces if they bother your lips or cheeks. Just don't forget to take it off when you eat something."

I wasn't able to eat dinner that night. I felt as if I had 500 pounds of pressure squeezing my teeth together through my gums. The pain eased up after a few days, and I was able to eat solid foods again, but had to chew carefully. I was thankful I didn't have to wear headgear like some of the other kids did.

My mom and I waited at Pier Twelve one windy afternoon for the arrival of the USS *John F. Kennedy.* The ship was a behemoth, slowly moving toward the pier with sailors standing in formation along the entire upper deck of the ship. We all stood and watched in awe. There was a TV crew aiming their cameras at the giant ship. As the crew started coming down the gangway, many wives and children ran to hug husbands and dads with tears of joy. Seven months was a long time. My dad came toward us, giving my mom a hug and then me. I hadn't realized until then just how much I missed him. He was carrying one suitcase and a large plastic bag. Instead of going straight home, we stopped in a little seafood restaurant for lunch, and to avoid all the traffic that was heading out.

"Did you get my postcards?" my dad asked.

It had been so long since we'd been together. I told my dad I kept them all in a big stack except for a few I had pinned on the wall above my desk. "I really liked the last batch you sent from the pyramids in Egypt," I told him. "I like the postcard with the camels in Alexandria, Egypt, too. Did you climb the pyramids?"

"Oh no. Those are extremely high."

I thought about the postcard he had sent with a picture of the Sphinx. I thought the statue, was strange-looking, like something out of a Sinbad movie full of cy-clops and giants. My dad told us about how he had gone on a tour of the tombs of King Tut and other pharaohs.

"I noticed your teeth turned silver," my dad teased. He knew I had braces put on. He was going to have to make a lot of payments on my orthodontics. I showed him my braces, smiling real wide before telling him about the wax I had to put on them to avoid cutting my lips and cheeks.

"Your teeth will be pretty when they take the braces off in a couple of years. It's well worth it."

I remembered the orthodontist saying the same thing.

As we headed out, the traffic had cleared quite a bit. At home, my dad liked the new carpet. While unpacking, he pulled out a large plastic bag from his suitcase and set it on his bed.

"Here," he said as he handed me a large jade-green beetle.

"What is it?"

"It's a scarab from Egypt." It fit perfectly in the palm of my hand. I turned it over. On its flat bottom, there were Egyptian hieroglyphics inscribed on its waxy body.

My eyes went wide when my dad pulled out from the same plastic bag an amazing twenty-four-inch-tall Spanish dancer doll, complete with a blue dress and shawl. Her arms were held above her head in a dance position above her black bouffant hair. My dad pulled out a second doll just like it, except with a pink dress.

"Choose which one you want, and pick a friend of yours to give the other one to," he told me.

I immediately knew who I would give the pink doll to. I went into my room to call Joanie right away.

"Hello?"

"Joanie! You have to come over! I have a J-Bird gift for you!" A J-Bird gift was a gift other than a birthday present or Christmas present. I was getting excited just anticipating the look on her face when I gave her the doll.

"Okay, I'll be right over."

When she saw the doll, she couldn't believe I was actually going to let her keep it.

"You're just teasing me aren't you?" she asked.

"No, really. My dad bought two of them and is letting me give you one. I know pink is your favorite color, so take her."

Joanie had tears in her eyes as she hugged me. "Thank you, thank you."

Later, Mrs. Ainsworth and Joanie called to thank my dad and I even more profusely.

Whenever Joanie and I got into an argument, she would always say "I suppose you want that pink doll back?"

"No, silly, that's *your* doll." Soon we would get along again.

Mrs. Ainsworth helped me with my English homework, and was the best tutor I could have asked for. Mrs. Ainsworth worked as an English teacher at a high school all the way over in Norfolk. She was kind enough to come over in the evenings after dinner to help me. We started getting into tricky stuff in English class at school, but she had a knack for explaining things that were utterly confusing to me, making them seem crystal-clear.

Mrs. Ainsworth inspired me to take a deeper interest in reading novels. I never was enthusiastic about reading books until she introduced me to a wider variety of novels. She would read out loud on our long drives up to the Williamsburg pottery. It was a pottery factory retail outlet store where we could buy ceramics, dishes, lamps and such. Mr. Ainsworth would drive, and Joanie, Morris, my mom, and I listened to Mrs. Ainsworth read passionately. She was an emotional person, crying easily and sometimes quick to become angry over things none of us really paid much attention to. When I slept over at Joanie's, Mrs. Ainsworth would read out loud to us as we played board games on the living room floor. She was a talented lady who wrote poetry, sketched, painted, played the piano, sang and acted in local plays at the Tidewater Little Theater. She would tear up sometime after immersing herself in a character. Sometimes she would become angry at how a character in a play would respond to a situation to the point that her face would turn red.

"She's over-emotional," my dad would always say, especially after getting into heated debates over politics with her. Mrs. Ainsworth's enthusiasm for life and people inspired me. She enabled me to look at things from a different point of view. Mrs. Ainsworth involved my mom in volunteering for the Meals on Wheels charity as well. Joanie and I loved going along with them, and found ourselves getting attached to some of the elderly people. The old folks usually had interesting stories to tell, and it was always nice to see how they were so appreciative of our help.

I'll never forget the time Joanie and I stood behind the curtains during a play at Mrs. Ainsworth's high school. Mrs. Ainsworth had volunteered to play the piano for one of her school's plays. Joanie and I stood backstage watching everyone come and go dressed in costumes. The school was old, dark, and spooky–it was rumored to be haunted. I was spooked while standing backstage in the dark. I felt a cold draft blowing behind me. I turned but saw nothing. I clutched the rosary that I secretly carried in my pocket, which made me feel safe.

The neighborhood was at peace once again when the Normans finally moved out. My last memory of them was waving good-bye to Marsh and Johnny Ray as they sat in the back of their old, beat-up pickup truck. Johnny Ray flipped me the bird as they turned the corner and went out of sight. *How typical*, I thought. A part of me felt sorry for them and wished them the best of luck, especially Marsh, but another part of me was glad they were moving out. I wouldn't miss their boisterousness and trashy ways. I went back inside to write Janie a letter letting her know that her old house was empty again. The place smelled of cigarette smoke and stale beer. One of the rooms was painted red—that was where they had filmed their porns. Oh how I wished Janie could move back in.

Young Teen

I dragged myself out of bed and looked at my ugly black, white, and red plaid uniform. I remembered that I hadn't set out a white blouse to wear with the jumper. I slid open my wooden closet door and saw my summer clothes still hanging. I wished I could just put on a shirt and pair of shorts and go for a bike ride. I was still half-asleep. I hadn't fallen asleep until late, sometime after midnight. Breaking summer vacation habits of sleeping in until 10:00 or so was always hard. My dad wasn't home. He had left at 5:00 AM to go to work, as usual. My mom was still asleep. *Lucky her*, I thought as I pulled out a short-sleeved white blouse. The weather was still going to be hot for at least another month. I got into the shower to wake myself up. I opened a bar of soap my dad had bought me in Spain. I was lucky to have a dad who brought me such unique gifts. The soap's red-and-black wrapper had a picture of a Spanish dancer on it. The label read *Maja* across the top. I wondered what that meant as I sniffed its spicy scent.

"Have a good day at school" I heard my mom say from her bedroom as I headed out the front door.

"I will! See ya!" I sat on the front steps waiting for my ride. We were car-pooling again that year. I could hear crickets chirping, which meant it was still early. The sun felt hot and the rose bushes my mom had planted next to the porch smelled heavy with the wet dew on the pink, delicate petals. I regretted not having sat out here more during the summer, if only to take in mornings like this.

A small car pulled up in the driveway. The driver tooted the horn. I got up and climbed in.

"Good morning, Junie" Mrs. Donovan said as Tori held the car seat up so I could squeeze in the back.

"Good morning" I politely replied.

"Are you all ready for school?" Tori asked, too chipper for me so early in the morning. Tori was a very astute, proper girl, and that got on my nerves sometimes. She was always talking about what was going on in the news or about her class work in a way that made me think she was trying to act much older than she was. I envisioned her spending the summer in a library and being happy about it. No wonder she didn't have a suntan. She was thin with pointy features and wore glasses. She had long brown hair that was fine like mine, except she kept hers combed nice. There were times I forgot to brush my hair. I had it cut short over the summer because I wanted to have that cute and sassy look everyone said Dorothy Hamill had. I looked like a little boy. As I sat listening to everyone chat on the way to school, I blinked hard, trying to stay awake. I should have had a glass of iced tea. I hadn't even thought to eat breakfast. It was going to be a long morning. I hoped that I would make it through to lunch.

Mrs. Scango introduced herself to her class. We were seated facing forward. There was one class of each grade in the small school, so my classmates were the same as the year before. Mrs. Scango was an overweight woman with dark brown shoulder-length hair and big brown eyes, reminding me of Mrs. Ainsworth. Chrissie and Stephie were in my class again. Even though we weren't friends, I'll never forget them. I was envious of their looks. They were the prettiest girls in the class, and they knew it. Chrissie had long, chestnut-brown hair that was silky and shiny. We couldn't help but notice, as she constantly brushed it. Chrissie had braces. She had cute features, looking much like her friend Stephie, except Stephie had short, flaxen-blond hair. There was Patty and Patricia, who always buddied around together, acting like eight-year-olds. Susan was nice, but didn't care to befriend anyone in our class. Melody and Cindy were the only two Asian girls, also known as the straight-A girls. There was Caroline, who had flunked sixth grade on her first attempt. The boys were typical teen boys. They teased me a lot, saying I looked like a boy or calling me "dog face" or whatever they could come up with. I agreed with their insults on the inside. They would really have fun teasing me about my newly-developed acne. I was fortunate not to suffer too much acne. I would get one huge zit in between my eyes, and another one on the middle of my chin. Add in the braces and one had the recipe for a geek.

I found myself sitting alone at lunch time. Everyone else had paired off, leaving me out. I missed Kim, who had sat with me during lunch the previous year. I had carpooled with Kim as well. She had decided to go to the public school so she could join band. I missed Tommy, Janie's little brother, who would sit with me during lunch sometimes. I was embarrassed and felt awkward eating alone. I had nobody to play with on the playground at recess. As the weeks went by, I would try to sit next to someone to start a conversation. They would just ignore me though, and call me "the geek" in the halls later. I resorted to eating alone while doing homework, which gave me more free time at home. During dinner, we watched *All in the Family* on the tiny six-inch black-and-white TV my dad had set on the kitchen hutch by our table. It was a comedy, and it made dinnertime more pleasant. The news would come on afterward. Jim Kincaid was the anchor, and he liked to tell stories at the end of the news broadcast. He called these stories his "notes from Elam"—Elam was the name of his farm. I enjoyed listening to his witty stories while I washed and dried dishes. He told short stories about the different seasons on the farm and how the leaves of his maple trees changed colors. I will never forget Jim's stories about his dog Murphy.

I was getting paid $10 a week for my chores after a conversation with my dad about earning an allowance. "I'll give you $10 a week for keeping your room clean and tidy—bed made every morning. Set and clear the kitchen table, and wash and dry dishes. When summer comes, you can mow the lawn and help your mom sweep up the grass. Also make sure the garbage can is set out by the curb each week for pick-up." I was more than happy to get paid $10 a week for my chores. That was a large allowance in 1979.

As the weather grew colder, I would sit in the living room to wait for Mrs. Donovan to pull up in the driveway.

I climbed into their little gray two-door car. "Good morning."

I was so sleepy on the way to school. As usual, I almost dozed off while listening to Tori and her mom chat about the Shah of Iran and the fifty-two American hostages in Tehran. I imagined being a hostage, tied up, with a gag wrapped around my mouth, and guns being pointed at me.

"Gosh, I hope they will get released," I said, joining the conversation for once.

"Yeah, me too," Tori answered, sounding pleased that I had finally joined in.

We prayed for the hostages during religion class, and then we prayed again during Wednesday's Mass. I also prayed silently for a friend. I was so alienated from my classmates that I could go almost an entire day without conversation. It was so comforting to hang out with Joanie or Neana after school. Morris and Mick were involved in sports again, which took up most of their after-school time.

One afternoon, while doing my homework in the quiet cafeteria after everyone had gone outside for recess, Sister Christine came in. She looked at me with her hands on her hips. I stood up. As a rule, whenever Sister Christine spoke or entered the classroom, we had to stand at attention.

"Junie, I appreciate your devotion to schoolwork. But you need to go outside and get some fresh air. Close your books and head on out!" she ordered.

"Okay." I was very obedient.

I went outside, planning to sit in the grass and study my weekly spelling words, but I noticed Susan talking with a group of girls. Susan was nice. I knew she wouldn't get an attitude if I walked up to her. She spent lunch period sitting with the older class. *I'll just casually walk up to them*, I told myself.

As I walked up, I heard Susan asking "Hey, did any of you get your periods yet?"

Everyone looked a little tongue-tied. "I did," she admitted.

This was a perfect opportunity to get in on the conversation. "Hi. I thought I'd take a break from homework. Guess what? I got my period last summer, right when I was invited to a pool party." I was waiting to be ignored.

"Oh no! That must have sucked," one of the seventh-grade girls said. She had gotten hers right at the beginning of summer vacation. "I felt horrified. The whole summer was ruined because of it."

The conversation slowly changed direction. We talked about how some of us had gotten braces over the summer, and how they hurt our gums. I began to feel comfortable talking to them. My confidence grew from merely talking with seventh-graders. No wonder Susan preferred to hang out with the older girls. Caroline also hung out with older girls. She was the class clown, preferring to joke around than to have meaningful conversations. Caroline would often take huge swigs of wine during Mass. I have to admit, we all took large swigs of wine during Mass. During lunch one day, we all admitted taking big drinks of wine to one another. We shared a big laugh. That was a funny Catholic schoolgirl bonding moment for us. I laughed whenever I heard the Billy Joel song "Only the Good Die Young," which contained a reference to something similar.

Making friends with the older girls taught me a life lesson. I had grown up over the summer, but most of the girls in my class hadn't. I had to keep in mind that I was a grade behind after all, having failed third grade. It wasn't *me* and it wasn't *them*; it was all of *us* and our age and maturity differences that had been keeping me alienated.

While the girls in my class played hopscotch, jumped rope, or just swung on the swing sets, I was standing with Susan and the seventh-grade girls discussing the love saga of Luke and Laura on the soap opera *General Hospital* or how cute we all thought Shaun Cassidy, Leif Garrett, and Donny Osmond were.

Talk of Ronald Reagan on the evening news seemed to calm my dad. He had gotten to the point of switching off the TV every time they so much as showed Jimmy Carter's face. We had a mock election in school, with two of my classmates imitating Reagan and Carter. My classmate Paul gave a terrific speech, sounding just like Reagan. After listening to my dad talk a lot about Reagan during dinner and listening to Tori talk about the hostages and the ayatollah, I started getting interested in politics. I earned respect during open debates about it all in history class. I spoke only from the knowledge I had gained from listening to my dad and Tori. Classmates came to me with their questions regarding the candidates.

With the holidays approaching, we were bombarded with homework. I had pages and pages of long division from math class, as well as English homework. *Yuck!* Mrs. Ainsworth came over twice a week after dinner to sit at the kitchen table with me and review conjunctions, prepositions, verbs, and adverbs. She tutored me, showing me how to use each part of speech in paragraphs. Mrs. Ainsworth helped with my spelling workbook assignments, having me write the words over and over, calling them out to me, giving me tips on remembering how to spell them. I thought she was a better teacher than any of my instructors at school. I ended up with a decent report card, which started Christmas vacation on a nice note.

For Christmas, Joanie got the vanity table she had been asking for. I liked sitting on the edge of her bed and watching her brush her hair and apply makeup, which made her go from cute to beautiful. She had her telephone on the vanity table and when someone called, she would pick the receiver up saying "Hello," changing her voice trying to sound older and provocative. That tickled me.

"Why don't you let me make your face up?" she asked one day while I was watching her apply mascara. "I bet you would be really pretty."

I didn't like the thought of having that inky stuff all over my face. Putting on eyeliner seemed intimidating, sticking a wand so close to the eye. On the other hand, the thought of looking *pretty* was appealing.

"Okay," I agreed.

Joanie rubbed in the base makeup. I think we had the same skin tone. She applied blue eye shadow, black mascara, and pink lipstick.

"Okay, look up," she said as she carefully drew on the eyeliner.

"Please don't get that in my eye," I said nervously.

"I won't. Sit still."

She was right about the makeup. When I saw myself in the lighted mirror attached to the vanity table, I thought I looked pretty for the first time in my life.

"Hey, Mom!" Joanie called.

"What is it?" Mrs. Ainsworth shouted back, probably busy crocheting or grading papers in her room.

"Come here!"

"Wow!" Mrs. Ainsworth said when she saw me.

"See?" Joanie said, proud of how she had transformed me. "Don't you look beautiful! I want to show your mom, c'mon."

"Okay."

We walked over to my house, crossing over the empty lawn that had once been the Normans'.

"Yeah, you do look pretty," my mom said when she saw my face. "Why don't you wear makeup more often?"

I wondered why she had never introduced me to makeup. I guess I was still a little too young. After watching *The Facts of Life* on TV, eating dinner, and washing my face, I said "Thanks Joanie" out loud as I laid in bed looking up at the silent airplanes going by in the dark sky. Watching the planes' tiny red and green lights, I fell asleep with the opening theme to *The Facts of Life* going through my head. *The boys you used to hate, you date, and now you'll have to investigate the facts of life, the facts of life ...*

I sat at my desk one Saturday afternoon, staring dumbfounded at a page in my math book. I had a blank piece of paper out and a pencil in my hand, but I couldnt write. I could hear the beat of a basketball being dribbled outside on the pavement and it was distracting me. I read the word problem a second time. "Jamie Smith ordered 5 ½ cords of oak."

Bam, bam, bam went the basketball. "The cost of each cord is $150.00. He also ordered 2 ½ cords of maple."

Bam, bam, bam, the basketball continued. It's February and cold out. *Why is someone dribbling a ball outside?* I thought. I put my finger on the word problem as I read it a third time, trying to concentrate. We were supposed to solve by multiplying fractions. *Who the heck uses this stuff anyway?* I thought, getting frustrated. *I bet the teacher gave us this homework just to ruin our weekend.* I didn't want to ask my dad for help, knowing he would only scream and holler at me when I didn't grasp the math the first time around. My dad couldn't teach math even though he knew everything about it, because he had no patience. In frustration, I slammed my math book shut. I sat staring at a picture of Mick, Joanie, Janie, Morris, and I that was pinned on my wall by a thumbtack. We were all smiling as we stood together at the beach. I started feeling better sitting with my elbows on my desk, chin resting on the palm of my hands, remembering that hot, sunny day. I noticed Mick's hair was a much lighter shade of blond in the picture. My parents and his were planning to go out to dinner that night. *I'll just have Mick show me*

how to do my math homework later when we all get back from dinner. I
pushed myself away from my desk, satisfied with both my decision and
the realization that the *bam, bam, bam* had stopped.

I watched my mom from the bathroom doorway as she stood in
front of the mirror putting on her makeup. My mom had black hair
that was then permed in small curls. I didn't know why all the moms
were wearing their hair styled that way. It made them look older than
they were. I had found some old black-and-white photos inside a large
cardboard box stashed in the bottom of the hall closet once. Some of
the pictures showed my parents years before. I thought my mom looked
like Mary Tyler Moore. My dad reminded me of Desi Arnaz from *I Love
Lucy.* I remembered watching my mom back when we lived in Norfolk,
how she would carefully roll her hair in pink rollers, sitting under a large
hair dryer that encircled her head. The dryer sounded like a miniature
airplane. Mom was attractive, and had a fairly high opinion of her own
beauty. She would often comment on other women, saying that she
thought they were too thin or too fat.

"Mom?"

She was applying eyeliner around her small brown eyes.

"Mom?"

"What is it?" she asked, blinking her eyes while looking at me out
of the corner of them. She always looked at me like that when she was
annoyed with me.

"Why do you perm you hair?"

"So I don't have to curl it and then have to sit under the dryer for
so long. Go get ready and put on something nice."

I went into my room and put on black dress slacks along with a nice
pink button-up blouse. I could smell Mom's Chanel No. 5 perfume
drifting from the bathroom. My dad bought her a bottle every year for
Christmas.

When we arrived at the seafood restaurant, I pulled my jacket
around me to keep warm. The restaurant was right on the beach, and
I could feel the cold wind blowing off the ocean. We met up with the
Ceavers at the entrance, where they were waiting for the hostess to
seat us. Mick looked nice in a white button-up shirt tucked into black
dress slacks. We were finally seated and handed menus. I knew our
parents would sit there for quite some time after dinner to enjoy a few

cocktails, which always annoyed me. I was glad Mick was there to keep me company.

"Do you want to walk around or somethin?" Mick asked when our parents ordered the first round of post-dinner drinks.

"Yeah, that sounds good."

"We're going to walk around," Mick told his mom. He stood up and pulled out my chair for me.

"Okay, but don't wonder too far, Mick."

We put on our jackets as we headed outside. Once we were outside, he immediately lit up a cigarette. I could hear the ocean waves and smell the salty air. It made me want to run through the sand to the ocean. As cold as it was; I still found the beach exhilarating.

"C'mon, Mick!" I said, walking down the sidewalk toward the beach. Mick followed. The ocean was beautiful. The moon's reflection shone across the black water. The waves' white foam seemed to glow under the bright moonlight. We sat down in the sand, which was warmer than standing in the cold wind.

"I wish it were summer."

"You can say that again," Mick said as he flicked his cigarette into the surf.

We watched as a wave sucked the butt out to sea.

"C'mon, get up." Mick said, jumping up and holding out his hand to pull me up. I jumped up with him, and followed his lead in walking along the shore.

I thought about Joanie making up my face and saying I was pretty. I thought about how all the boys at school made fun of me for being so skinny and plain-looking.

"Hey, Mick … do you think Im pretty?"

"What?"

"Do you think I'm pretty?" I figured he would be honest. Because he was a guy, his opinion would matter in a different way than Joanie's or my mom's.

"Why do you care what I think about that?"

"I just wonder, because the boys at school call me names and stuff."

"Girl, I've known you since you were knee-high to a grasshopper. I don't care how you look."

"Oh," I said, looking down.

"Look, you're a cute girl who I know will become a bright and blooming young lady." Mick stopped and reached down, picking up something white in the sand.

"Look," he said, holding it up. "It's a shark's tooth."

"Neat! Can I have it?"

"I don't care." He handed it to me. It was flexible and sharp on the tip.

"Girl, let's head back in. This cold air isn't fair to my skin."

"C'mon, I'll race ya!" I said, taking off through the sand. I almost beat him to the restaurant. As we headed back inside, Mick gave me a bit of advice.

"If anyone calls you a name, tell them to kiss your ass."

I laughed out loud as he held open the door for me.

"And if they still call you names, send them to me and I'll kick their ass."

I laughed again as we headed back to our parents' table. They were finishing up with their drinks and my dad was going over the check.

"Weren't you cold out there?" My mom asked, looking at my cheeks, red from the wind.

"Yeah, but the waves were pretty, and look!" I held up the shark's tooth.

"What is it?"

"A shark's tooth."

"Wow, imagine that," she said, looking at it quizzically.

On the way out, I asked Mick if he could help me with my math homework.

"Sure, bring it over tomorrow." It was getting late and his parents wouldn't be going back over to my house for more cocktails. "And remember what I said," he told me as we headed across the parking lot.

"I won't."

I knew Mick's advice meant: stand up for myself. I knew he would look out for me if anyone tried picking on me. I couldn't stop thinking about his reassurance that I would grow up to be a bright, blooming young lady. I liked the sound of that and it gave me a sense of hope. "Thanks Mick," I said to myself. I looked at the shark's tooth on the way home, holding it up to the rear window, letting the streetlights give me a better view of it.

On Sunday, I brought my math homework over to Mick's house after church. We sat at his kitchen table drinking sweet iced tea while going over the word problems together.

"Why didn't you bring something easier over?" he teased before we started on the third problem.

James walked into the kitchen, opened the refrigerator door, and pulled out the olive-green Tupperware pitcher of iced tea. He looked at us, leaning against the kitchen counter. I took notice again as to how tall James was and thin like Mick, with the same sandy blond hair. But he wasn't cute like Mick. James had his dad's large ears, which made him sort of quirky-looking.

"What are y'all doin' now?" James asked.

When I told him we were learning fractions, he shook his head in disgust.

"No thanks, I don't miss doin' those. You need to hurry, Mick. We're heading out soon," James said as he left the kitchen.

"Where are y'all goin'?" I asked as Mick took my pencil and swiftly finished off the rest of the problems.

"Down to Carolina to visit my grandparents."

"Lucky you. You get to miss school."

"I'm not too lucky. I've been suspended for a few days again for fighting."

"Really?"

"Yeah," Mick said, with his chuckle that always sounded nervous, even though it wasnt. "Okay … there. I hope theyre all right," he said, closing my notebook and sliding the work back across the table to me.

"Thanks, I owe you one." I got up, as did Mick.

"See ya."

"See ya."

Later that evening, Joanie called to tell me that we had new neighbors next door.

"When did they move in?"

"My dad said he saw a moving truck parked out front all day Friday. I haven't seen anyone though. Have you?"

"No," I answered peering through my curtains.

"Well, I have to go. I have lots of homework to finish," Joanie said. We hung up.

Bam, bam, bam. I heard the basketball being dribbled again. This time I saw who was dribbling it. I watched the new boy next door bouncing the ball in his driveway before stopping to make a shot at the basketball hoop they had just installed above their garage. He looked to be about my age, with short black hair and fair skin like mine. He was tall and lanky like me, but he was handsome. I didn't call Joanie back to tell her I had seen our new neighbor. For some reason, I felt this was one new neighbor I wanted to meet on my own.

During recess on Monday, I told the group—Susan, Caroline, Stephanie, Deborah and Laura— about my new neighbor as we stood in our usual circle on the playground.

"He's *so* cute. I don't know what to say to him, though."

"What you should do, Junie, is get yourself your own basketball to dribble around in your driveway," Stephanie said.

"Yeah," Deborah interrupted. "Then you'll have something in common to start off a conversation with."

"You know, that's a great idea," Susan said.

When I got home that afternoon, I dug through a big cardboard box in the garage. I rummaged through piles of old toys, roller skates, tennis racquets, my skateboard and more.

"Aha! I knew I had a basketball in here!"

I should be doing my homework, I thought as I drudged the basketball out of the assortment of old toys. I bounced it on the cold cement garage floor, but being slightly deflated, it only rebounded about an inch. I grabbed the tire pump that we kept by the door and found the basketball needle in my dad's work-bench drawer. I pumped the ball, stopping every few seconds to see if it was firming up.

Finally, the ball was inflated and ready to go. I took it out into my driveway, looking out of the corner of my eye to see if *he* would come out. I was hoping my ball could be heard the same way as his. I remembered the echoing sound it had made between the brick homes. With it being winter, all the trees were bare. Birds were hibernating, and there was less activity throughout the neighborhood, which made it easier for sound to travel. I remembered sitting behind Mick's house one day waiting for him to finish with his dinner so he could come outside. I kept yelling "Hey!" and listening to my voice echo back to me. *Hey, hey, hey.* When Mick finally came out, he looked at me like I had twenty heads wondering what I had been yelling at the entire time. "Oh" was all he said with his chuckle when I had told him.

My fingertips were starting to go numb in the winter air. As I turned to go back in, *he* came out. He had opened his large garage door, which grabbed my attention. I noticed a younger boy with the same black hair walk out with him. They started shooting hoops. I became instantly shy and ran inside. I went to my room and watched them through my sheer curtains. Joanie was heading down the street toward their driveway. I ran down the hall, out the front door, and then jumped down over all four steps. I landed at the bottom, hidden behind the arborvitae planted next to the bottom step. I composed myself before walking over casually.

"Hi," I said. I was glad that Joanie had come over to meet them.

"This is my friend, Junie," she said, gesturing toward me. "This is Shaun and his little brother Chris."

"Hi," Shaun said. I was glad to see he had braces just like mine. It turned out he was my age as well. I was relieved to have Joanie with me. She wasn't shy like me and knew how to start a conversation.

"Where did y'all move here from?" she asked.

"Germany. My dad is in the air force."

"Germany? That's where a friend of ours moved *to*. She used to live in your house," I said, thinking of Janie.

"Junie?" I heard my mom calling from our front porch. "Dinner's ready."

"Okay, Mom, I'll be right there."

"Well, nice meeting you," I said as I turned to go.

"Hey!" Shaun called to me.

"Yeah?"

"Was that you I heard dribbling a basketball around earlier?"

"Oh yeah, it was. I'm thinking about going out for the basketball team," I lied.

"You are?" Joanie asked.

"Yeah, remember?" I said, pressing my lips and widening my eyes, hoping she would catch on.

"I'll call you later," she said as I ran inside, not wanting to get embarrassed by my mom coming out a second time.

"Come over after dinner and we'll shoot some hoops," Shaun yelled back.

"Okay. See you later." *Forget homework*, I thought as I went in for dinner.

First Crush

I remember those difficult years of being hormonal, emotions racing out of control, not understanding why and not understanding my feelings. Shawn and I played basketball almost every day after school. I liked his mom, who seemed to be very understanding of teenagers and kids, unlike my parents. God knows my mom tried. But she had grown up barefoot on a farm in the country down in Florida. There was quite a generation gap between my parents and me. They could remember World War II. I went through puberty at the same time my mom was going through menopause. We screamed at one another a lot, and had little to no understanding of one another. I was expected to jump when my dad commanded that I do something. He would yell in a loud, booming voice, intimidating me. My mom always took his side.

When Shaun's mom interrupted one of our basketball games to tell him to take out the trash, I was taken aback when he expressed frustration towards her. I thought (but didn't say) *You ought to have my parents if that's all it takes to frustrate you.* My parents fought constantly, and the conflict trickled down on me. With constant screaming and yelling, it was hard to concentrate on schoolwork. Their fighting was embarrassing when friends were over.

My grades dropped, so I was given lots of extra credit assignments to bring my grades up. The lower marks were my fault, and resulted from spending so much time and energy concentrating on Shaun. The rule at St. Matthew's about staying after school to complete late homework had been changed, because some of the parents had complained about it. I didn't finish all of the extra-credit assignments and ended up with two Fs on my report card, one in math and one in history, the two classes I

178

loathed the most. On report card day, I went over to Shaun's. I sat in a chair next to him as he sat at his desk.

"I'm going to be sent to the death chamber when my dad gets home," he told me.

"Why?"

"I got two Fs on my report card."

"Really?" I couldn't believe he was in the same boat as I. "In what subjects?"

"Math and science."

"I guess I'll be right behind you then. I got failing grades in math and history."

We both laughed at our awkward situation. Right before Shaun's mom came in to send me home because his dad was home, I remember noticing how blue his eyes were. They seemed bluer and more beautiful than at any other time I had looked at them.

"I'll see you later if my dad doesn't kill me," he said.

"Yeah," I said, chuckling. "Good luck."

Shaun laughed. "Good luck to you too."

I felt somewhat at ease knowing I wasn't the only one who would be getting into trouble over bad grades. The last A I got was on the math homework that Mick ended up doing for me. I never quite got the hang of math after that. I had been so neglectful with Shaun living next door.

"No more going out to play basketball after school until homework is done and we've checked it," my dad said, looking at my report card. I was relieved that was all he said on the topic.

"Oh, I will," I promised, thankful to not be yelled at. Shaun ended up not getting a death sentence, but was given the same rule as I. It worked out nicely, because we could still play basketball in the evenings. We would call each other when homework was done, and would meet in Shaun's driveway. I hated cold weather but didn't mind when it came to being with Shaun. Basketball was a great excuse to hang out and talk.

I had neglected my friends in the neighborhood. Shaun was all I could think about. We would stay up late and tape-record songs played on a local radio station, K-94. I taped "Call Me" by Blondie, and played it over and over. I also taped "You Shook Me All Night Long" and "Back in Black" by AC/DC. Shaun taped "Whip It" by Devo, and let me borrow his tape. He moved his bedroom to the room over their garage, giving him a view of my room. We could signal with our flashlights to say goodnight after we were finished taping songs. On Saturday afternoons, when one of our moms would drop us off at Military Circle Mall, we would head straight over to the record store to buy the top hit albums. Foreigner's *4* and REO Speedwagon were some of our favorites. I cried myself to sleep each night, like some love sick cow, thinking of Shaun while listening to REO Speedwagon's "Keep on Loving You." It seems so silly looking back, the way I tortured myself playing that song over and over, knowing it would make me cry. I had never cried over a guy before, therefore I had to be in love, I thought. I let Shaun borrow my copy of the Olivia Newton-John album *Totally Hot* so he could tape songs off it, and so I would have another excuse to go over to his house.

I knew every word to every song on that album. Neana and I would sit on my bedroom floor, holding hairbrushes up and singing into them as if they were microphones. The lyrics to each song were written on the back of the album sleeve, and we read along as we sang. Neana's mom bought her a baton like mine, so we both could twirl them while talking in our rooms or while playing outside. I showed her some moves that I had learned in baton class.

Joanie had quit cheerleading to twirl rifles in the junior high school's band. They no longer had majorettes, which was disappointing to me because I had dreamt of becoming a majorette once I got to junior high.

"The majorettes always bring our scores down when we have band competitions," Joanie had explained to me one day. "Now we have rifle girls and flag girls."

"What's the difference?"

"They still *twirl*. The rifles are less frivolous-looking and sturdier, and the flag twirlers give the color and pizzazz that the majorettes used to give."

"They're not real rifles, are they?"

"God, no, Junie! They're just shaped like them. They're solid wood."

Joanie being in band took up all of her spare time. She had joined the debate team as well, and, of course, was one of the best debaters. I missed hanging out with her after school. St. Matthew's didn't have any extracurricular activities, so some of the moms got together and volunteered to teach us different hobbies. We had to choose only one activity. There was golfing, which one dad volunteered to teach, or crocheting, painting, sketching, or cross-stitch. I signed up for cross-stitch when I found out Susan had signed up for it.

May arrived out of nowhere, it seemed. I would inhale the air deeply after a heavy rainstorm to smell the heavy scent of daffodils, tulips, and roses. Mrs. Ainsworth's lavender, blue, and white hydrangeas wouldn't have blooms until late summer. I loved those flowers but had forgotten that they didn't bloom in the spring. My dad had planted pink and white azalea bushes along the side of our house under my bedroom window. I kept my window open to smell their sweet blooms if the humidity was low. I remembered how our azalea bushes grew up high around our house back in Norfolk, touching the windows, and my dad taking a picture of me standing in front of them. I was wearing a pink sundress that matched the flowers, camouflaging me with the pink blooms behind me. George Town was beautiful in the spring. Everyone's yards turned green again and the trees had blooms on them after the colorless, cold winter retreated.

Time sped by after Shaun moved in and changed my life. I no longer woke up in the morning to run across my lawn into the cul-de-sac to play jump rope or jacks. I didn't concern myself with playing Barbies or dolls with my friends on their lawns, or even flag football or kickball for that matter. Shaun popped into my mind when I awoke each morning.

I was so excited when he called one day to ask me to the movies. I never had a boy ask me to go to the movies before, except for Mick, Morris, and Teddy, but that didn't count; they were like brothers. Shaun's mom dropped us off at the mall, telling us she would be back at 3:30 PM to pick us up. I liked how she looked, with her red hair cut into a short mullet, reminding me of the mom in *The Brady Bunch*.

We saw *Popeye*, starring Robin Williams. It wasn't animated like the cartoon. Shaun and I were curious as to how they were going to portray the characters. We ended up thinking the movie was pretty good, considering it wasn't a cartoon.

Shaun's family was one of the first in George Town to buy a VCR. I spent one evening with Shaun on the living room floor watching *Saturn 3* starring Farrah Fawcett. I was too scared to walk home alone when it was over, thinking of the scary, evil robot in the movie that killed everyone aboard the space ship. At least Farrah got away. Shaun walked me home when it was over. As soon as we reached my front porch, he dashed back to his house. *He is just as scared as I am*, I thought. The following weekend, we decided to watch a comedy instead. It was easier walking back home after watching *The Blues Brothers*.

My dad yelled at me one day and put me on restrictions after my teacher called to let him know we had a major science fair coming up, which was going to be the biggest part of our grades. I was supposed to hand in an outline of what I was going to do my project on, but never did. I had honestly forgotten about the whole thing.

"The assignment was given three months ago," Dad told me when he got off the phone with Mrs. Scango.

My dad came home the next day with a twelve-inch, U-shaped magnet. He set a plastic bag full of tiny metal beads on the table next to the magnet. "You're going to do your report on magnetism," he said.

I sat reading through books and writing my report until midnight. I had to give an oral report as well as a demonstration. My dad typed up information on index cards for me to read in front of the class. We put the magnet in a cardboard box, and glued index cards all around the box.

At the science fair, everyone walked around and looked at the projects from all the classes. Mine was obviously the most popular. Most of my classmates couldn't stop bouncing the tiny beads off the table and watching the magnet's strong gravitational pull suck the beads in. I would have received an A, but Mrs. Scango had to give me a B because I started the project so late. *Thanks, Dad* I thought to myself. I would have flunked if he hadn't stepped up.

During the first week of summer vacation, Morris asked me if I wanted to go to the mall with him. They were having Volkswagen races in the parking lot. Shaun was going to be away on vacation for the week. Morris had just gotten his driver's license. He'd saved enough money to buy himself a two-door olive-green Duster, with a sporty black stripe going down the side. It made me think of the white stripe going down the side of the red sports car in *Starsky and Hutch.*

My dad said it was okay to go. Morris was a responsible driver. As we headed down Providence Road, I turned on his radio. When we heard the first song that came on, we both instantly started singing, looking at each other as if its lyrics harmonized with our young lives. "It's a Heartache" by Bonnie Tyler was playing, making me think of Shaun. Morris always had a girlfriend. *Did his heart ache, too?* I wondered. We stopped in a 7-Eleven along the way to buy a couple of Coca-Colas before heading to Military Circle Mall.

In the parking lot, we sat on the hood of his car and chuckled as all the souped-up Volkswagens raced, going really fast and sounding extremely loud for such little cars. They looked silly, because they were cute, round cars, not tough sporty ones. "W-w-which one do you think w-w-will win?"

"I think the red one. It looks pretty fast."

"Yeah m-m-me too."

Sure enough, the little red car won.

"They looked like a bunch of jelly beans," I said as we headed home.

Morris chuckled. "I w-w-wish I had one of those th-th-though. They are some bad little cars w-w-with their engines souped up l-l-like that."

I pictured Morris and I racing against one another. "I bet I would beat you in a race," I couldn't help but tease.

"Uh-uh, no way."

"I know how to drive."

"Well, I-I-I have a driver's license."

"Yeah, but I've known how to drive since I was ten."

When we pulled onto our street, I thanked Morris for taking me. "Sure, anytime."

Teddy came over one afternoon, much to our surprise. Joanie and I were sitting in my bedroom talking about a guy she was dating named Darren. When the doorbell rang, we both jumped up, curious as to who it was. My dad was out to sea, but my mom was home. She got to the door before Joanie and I. It was a pleasant surprise when she answered the door. There stood Teddy, with his familiar grin spread across his face. He had his driver's license now, and had taken it upon himself to drive up to see us. While sitting in the living room chatting about life back in Norfolk, we decided to go out for pizza.

"You come along too," he said to Joanie.

"Okay," she said, impressed by his friendliness, charisma, and humor (as was I).

We all sat in a crescent-shaped booth with red vinyl cushions at Milton's Pizza. Even though Teddy was only sixteen, he seemed so much more mature. He spoke with my mom like a fellow adult. I thought he was handsome with his sandy blond hair cut short and parted on the side. He seemed like such a happy guy. His blue eyes sparkled as he spoke, just how I remembered when we were little. He hadn't grown very tall, though. I was the same height as him now. Teddy explained how he was attending a private school in Norfolk and taking Chinese as an elective.

"Chinese isn't a common foreign language for a school to offer, so I chose it."

While we ate our pizza slices, he occasionally would make a funny face and say something in Chinese. He had us rolling in laughter. He had also learned to play the banjo. When we returned home, he brought his banjo in. We sat on the couch watching him play. He had on a short-sleeved blue-and-red-striped shirt with a white collar and blue jeans. Every now and then, he would stop playing and say something in Chinese, again making us burst out laughing.

"How do you say hello in Chinese?" I asked. "*Shang how*!" he answered, once again making us hysterical with laughter.

Teddy had taken up clog-hopping as well. As he left to go home, he clog-hopped to his car, putting on a goofy face and flapping his arms like a chicken. My stomach literally hurt from laughing so hard. I remember wishing he lived in George Town. We would have had so much fun. I sure did miss him.

I missed Shaun too, and was excited when he returned home from his trip to Ohio after visiting relatives. My fondness for Shaun had grown quite a bit. Did he like me back as much as I liked him? That thought played over and over in my head and frustrated me. I would never ask him, of course. I would never be brave enough. *How do you know if someone likes you back the same way?* I wondered.

Joanie started to shoot hoops with us in Shaun's driveway, annoying me a bit. Her presence interfered with my time with Shaun. Jealousy grew inside me when Shaun started giving her just as much attention as he gave me. I kept my feelings tucked down inside, trying not to show them. But I could feel a slow burn growing.

Shaun's parents invited us and the Ainsworths' over for a cookout one afternoon. Shaun's dad, Mr. Armstrong, grilled hamburgers on the grill while we sat around on their back patio. Their back patio was nicely shaded during the summer months by their large maple trees. We brought over our own lawn chairs. After we ate, Mrs. Armstrong brought out beer for the adults. The five of us kids went out front to play hide-and-seek. As the sun dropped and the moonlight shone, Morris, Joanie, Chris, Shaun, and I sat in the front yard talking with the sound of crickets all around. I don't know why Joanie suggested it, but we ended up playing Truth or Dare, a game Joanie had learned from the Normans, no doubt. We asked silly questions, which had to take the form of a revealing question or a dare.

"I dare you to run around the house three times"

"Have you ever farted out loud in class?"

I was astounded and peeved when Chris dared Joanie to *kiss* Shaun. I sat watching, hoping she would give Shaun a quick peck on the cheek or forehead, which to my relief she did. It was now Joanie's turn. She turned to Shaun.

"Truth or dare?"

"Dare."

"I dare you to kiss Junie."

"Hey, Shaun?"

We heard Mrs. Armstrong's voice coming from around the side of the house, but couldn't see her in the dark.

"Yeah?"

"I need you and Chris to come in and load the dishwasher and take out the trash."

"All right." Shaun and Chris jumped up and headed inside. Joanie, Morris, and I went to sit on the front porch in the soft, yellow glow of the porch light.

Mr. and Mrs. Ainsworth made their way across the lawn, saying it was time to go home.

Morris and Joanie traded "see yas" with me.

I was about to head home when Shaun came walking up out of the darkness. He told me my parents were heading home and that I was supposed to go too. But before I started down the steps, Shaun walked right up to me kissing me right on the lips! I didn't know what to say. I was shocked.

"Good night," Shaun said. He walked around me, heading through his front door. I ran home, feeling exuberant and alive. *I am in love and I think he loves me back*, I thought, feeling giddy. I went to bed playing "Keep on Loving You," this time without crying.

I felt disappointment over the course of the days that followed. Shaun never said anything, and never treated me any differently. It was as if the kiss had never happened. When we went to the beach with our moms and body-surfed the waves or built sandcastles together, I would bump his hand or arm on purpose. I remember trying to bump his hand on purpose as we placed little seashells on the sandy towers of the castle. I was always hoping he would kiss me again or hold my hand while walking along the shore. Our friendship just stayed the same. It frustrated me, leaving me venting to poor Neana, who had to listen to my whining. She tried valiantly, but didn't fully understand my feelings.

"Should I tell him how I feel?"

"I don't know," she would reply. I knew if I told Joanie, she would tell Shaun, and I didn't want that.

Neana was only nine, but I appreciated her friendship. She helped me take my mind off my worries and let me ramble on and on, always lending a solid ear. I think she looked up to me as a big sister. She would call to tell me things, like when she got her ears pierced and couldn't wait for me to see them. She called another day just to tell me to come down and see her new short haircut. I had let my hair grow out longer, and by then it reached just below my shoulders. I wasn't brave enough to get my ears pierced. I was proud of Neana getting hers pierced, and how she carefully applied ear cleaning solution while rotating the studs to keep her ears safe from infection.

My thirteenth birthday arrived on a day where everyone happened to be out of town for one reason or another. It was nearing the end of summer, and everyone wanted to get that last-minute vacation in. Neana was the only one who could attend my birthday party. We had planned for everyone to come over for cake and ice cream before heading to the beach. I was glad at least Neana could make it, even though it wasn't the same without the whole crew.

Shaun gave me a Kool & the Gang album, featuring their latest hit song "Celebration." Joanie and Morris bought me the singles of "Bette Davis Eyes" by Kim Carnes and "Jessie's Girl" by Rick Springfield. They brought the records over to me a few days before heading out of town.

Rain poured all day on my birthday, leaving condensation on the windows because of the air conditioner running inside and the high humidity outside. The clouds made the sky so dark that the streetlights came on. I decided to go see a movie for my birthday instead of a beach trip, as the weather was so wet and gloomy. After Neana and I had cake and ice cream, my mom took us to see *The Blue Lagoon*. I was captivated throughout the entire film. The beautiful, breathtaking scenery of the tropical island was so romantic. The water was a crystal-clear turquoise blue, with white-sand beaches and palm trees lining the shore. The music made my heart ache, making me think of Shaun and I on the island, instead of Brooke Shields and Christopher Atkins. I didn't know there was such a place, with water *so* clear and sand *so* white. *Someday I'm going to a place like that,* I thought. *Someday before I die, I'll go to a South Pacific island and maybe never leave.*

After school started again, I was back to the old routines of getting up early each morning, and making sure homework was done before going outside after school. *Yuck.*

I was studying my list of twenty-five spelling words for the week when I heard my mom answer the doorbell. I heard Mrs. Ceaver's voice. I was happy to know she came over for a visit with my mom. I found her presence calming. Mrs. Ceaver would often bring a gift for me from Avon. She had always wanted a little girl. That time she brought me a white imitation alligator-skin clutch. I opened the snaps and looked inside. There were six bottles of fingernail polish inside.

"Thanks, Mrs. Ceaver."

"You're starting to grow up now, so I thought I would give you a gift that's a little more *mature*, instead of a toy." It was a belated birthday gift, as they had been down in Carolina on my birthday.

My mom came into my room after she and Mrs. Ceaver finished drinking a pot of coffee and gossiping.

"Mrs. Ceaver told me that you should be careful hanging around Mick," Mom said.

"Why?" I asked, fearing they might have caught him smoking.

My mom sat on my bed. I turned sideways in my desk chair to listen to what was wrong. "Well, Mrs. Ceaver was very upset. They caught Mick stealing. So watch out. He has sticky fingers."

I felt disappointment as I looked over at the stack of records Mick had recently given me. I wondered where he had gotten them. They had obviously been used. I remembered him saying a friend gave them to him. The Steve Miller Band's "The Joker" and Vicki Lawrence's "The Night the Lights Went Out in Georgia" were probably missing from someone's record collection. *Oh, come on Mick, don't go down that road,* I thought.

"One more thing. They found drug paraphernalia in his room too. So Junie, I don't want you going over there if his parents aren't home. If he ever offers you drugs, you come and tell me."

"Okay," I said, feeling a little perturbed. Mick would never offer me drugs. He would kick my butt if he caught me with drugs.

"Mom?" I said before she got up to leave me to my homework.

"Yes?"

"Mick is my friend. He would never give and has never given me drugs."

"You never know, Junie. Just remember you can't trust anyone out there. Not anyone, *especially* guys."

Sister Christine announced that St. Matthew's was starting a basketball team over the loudspeaker one morning before classes. "There will be a boy's team and a girl's, for seventh and eighth graders only. So sign up in the office after school."

All of the Catholic schools had gotten together and formed a league of teams, drawing players from more than one school onto each team. I didn't sign up after thinking about it. I became angry when my mom took it upon herself to sign me up. I was angry at her at first because she didn't ask me if I had wanted to play. She just went ahead and did it. *Dammit*, I thought. I know she had my best interests in mind, but I felt too shy and awkward to play in front of a crowd of people.

When I met our coach, Mr. Mike, I felt a little more at ease. He was very friendly and had a good sense of humor. I had pictured him being stern and yelling, like the football coaches did on TV. Susan refused to play. I was relieved when I found out that the two new girls in school were going to be on my team, meaning I wasn't going to be the only girl from St. Matthew's on the Blue Devils. *What an odd name*, I thought. The Blue Devils from Catholic schools. One would think we would be called the Blue Angels instead. I envied the players from the Catholic school Star of the Sea. Not only did I like their name, but their team was lucky enough to go to a school located right on the ocean. Their school even had stained glass windows.

Laura was our most valuable player, scoring the majority of our points. She wasn't shy and helped me tremendously with my position. I was to play center, because I was one of the tallest on the team. I knew nothing about basketball and its rules or positions. Shaun and I had only dribbled the ball around, making shots at the basket whenever we felt like it. We never got technical about it. At least my lie about joining the basketball team was now true.

During our first scrimmage, I embarrassed myself and the team when I became so nervous that I forgot to dribble the ball. I *carried* it. The Ainsworths came to most of my games to cheer me on. Shaun played basketball for Indian River Junior High, and all of his games were on the same days as mine, so we never got to watch each other play. Thank God. I would have died if he came to one of my games. I would have fumbled and stumbled so badly. At the end of basketball season, we had a ceremony in the cafeteria at St. Matthew's. Coach Mike gave a speech, mentioning something special about each player. He called up Laura handing her a trophy as our MVP. *I wish I could get that*, I thought.

"I've never seen a person able to do a right handed and left handed layup perfectly. Nor have I seen a young lady come such a long way. Junie?"

Coach Mike was calling me up, looking at me with a wide smile. I was stunned. *Did he just call me up there?* I asked myself.

"Junie?"

He had. I got up out of my seat, hoping not to stumble and fall on my face with my black high heels on. I had on a blue dress, almost the color of our team's jerseys. I shook his hand as he handed me a trophy that read *Most Improved*. I *had* improved, and was proud of the trophy, considering how I knew absolutely nothing about basketball when I first started. Everyone else on the team received certificates, stating the year we played with their name printed across the top. We never won a game, but the experience was educational and gave me confidence.

I never thought much about John Lennon until Shaun talked about how much he liked Lennon's latest song. *I'm just sittin' here watchin' the wheels go round and round/I really love to watch them roll,* John Lennon's smooth voice sang on the radio. I can recall Laura from the Blue Devils talking about John Lennon all the way to basketball practice one evening. She had said her brother was a huge fan. When John was gunned down in December 1980, it made a lot of fans very sad. Laura had tears in her eyes as she spoke about John and her brother Jack's love for the late musician. Seeing how people loved the singer so much changed my perspective. I took a newfound interest in his music and the Beatles.

I was growing unhappy at St. Matthew's. The two new girls who had played on my basketball team were bigger than the rest of us girls and bullied us. Joanna and Sue Anne buddied around together, trying to act like tough girls. They were nice while on the team, but in class they would make fun of me by mimicking me every time I said something. They would shove me or the other girls while playing volleyball in gym class when the teacher wasn't looking. Joanna and I got into a shoving match one day and had to spend recess sitting in the library for a couple of days as punishment. My heart sank when Susan moved away, followed by Caroline, leaving me isolated once again.

"When the school year is over, I want to go to Indian River" I told my parents during dinner one night.

"Why? What's wrong with your school now?" my mom asked, sounding exasperated.

"Oh, I would just like to go to a bigger school."

"Well, that's fine, if that is what you want," my dad said. I was glad he didn't object. "It will save me money anyway."

For our final grade of the year, we had to pick a foreign country to do a report on. We had to provide pictures and were expected to give an oral report as well. I chose Iceland. Not only was it the most recent country my dad had been deployed to, I also found the island nation intriguing. My dad had sent many postcards from Iceland, as well as a beige-and-brown wool purse that was hand-woven in Reykjavik, Iceland's capital. My dad had also brought me a necklace made from pewter. It was heavy and gawky, but interesting. There was an emblem of an ice princess carved on the largest piece of the necklace.

I surprised myself with how well my oral presentation went. I remembered everything I had planned to say, and the class seemed intrigued. I spoke about the natural hot springs in Iceland, showing a picture of elderly people sitting in one of the hot springs with snow all around. An old man was sitting in the middle, holding up a thermometer with his toes. I couldn't read the thermometer, but I could tell the water was warm, as it was steaming. I received an A for my final grade. When school let out, I was thrilled about not having to return again after summer vacation. No more wearing uniforms and no more carpooling with overzealous people so early in the morning.

After a barbecue at the Ainsworth's, Shaun, Chris, Morris, Joanie, and I played freeze tag in their front yard. Our parents did the usual, chatting while sipping beer or cocktails in their lawn chairs. We ended up playing Truth or Dare again when the sun fell. Once again, I felt my jealousy boil over when Chris dared Joanie to kiss Shaun. This time she not only gave him a peck on the lips, but started French-kissing him! My eyes bulged, and I didn't know how to react. I was angry and green with jealousy. It was only a game, but Shaun was kissing her back. I wanted to punch Joanie over and over again. *How could she?* Shaun was *my* friend, who *I* loved. This would be the end of our friendship. I would never be able to speak to Joanie again, and maybe not even Shaun! I began to ignore them both, spending all my time in my room reading and sketching, or taking bike rides alone.

Mrs. Simons called and asked to speak with me one day. I was curious as to why she was calling for me.

"Hi, Junie. I need a babysitter, and now that you're thirteen, I thought you would like to sit with Neana and Jake for a few hours this evening."

I had never babysat before, but I figured I could handle it. I wasn't doing anything of importance at home, after all.

"Okay. What time?"

"Can you come over around 7:00?"

"Sure." I knew my parents wouldn't mind, and would even be proud of my making some money.

Mrs. Simons explained everything I needed to know, and wrote down where they would be and a phone number where they could be reached. She was dressed nice and had her red hair permed in waves. She was a petite lady, standing at the same height as me. Mr. Simons was tall, well over six feet, with black hair and features that reminded me of Johnny Cash.

"Jake, Neana, in bed by 9:00, no later!" she said sternly before heading out. Mr. Simons was waiting in the car.

Neana watched TV while I played with Jake, keeping him entertained as we sat on his bedroom floor. He had his *Star Wars* dolls and space ships out. Jake was obedient, going to bed when I told him to. I was glad he fell asleep right away. I let Neana stay up as late as she wanted, but she eventually grew tired and went to bed around 10:00. I decided to sit in their rocking recliner. It was so comfortable. I could rock for hours in that chair. I didn't know how late the Simons would be. I was hungry. I went into the kitchen and opened the olive-green Tupperware canister on the kitchen counter and helped myself to some cookies. Mrs. Simons made the best sugar cookies. I poured myself a glass of Kool-Aid and went back into the den to watch TV. I didn't want them to come home and find me sleeping. Neana had told me how they no longer called on Joanie to babysit because they always found her fast asleep on their sofa when they got home. I wanted to be a responsible babysitter. Finally they came home around midnight. Mrs. Simons gave me $7.

"Thanks" I said.

"No, *thank you*. How did everything go?"

"Oh just fine. They both behaved very well."

"Well good. Can you babysit next Friday night?"

"Sure." Even though their house was just down the road from mine, Mr. Simons gave me a ride home because it was so late.

My mom was sitting on the couch watching *Goldfinger* on TV when I came in.

"How did it go?"

"Fine. Kind of boring. But at least I got paid."

"Good," my mom said. I headed down the hall to my room. I went straight to bed, falling into a deep slumber. Babysitting had taken my mind off Joanie and Shaun for a while.

When I awoke, my mom was packing up her beach bag. I could hear her pulling towels out of the linen closet and digging around in the bag, suntan lotion bottles rattling.

"*Junie*, are you up?"

"Yeah."

"When you get up, I thought we could spend the day at the beach."

I thought of Shaun and felt depressed. I'd been ignoring Joanie and Shaun for over a week now, making excuses when one of them called. I became enraged when I saw Joanie shooting hoops with Shaun. That was what Shaun and I did. I thought that she was a backstabber, Shaun too, for that matter. Couldn't they see I loved him? If Joanie loved a boy I wouldn't impose coming in between them. I got up and put on my bathing suit.

"Can Neana come?"

"Why don't you ask Joanie? Neana is so young, and she gets on my nerves."

"What does she do?" I asked. I considered Neana a good friend. She and I had the same age difference between us that Joanie and I had. *What difference did it make?* I thought. Reluctantly my mom let me invite Neana to go with us, which made Neana's day. I did notice how Neana could get on my mom's nerves. She asked my mom one question after another.

"How long until we get there?"

"About twenty-five minutes."

"Why?"

"Because of traffic and the miles."

"How many miles?"

"I don't know for sure. Can you please stop with all the questions?"

"Why?"

"My mom needs to concentrate on driving," I intervened, putting a finger over my lips so Neana would hopefully quiet down. We enjoyed the day at the beach. The sun was bright, making the waves sparkle as I showed Neana how to bodysurf. While the three of us made a huge sandcastle; I couldn't help but think of Shaun. My heart sank again. I let out a heavy sigh.

This is the worst summer of my life, I thought as I lay in bed the next day, staring up out the window at the beautiful blue sky. I didn't feel like riding my bike. I didn't feel like swimming, roller-skating, reading, or sketching. My Barbies bored me. They were packed in my closet. Usually on hot summer days when we weren't going to the pool or beach, we would go to the movies. Or Joanie and I would cool off in my sprinkler before laying out in the sun on beach towels in the backyard. I felt so let down by Shaun and Joanie's hanging out together.

Things felt worse when Janie came to town for a visit. She spent twenty minutes sitting on our couch, mainly speaking with my mom. She seemed so grown up, sitting with her legs crossed and wearing makeup. She acted like she was too old to pay attention to me.

"My dad is going to do another term in Germany" she said. "Ruth is going to college over there."

"How is Tommy?"

"He's doing fine, playing a lot of soccer."

"How is your mom?" my mom asked.

"She's fine. She's teaching again on base. Well, I have to go," Janie said, looking at her watch. "I'm sorry I can't visit longer, but we've got relatives to visit as well." Janie and Ruth had flown over and were staying with their grandma she had said. "I visited with Joanie awhile today too," Janie mentioned as she got ready to go.

"I wish you could stay, Janie. I really miss you," I said. We hugged each other good-bye.

"I miss you all too, Junie."

"I wish we could hang out like old times and be the J-Birds again," I said, forgetting about being mad at Joanie and suddenly missing her friendship as well. Janie headed out the door and got into a car that had been sitting in our driveway. The lady behind the wheel looked familiar, but I couldn't place her.

Later that day, I was surprised to hear Joanie's voice on the other end of the phone when it rang. Joanie asked me if Janie had visited.

"Yeah, but she didn't stay very long. I wish we all could hang out again like old times," I said, forgetting again about being angry and jealous.

"Me too. I miss hanging out with you, Junie. Whatcha been up to?"

"Oh, nothing much."

"My mom is going garage sale-ing tomorrow. Do you want to go along?"

"Sure."

"Tell your mom so she will come too."

"I will."

We got up early to hit the good sales before they got picked over. We loved garage sale-ing during the summer months. I realized how much I missed Joanie and let go of my jealousy.

When we got back home; Joanie and I decided to ride our bikes.

We passed by a chubby girl with short black hair who was riding her bike as well.

"Hey" Joanie called to the girl.

"Hey," she replied, stopping her bike.

We stopped too, putting our feet down for balance.

"This is Susan. Janie used to take acting classes with her," Joanie said.

"Oh, hi," I said. I remembered having seen Susan around, but had never spoken to her. She lived in George Town, but on the other side.

"Did you visit with Janie?"

"Yeah, we just dropped her off at the airport. She spent a week with us," Susan said.

Joanie and I looked at each other in surprise.

"What?" we asked simultaneously.

"Didn't she tell you? She and Ruth stayed at my place."

"No, she didn't," I said. I pedaled off with Joanie following. We didn't know what to say. Janie, our fellow J-Bird, had snubbed us. Joanie and I both felt betrayed over Janie's decision to choose Susan's friendship over ours. I knew Janie and Susan were friends at their school and participated in all of their acting classes together. We even went to see a couple of their plays. It had never crossed Joanie's or my mind that Janie didn't feel as strong a bond to us as we felt to her. We were the

J-Birds. We had been inseparable. I guess people change. We lost touch with with Janie after that, which hurt our feelings even more.

After that shock, I made the decision to just be honest and confide in Joanie that I had felt hurt and jealous over her kissing Shaun the way she did. Seeing as we were talking about hurt feelings anyway, I thought it was an appropriate time to bring him up.

"It was *just a game*," she said, sounding annoyed.

"Yeah, I know but …" I was trying to explain my feelings without letting her know just how fond of Shaun I was. She knew I had never had a boyfriend, and that Shaun was the closest thing to one Id ever had. Or did she?

"Shaun and I are good friends, and you don't even like basketball, so why would you play with him knowing that?"

"*You don't own him.*"

I felt angry and hurt that she wasn't accepting what I was saying. She had always listened intently whenever I had confided in her in the past. But not now. I turned to go home.

"Where are you going?"

"I have to go. We're not seeing eye-to-eye on this."

"On *what*? Like I said, you don't *own* him!"

I thought what she was saying was incredibly insensitive. "Do you like Shaun, Joanie?"

"As a friend."

"How would you like it if you had a boyfriend and I refused leave him alone? If I was always in the way of you two hanging out?"

"Is Shaun your boyfriend?"

"Well, no, not technically but …"

"So he's not even your boyfriend?"

I spun on my heel and walked home, completely outraged.

I still hung out with Shaun after my argument with Joanie. But if Joanie came over to join us, I would leave. The boiling anger and jealousy that simmered down was now back.

His mom asked to speak with me one day, inviting me in for a soda. I sat with her at their kitchen table. I had talked privately with her. She had overheard my mom and I screaming at each other one day, and was concerned by it.

"I remember what it was like being a teenager and not getting along with my mom. You can talk to me anytime you need to get something off your chest," she had said.

I felt comfortable around her but didn't know how to tell her my true feelings for Shaun. He was her son, after all.

"I just wanted to let you know that while doing laundry, I found this note in Shaun's jeans pocket. He must have forgotten to give it to you."

I was pretty sure she and Shaun were together on this, but she wanted to keep him from being embarrassed. I felt flattered that he had written me a note, and was curious as to what it said.

"Do you want to read it in privacy? I already know what he wrote, but I promise to keep it a secret."

"Thanks. I'd like to read it alone."

"Okay." She was refreshing to talk with. As she sat looking at me from across her kitchen table, I noticed she had big yellowish eyes, not blue like Shaun's. "Remember now, come over anytime you need someone to talk to."

"Thank you. I will."

Shaun was lucky to have a mom who was so understanding. My mom would have made inappropriate and unfair accusations if she found a note I wrote to a boy, no matter what it said. I went straight home to my room. I closed the door for privacy and then sat at my desk to read the note.

Dear Junie,

I like you very much as a friend. I also like Joanie and can't be friends with only you or only her.

From Shaun

I had my answer. He had platonic feelings for me. Damn. Even worse, he wanted Joanie for a friend too. I was still angry with her for her insensitive reaction to what I had said. I decided to write him back, but couldn't. When he called for me to come over and shoot some hoops out front, I went over. When Joanie came over, it infuriated me even more. *She has some nerve!* I thought. But I didn't leave this time, trying to act as if everything was okay. When Joanie gave him a pat on the butt for making a shot or he passed the ball to *her* every time, ignoring me, I felt my jealousy grow. I couldn't help but to make pointed comments, pretending to be just kidding around.

"Pass it to your girlfriend."

"Aren't you going to grab his ass again? He made another shot."

I could tell I was annoying them, but kept up the act for several days. I was only going over to shoot hoops to take my anger out on them. One day he said "stop" in the middle of the game. He gently rolled the ball into his garage and went inside. Joanie had the audacity to follow him in.

All three of our moms were chatting inside, sitting around Mrs. Armstrong's dining room table. It was dark out. The sun seemed to have dropped so fast. I stood under the open window to hear what was being said.

"You all need to learn to get along." Shaun's mom said.

"*We can't*!" I heard Shaun say, his voice upset. "She keeps making comments then says she's just kidding."

I didn't realize I had upset Shaun this much. I sure had caused some drama. I really *did* want to get along. I was just mad at Joanie, who seemed to be ignoring my feelings. I just didn't know how to handle friendship with a guy that I had a crush on, especially with Joanie also being his friend. My emotions were spinning out of control. I felt tears welling up in my eyes. I knew I was going to cry, the kind of crying that would require me burying my face in my pillow to keep the whole neighborhood from hearing me. I ran home, feeling humiliated that they were talking about me. After letting my tears flow and screaming into my pillow, I decided to write them both notes.

Dear Shaun,

Of all of the friends I've ever had, I am the fondest of you. Joanie and I have always been friends, but I think the three of us together is just too crowded. I think you are a jerk for being friends with Joanie, a real JERK!

Sorry.

Junie

I wrote the same to Joanie, except I called *her* the jerk. I hand-delivered both notes to them the next day. When my parents went over to Shaun's for a cookout, I sat at the picnic table on their back patio with my dad and Mr. Armstrong, feeling angry and embarrassed. I was pretending to be interested in their navy talk. I was way too uncomfortable to go inside and find Shaun.

My heart jumped when I saw him walk past the screen door. He glared at me. "Scuzz," he said under his breath but loud enough that I could hear it. He was glaring at me so hard it made me want to cry. I focused in on our dads talking about aircraft carriers to control myself.

I ate in silence and went home instead of going out front to play with Shaun like old times. I sat in my bedroom crying, relieved that my parents were over there and not in the house to hear me. As the evening grew dark I could see Joanie and Shaun walking back and forth outside. They never even bothered looking for me. I guess I really was scuzz.

Mrs. Ainsworth called the next day and told my mom about the note I had written to Joanie. My mom got off the phone and told my dad.

"Well, go visit with them and get to the bottom of everything." Dad said.

They would never ask me for my side of the story.

"You know how Mrs. Ainsworth can get so dramatic." Mom said as she let out a sigh.

It was true. Mrs. Ainsworth really could be dramatic over the slightest thing, especially when it came to her kids.

We all sat down at the picnic table in Shaun's backyard, Joanie, Shaun, and I, and all three of our moms. Sure enough, Mrs. Ainsworth became dramatic. With a red face, she told my mom how I was the instigator of all this trouble.

"The reason the kids have been a triangle is because your daughter started it all!"

I felt like I was on trial for murder. I honestly loved everyone at the table and didn't want any of this. I wanted to find a way to make things work. I wanted to be understood! Why couldn't they see that?

"Well, I say this is the kids' business. Let them handle it," Shaun's mom said, to my relief.

"We did let them handle it and now Joanie feels like she can't play next door with Shaun," Mrs. Ainsworth yelped.

"Why? She knows she's welcome over any time!" Mrs. Armstrong said.

My mom looked down before finally speaking. "Well, I don't know. I didn't know my daughter was such an instigator. She's an embarrassment. I don't think I even want her now."

Shaun's jaw dropped. He looked at my mom in disbelief. I was embarrassed for him to see how my mom could be.

"Okay, we all had our say. It's time to go in," Mrs. Armstrong said. She motioned for Shaun to come with her.

"I'm sorry," I told him as he went in.

"I'm sorry, Mrs. Ainsworth, I don't know what's happening or how things got to this point."

As I got up to leave, I could hear Mrs. Ainsworth telling my mom through clenched teeth that I was a liar. My mom came in behind me. I had never felt so humiliated in all my life.

That night as I lay in bed crying my eyes out, thinking I no longer wanted to live. My dad came in and sat on the foot of my bed. "I heard what was said tonight. I listened through your window. And I am here to tell you *not* to feel bad. You were publicly humiliated, and your mom did nothing to defend you. I'll talk to her though, so don't worry. I love you. Know that we are here for you, okay?"

"Okay," I answered. I felt a little better, and was relieved that my dad was defending me.

My dad called Mrs. Ainsworth the next day. Using his sternest voice, he forbade her to ever come over or even speak to us again without apologizing.

What a dreary summer, I thought. I could only look up out at the blue sky and feel blue myself. I spent all my time in my bedroom. I didn't know I could feel so down.

Part Two

I remember gazing out my bedroom window at night. I could see airplanes high up in the sky, heading west. I always imagined myself flying on one, going somewhere, someplace different. If I was sad or depressed, the sight of the jets in the beautiful sunset or night sky always gave me a sense of hope.

I've always enjoyed a beautiful sunset, and as a teen, I often glanced through the back windows of our house in the hopes of seeing one.

I would gaze past the tops of the pine trees, looking at pink, orange, and yellow sunsets, moments of beauty that eased my mind and gave me hope while growing up in George Town East. I'll never forget those sunsets.

With our families not speaking and Shaun ignoring me, I was once again isolated, a feeling I hated. I wanted to run to Morris and tell him my true feelings, so he would know that I wasn't an ogre. I knew Mrs. Ainsworth would give him her own version of the story, leading him to take her side. I let it go. Morris was never around anyway, between school and work. He found a job over the summer, but I can't recall where. *I wish Mrs. Ainsworth would learn to keep it cool when it came to her kids,* I thought. Her overreactions had happened before, and had resulted in other families getting written off, or writing her off. The Ceavers alienated her as well. I never knew why, but Mrs. Ceaver loathed Mrs. Ainsworth. I remember Mrs. Ceaver ignoring Mrs. Ainsworth during Christmas and New Year's Eve parties, actually turning her head with her nose in the air. I had never given it much thought until my spat with Joanie.

My mom told me one day that I wasn't allowed to hang around

Mick *at all*, due to his continued drug use. *Oh great, another friend lost*, I thought sarcastically. *Just what I needed.* There were rumors that Mick was getting involved in the Mob as well. I still called him on the phone late at night when I couldn't sleep. I would pull the phone under my covers and push the illuminated buttons.

"Yello?" Mick would answer. I imagined him sitting at his kitchen table, drinking sweet iced tea. He always seemed so laid-back and easy to talk to, just like his dad.

"I don't like losing my friends. I feel lonely."

"You've still got me, girl."

"Thanks."

"You don't have to thank me. We've always been friends. I've known you since you were knee-high to a grasshopper."

"Yeah, but I'm not supposed to hang around you anymore."

"Your parents don't like me, because I'm a bad influence on you."

"I think the decision should be left up to me. I've known you've smoked for years, and it doesn't make me want to smoke," I said, not wanting to bring up drugs or the mob.

"Yeah, but I do other things, too."

"Like what?"

"I like to party."

"What's wrong with that?"

"There are drugs at parties."

"Do you really do drugs?"

"Yeah."

"Why do you do them?"

"I don't know, I like getting high."

"What's it like?"

"Sometimes I feel high. Sometimes it's a weird trip."

"Weird trip?"

"Yeah. Can you believe I saw the walls breathing once?"

"That would scare me. Thanks for telling me that. Now I really won't ever try drugs."

"You'd better not. I'll whoop your ass." I heard him take a sip of tea. "You know I've been expelled from school, right?"

"Expelled? Really?"

"Yeah," he said, with his familiar, nervous-sounding chuckle, even though he wasn't nervous.

"What did you do now?" I had heard that once he had turned on all the gas handles in chemistry class, and they had had to evacuate the school.

"I got caught making out with my teacher."

"Why did you do that?"

"She's kind of cool. She likes to party."

"How old is she?"

"I think she's twenty-four."

"Mick, does she know you're only fifteen?"

"Yeah, but she thinks I'm mature for my age."

"What are you going to do now?"

"Ill be sixteen next spring. Then Ill get a job and my GED ... So wheres your boyfriend?"

"He's not my boyfriend. Joanie took him away."

"How did she do that?"

"I don't know. I told her I didn't like her imposing on my friendship with Shaun, and she imposed even more. Now none of us are speaking."

"Really?"

"Yeah."

"Hotel California" was softly playing on my radio.

"That's a bad song there. Turn it up," Mick asked.

"You can hear that?" I asked. I hoped my parents couldn't hear me talking. I thought that the radio would help drown out my voice. I reached down to turn it up a little.

"The Eagles. They're the best," Mick said.

"What time is it?" I asked, feeling a little drowsy.

"Its ..." I could hear Mick leaning back in his squeaky, vinyl kitchen chair to see the clock. "Its almost midnight."

"I better go. I'm getting sleepy."

"All right. Remember something."

"What?"

"You can always make new friends. You're getting older. Aren't you going to the public school next year?"

"Yeah."

"You'll have all kinds of new friends and boyfriends."

"Thanks, Mick."

"No problemo. Now get some sleep."

I felt better after I hung up. Another Eagles song was on the radio, "New Kid in Town." *I guess the station is playing an entire album of the Eagles tonight*, I thought. Sometimes when they did that, I would tape the albums. It made me miss recording songs with Shaun. I was too tired that night to record anything. I turned off my radio and fell asleep.

My mom took Neana and I to the movies to see *Xanadu*. We had wanted to see that movie after seeing lots of previews for it on TV. It starred Olivia Newton-John, who we idolized. It was a low-budget film, but the music was awesome. The soundtrack featured lots of Electric Light Orchestra's songs, with Olivia singing some of them. Neana and I both bought the soundtrack to the movie. We played it over and over, memorizing each song.

My dad picked the perfect summer for us to take a long vacation. He took a whole month off from work. He had mapped out a trip around the country to visit most of our relatives. This was a good time to get away from everything. Even though we would be gone an entire month, my mom and I packed as if we were permanently leaving. My dad hired Shaun, of all people, to bring in our mail, feed our cat, and turn on the sprinklers every now and then. I knew my dad would pay him well. Mr. Shirrell would mow our lawn.

I spent most of the drive down to Florida wearing my headphones, listening to all the tapes that I had recorded songs off the radio over the past year. I gave a sigh of relief once we crossed into North Carolina. *Just leave everything behind and forget everybody for awhile*, I thought to myself.

My parents sat in the front seat and I sat in the back with blankets and a pillow. When we reached Florida, we took a different route than on previous trips, because Aunt Nora and her new husband had built a ranch out in the country. The road that led to their new house didn't even have a name. We had to memorize my aunt's directions. "Take the first dirt road on the right past the gas station," she had said. After following along the dirt road for quite some time, we saw their ranch, with cows grazing out in the green pasture that sprawled in front of it. The long dirt driveway leading up to the house was lined with trees. I was amazed at how quiet it was when we got out of the car. The air was so fresh and sweet-smelling. Aunt Nora came out of the house and gave each of us a big hug. She had short black hair and large brown eyes. I thought she looked great for her age. She was older than my mom. It would take me a while to get used to her new husband. Uncle Elvin spoke with a long Southern drawl. Their house was icy cold as we entered, which pleased my dad; he hated the heat and humidity of Southern summers. Her house was homey, decorated with country-style curtains, bedspreads, and new carpeting throughout the house. The carpeting felt soft and cushiony because of its extra padding underneath. Her kitchen counters were beautiful, decorated with unique blue tiles imported from Mexico. I'll never forget drinking sweet iced tea from her gorgeous blue glasses shaped like tulips. I stayed in a small guest bedroom that had a large window, giving a view of the pasture and cows. I thought the cows were cute as they chewed grass, and comical as well, the way the animals would stare every time I walked past.

I had a hard time falling asleep that night because of snoring. I could hear Spike sleeping on the porch under my bedroom window. I never knew a dog could snore like a human. Spike was a friendly old bulldog. He followed me everywhere, keeping me company the next day as I took a walk around. We walked down the long driveway onto the sandy road. Not a neighbor in sight. The sun felt so intense, beating down on my back as I walked. I was sweating from the humidity as well as sheer heat, and decided to head back. I cooled off in the rocking chair on the front porch, rocking in the shade with a glass of iced tea. I listened to the sway of the pine trees that surrounded the house. I could hear the sound of cows swatting flies with their tails every now and then. I took a deep breath and exhaled slowly, letting the sadness and anxiety that I'd been harboring all summer dissipate.

All of a sudden I noticed a scorpion slowly making its way across the sidewalk. I had never seen one in person before. I got up and walked over to get a good look at it. With its curved tail, it looked just like the ones I had seen in science books. It wasn't very big, only about an inch long. I wandered if it was poisonous. "C'mon, Spike," I said, moving away from it and hoping Spike wouldn't try to sniff at it too close. I walked inside through the front door, finding the cold air welcoming.

I stopped in the dark tiled foyer and looked inside the display case there, which had glass doors and mirrored shelving. A light was shining down through the glass shelves, illuminating the contents of the case. My aunt's glass Avon perfume bottles (that I called Avon dolls) seemed to look back at me as I stared at each one. She had been collecting them for years. I examined each one, staring at their intricately detailed faces. Each one wore a dress from a different era, and all were made from frosted glass. I stared in awe at their different dresses. One doll was pink and held an umbrella; another was a blue fairy holding a wand that glowed in the dark.

"Junie darling, come in and have some lunch," Aunt Nora said when she saw me looking at the Avon dolls. I went into the kitchen where she and my mom were making tomato sandwiches.

"I love those dolls."

"Honey, I know you do. I remember you liking them the last time you came to visit. I'll tell you what. When I die, I'll make sure they are left for you."

I felt a little embarrassed, because that wasn't why I had told her I liked them.

"Which ones are your favorites?" I asked, trying to shift the conversation from her dying and me being in her will.

"I think the Ms. Muffet one with the spider. She's *all white*. Did you see her?"

"Yeah, I like her too."

Elvin and my dad walked in, looking hot and sweaty from the heat. After eating, I went and put on my bathing suit. The adults had made plans to go to the country club for a round of golf. I would be spending my time by the pool.

On our third day visiting, I found myself in the rocking chair on the porch again, letting the warm breezes caress my skin. Off in the distance, black, billowing clouds rolled in our direction. I could hear distant thunder. I had never seen rainstorms like they had in Florida. As the clouds rolled in, the wind picked up. I saw a huge bolt of lightning go straight down. *It had to have hit something*, I thought. I could feel the thunder's vibrations under my feet as it became louder and louder.

A few big drops of rain hit the sidewalk, and then it came down in bucket loads. I went inside, hoping a tornado wouldn't come. I had only seen them on TV, and thought they looked terrifying. Aunt Nora had told me how a tornado took off the end of their house while they were building it, setting back the construction.

Fortunately, this storm passed over within half an hour and the sun came back out, seemingly even more intense. Steam rose from the sidewalk and the air felt muggy. It had rained several inches in that short amount of time. I loved afternoon thundershowers in Florida. *One could set their watch to them during the summer,* I thought noticing how they seemed to pass through at 3:00 PM on the dot every day.

Day four found us packing our suitcases into the trunk of the car.

"It was so good to see you again," Aunt Nora said while hugging me good-bye.

"Y'all take good care now, ya hear?" Uncle Elvin said as we got in the car.

We were back on the highway in no time. I didn't worry about getting lost with my dad driving. I knew he could read a map and follow directions. However, I did worry about his constant road rage. He could never drive anywhere without cursing and yelling at people. My dad thought he was the only one on the road. It was terrifying when he would get right up on somebody's bumper. We could easily run into them if they stepped on the brakes even the slightest bit! I laid down with my headphones on, listening to Chicago, Styx, or Rush. I looked up at the clouds in the sky. My thoughts went back to George Town and Shaun. *Was he glad that I was going to be gone for a month?* I wondered.

After driving all day, we finally reached my brother's house. They had bought a small house since the last time we visited. *My nephew would be a lot older now,* I thought as we pulled up in the driveway. Louisiana was even hotter and more humid than Florida. It was a wet, muggy place. Virginia could get like that, but such extremes didn't last long. During our stay, my nephew and I mostly rode bikes around his neighborhood. Chris was a cute little boy with blond hair and blue eyes. He seemed so happy, and seemed to wear a constant smile. I found his company a delight. Chris was interested in everything. "Look!" he'd say, pointing to bugs crawling on tree limbs or in the grass. Once he scooped up a bullfrog, cupping it in his hands while giggling. "I'm gonna scare my mama." Sheila jumped, screaming as Chris held up the toad close to her face. She ended up laughing, telling him to put it back outside and to wash his hands.

As we rode our bikes around going through mud puddles, I noticed people in Louisiana were a lot friendlier than people in Virginia. Everyone greeted us as we rode by. In Virginia, most people just stared at the ground while passing a stranger.

After a couple of days, we were back on the highway again. I was getting tired of all the driving. My dad only stopped for gas and food. Texas seemed like it would never end. I'll never forget how exhausted we were from driving all day and trying to find a hotel to stay in. I bugged my dad each evening to please find one with a swimming pool.

One evening of our trip, the sky was turning orange as the sun started setting. On the left of the highway we saw a huge, ugly, gray warehouse with a sign that only read *Hotel*. My dad slowed before turning to pull up to it.

"What a funny looking hotel," he said, not caring to find another place to stay, because he was very tired.

My mom and I sat in the car waiting for my dad to sign us in.

"Wait until you see the inside, you'll get your pool" he said excitedly when he walked back out toward the car.

"Wow!" I said as we entered. It was a tropical oasis. The entire inside of the warehouse looked like a tropical island. Tall banana trees, palm trees, yucca plants, and hibiscus were planted everywhere. There were stepping stones leading up to our hotel room's door, as if we were outside. The swimming pool was in the middle of it all, with a slide going into the water. There were restaurants surrounding the pool, like tropical outdoor cafes. All of a sudden I wasn't tired. I couldn't wait to get my bathing suit on and swim. The tropical setting and the pool made me feel like I was in the movie *The Blue Lagoon*!

I hated leaving the next morning, even after a good night's sleep. I could have spent the entire summer in this hidden oasis of a hotel. Texas was not only a huge state it was a hot and sandy one. It took us three days to drive through it. I didn't like the dry heat. It felt harsh, as if it was stinging my skin rather than caressing it. I was looking forward to California. I hadn't been there since I was a baby, and couldn't remember any of that visit. I only knew what I'd seen on TV. I was hoping to see movie stars and rock stars like Rod Stewart and the Rolling Stones. *I would love to run into Magnum, P.I. He lives in Hawaii though*, I thought. I had always wished we could go to Hawaii. "No!" My dad would say whenever I asked if we could visit there. "It's no good there." I never understood that. How could any place with crystal-clear water and sandy beaches surrounded by palm trees be no good?

The constant driving was gruesome. I tried passing the time by writing in my Mad Libs book. When I grew bored with that, I pulled out my Spirograph, but making spirals with my pen going around in circles on paper was too awkward to handle in the car. So I put it back in my bag. I found the magnetic Wooly Willy I forgot I had packed and gave that a shot, trying to give him hair and a beard. Time seemed to stand still. The countryside passing by outside my window could have been just turning in circles, I imagined. Maybe we weren't really going anywhere, like being caught in the Twilight Zone.

Finally we reached California. As the orange glow of the setting sun appeared in the sky, we found another hotel with a pool to make our stop for the evening.

My dad woke us early the next morning to get on the road up to Sacramento. My dad's sister Linda and her husband Bruce lived there. They had a son around Chris's age named Sean. The name "Sean," even spelled differently, made me think of Shaun back home in George Town. I pictured him shooting baskets in his driveway. I quickly pushed the thought of that out of my head when I pictured Joanie shooting hoops with him.

When we arrived, I was happy to see that Aunt Linda had a pool in her backyard. It was only an above-ground pool, but that was good enough. It was a large one, too. We were exhausted from another long drive, but I knew a few laps in the pool would wash away any fatigue or stress. Their house was small, with only two bedrooms, so I ended up sleeping on their sofa. It was actually soft and comfortable, and I slept quite well. During breakfast, Aunt Linda spoke of how she had visited us when I was little, back when we lived in Norfolk. I had no memory of her or Bruce, but I liked them. They were a nice, quiet couple, and easygoing, unlike my dad, who was always so rigid and stiff and took everything too seriously. I mostly noticed this problem of his when I was around people not like him.

Linda and Bruce took us to the movies inside a huge shopping mall. We saw the new James Bond movie, *For Your Eyes Only*. After that, we drove around and stopped to look in some model homes being built in a new development. Looking at model homes was something my mom and I had enjoyed doing with the Ainsworths after church on many Sundays. I'll never forget one particular home in Sacramento. The whole entire living room wall was one giant stained-glass window, depicting a red rose with green petals all around it.

"Wow, just imagine living here, leaving for school in the morning with the sun shining through, splashing colors all over the living room," I said.

"It is quite magnificent, isn't it?" Uncle Bruce replied.

That evening, I pushed Sean in his swing set. He giggled happily. The adults grilled steaks for dinner. They were sitting around in lawn chairs on the shaded back patio. I pictured my nephew Chris playing with Sean in the backyard here with the tall trees all around, Sean swinging on the swings and Chris scooping up bugs, making Sean laugh.

Over the next few days, our gruesome, tiring drive took us through Napa Valley, stopping along the way in each winery and taking tours. This *bored me to death*. My dad had become quite the red wine consumer on his tour of duty in the Mediterranean. He bought a case of St. Michele wine, the value of which went up over the years.

If I was an adult, I would have appreciated this trip much more, but as a teen nothing interested me. I was with in California. I didn't see any movie stars or rock stars. By the time we reached San Francisco, I was dissatisfied with the fact that it was July and only sixty-eight degrees. I shivered miserably after getting out of the car near the Golden Gate Bridge to have my picture taken at my mom's insistence. I was surprised at how clean San Francisco was as we walked up its steep streets, looking at all the tall buildings and admiring their architectural designs.

At the time, I didn't like how there were only foreign-cuisine restaurants everywhere. I was craving a McDonald's cheeseburger, but I knew if we actually did find a McDonald's, my dad would never eat there. My mom and I followed my dad around Fisherman's Wharf.

He took his time comparing prices of lobster, crab, salmon, and other seafood. He drove us down Lombard Street, telling us it was the most crooked street in the country.

"It was made that way to help cars go down, because it was on such a steep hill. See the wheels and how they all are turned sideways on the parked cars?" he pointed out. "They'll get a parking ticket if they don't do that."

"Why" I asked.

"Because it's a law they have to abide by on such steep streets."

I imagined going down such a street on my skateboard, or on Morris's moped.

"Look," I said, pointing. "A wax museum! Let's go there!"

"No," my dad said.

That made me angry. I sat back against the car seat and put on my headphones to listen to "Jessie's Girl" by Rick Springfield. It made me think of Joanie and Shaun, so I changed it. I closed my eyes, picturing myself being back home, sitting on the Chesapeake Bay, staring out over the water. I felt calmer.

We would have stopped in Prescott, Washington, to visit my dad's parents, but they had both died within the past few years, leaving me with only vague memories of my paternal grandparents. Instead, we headed out to Mt. Rainier, staying in a lodge that had fireplaces large enough for a person to stand in. I remember having the best prime rib dinner in that hotel's restaurant. We hiked on trails, where snow was on the ground. I thought it was neat how I could wear shorts while snow still covered the ground. The temperature was eighty degrees! At night, we watched skiers come down the mountainside carrying lit torches. It was pretty. I wished my friends were with me to see it.

I was relieved when we finally arrived in Libby, Montana, after another long drive. We were visiting my dad's other sister, Aunt Diane, and her husband, Uncle Marvin. They had two kids close to my age, Colleen and Kenny. I enjoyed listening to Uncle Marvin talk, with his loud but friendly voice and his odd Northwestern accent. He emphasized the letters O and R, which tickled me, making me think he sounded like a pirate. Colleen, Kenny, and I spent the days floating in tubes down Libby Creek. I had never felt water *so* cold. I wore my tennis shoes in the water to help keep warm. I was intrigued by the creek's rock bottom. I spent lots of time searching for unusual rocks with unique line patterns on them—yellow, black, gray, or white. I put some in my suitcase to show everybody at home. I was in awe at how massive the mountains were. I stared up at them every time we went outside.

One day I went with Uncle Marvin, Colleen, and Kenny on a drive up a mountainside trail through thick forest. What I thought was an elephant jumped out in front of the Jeep.

"That's a bull moose!" Uncle Marvin said.

The moose's rear was up above the Jeep's hood! I had never seen an animal that big in my life.

"Are you sure that's not an elephant on the loose or something?" I asked, shocked at its enormous size.

"No. See its legs? They're not big and round like an elephant's," Uncle Marvin explained right before the moose took a sharp turn to run up the hill. *Wow*, I thought. I had always thought moose were the size of horses.

I thought about the moose that night lying in bed. *I sure will be glad when we finally head out tomorrow.* I was getting homesick and wanted to get back to normality.

On our drive back, we passed by a huge rock formation called Devil's Tower, where the movie *Close Encounters of the Third Kind* had been filmed. We stopped to take pictures. My dad and I had loved that movie so much. We went back and saw it a second time.

I was full of excitement as we made our way back into Virginia. I was sitting up in the back seat, resting my arms over the front seat. I looked at the familiar Interstate 64. *No more mountains*, I thought. *I can finally see the beautiful sky again. No more intimidating huge trees. No more animals bigger than a car to jump out in front of us and startle me. No more strange foreign foods. No more dry, desert winds to whip my face, or heavy humidity to weigh my hair down. I was back to the soft air that kissed my skin. Last but not least, no more long, tiring drives that never seemed to end.* My heart raced as we turned onto Dunbarton, passing the signs reading GEORGE TOWN EAST. My anger and jealousy had melted away. I just wanted to be with my friends again.

I sat on my front porch with my chin resting in my hands, elbows on my knees. It was a hot July morning, and the dew was still glistening off the blades of grass. I jumped when Shaun suddenly appeared from around the arborvitae. I think my presence startled him as well.

"Is your dad home?" he asked.

"Sure, come on in," I said, trying to sound friendly.

After my dad paid him for house-sitting, I asked him if he'd like to shoot some hoops later.

"Sure."

After dinner, I could hear the familiar sound of the basketball being dribbled. *Bam, bam, bam.* It was echoing in between the houses. I went out to join Shaun. As we took turns making shots at the basket, I told him about my vacation.

"San Francisco's weather sounds like Germany, always cold, windy, and rainy. I'm glad that when we move again, we're not moving there."

I didn't think about him moving until that night, when I was lying in bed staring up at the stars out my bedroom window. *If Shaun moves, what will I do?* I thought before crying myself to sleep once again.

When the day came that Shaun told me that they were moving away in only a couple of weeks, I cried again. I didn't cry in front of him though.

"Where are you moving?"

"On base, into officer's housing."

"Oh, well, you'll have to stay in touch, okay?"

"Sure. As soon as we're settled in, I'll give you a call."

I cried every time I saw his empty house and the empty spot where his basketball hoop used to be. They had moved it with them. I wondered if he would have a place to hang it outside his new home.

Neana tried to console me whenever we rode our bikes past Shaun's old house. I hated the fact he wasn't next door any more. At the age of thirteen, I thought it was the end of the world. He did call every so often during the remaining days of that summer. We would mostly talk about the latest songs or movies. I didn't tell him my favorite song was "Endless Love" by Diana Ross and Lionel Richie, because it made me think of him. We eventually lost touch with one another when they moved again. Shaun never called or wrote me to say where they had moved.

One afternoon, I jumped on my bike, trying to embrace the last couple of days of freedom before school started. There were days I preferred to be alone, to absorb the world through my own eyes. No one could taint what I took in from my surroundings when I was alone. I followed Dunbarton out of my neighborhood all the way to Military Highway. I wasn't supposed to ride up to the highway, but I knew how to be safe; after all, I wasn't a little five-year-old anymore. After riding a ways, I stopped, putting my foot down to support my bike while glancing across the empty highway. I looked at the dirt road on the other side, which now had a street sign up. It read "Greenbrier Parkway." *Funny name for a dirt road*, I thought as I crossed the highway to the dirt road. I could hear the locusts buzzing all around me, telling me it was a hot August day. After riding about a mile or so, I heard something strange. I stopped to look and take a rest. I saw several dump trucks, excavators, and backhoes in a pit below the road. They were busy working, reminding me of carpenter ants roaming in different directions. *What could they possibly be building out here in the midst of blackberry bushes, arborvitae, and sandy-bottomed streams?* I wondered. I felt excitement and wonder as I pedaled back home, wishing I had had someone with me to see what I had seen. I went straight home.

I found my mom putting in a load of laundry in the utility room. I stood in the doorway watching her, thinking of a way to ask her to ride to the construction site with me without her knowing I had gone up there alone. As I watched her, I noticed how our utility room looked pretty. My mom had painted it. She hung beige country curtains with frilly edges and placed a small table with a green fern in front of the window, so the plant could soak up sunlight. There were curtains on the door's windows as well. My mom had painted the room yellow, which complimented her mustard-colored washer and dryer.

"Hey, Mom?"

"Yes?"

"Do you want to go for a bike ride with me?"

"No, not until later on."

"After dinner?"

"Okay, after dinner."

After dinner, my mom and I pulled our bikes from the shed and rode down toward the highway. I rode slowly beside my mom. She wasn't very coordinated, and I felt like I needed to look out for her when she was on her bike. My mom had trouble pedaling backward when she needed to brake. "Just pedal backward then put your foot down, Mom," I'd tell her. We finally made our way out to the construction site. The work day had ended, and all the equipment sat quiet. Some of the dump trucks and excavators looked as if they were resting.

"They're building something, but what?" my mom asked.

"I don't know. What's it going to be? A new neighborhood?"

"Maybe."

There was a huge mound of dirt and sand that looked like a miniature mountain. It must have been a couple of stories high. I felt it was packed firm as I ran up the side of it.

"C'mon up!" I yelled down to my mom.

She slowly started to climb up. I sat down, feeling the soft breeze while taking in the panoramic view, trees as far as the eye could see.

My dad had once told me during one of our bike rides that this area was one of the largest tree nurseries around. I was full of excitement as I sat on top of the dirt mound, wondering what was going to take place here. My mom finally reached the top, sitting down next to me to catch her breath.

"We can see the highway over there," I said, nodding toward our left.

"Look at all the pine trees," my mom said as we gazed around enjoying the soft warm breeze. After a few moments, my mom stood, wiping sand off the back of her white shorts.

"Well, we better get started back. I have some things to finish up at home," she said.

We carefully climbed back down to our bikes.

That Saturday morning, we sat around the kitchen table. It was the usual routine: my dad read the newspaper while my mom placed the food on the table in between the dishes I had set out. We usually had bacon, eggs over easy, and cheesy, buttery grits. However, on this particular morning, my mom decided on delicious, golden-brown pancakes.

"Here's your construction site," my dad said, still looking down at the paper.

"What's it gonna be?" I couldn't wait to hear.

"A shopping mall."

"A shopping mall? No! Really?" I was thrilled at the thought. "Wow, won't that be cool? We will be able to just ride our bikes there! It will be so close!"

The other shopping malls were a good thirty minutes away, with traffic light after traffic light en route. I couldn't wait to tell Neana, as I drowned my pancakes in golden maple syrup.

After breakfast, I washed the dishes as fast as I could, leaving them to air-dry in the dish drainer. I ran into my room, got dressed, and jogged all the way to Neana's. I rang her doorbell. Paul answered.

"Hey, how's it goin'?"

"Neana!" He yelled, holding open the door for me.

"Guess what they are building up in the nursery?"

"What's that?"

"A shopping mall!"

"Oh, so that's what is going on. I saw all of those trucks going back and forth in there."

Paul had recently been hired to work for a fencing company that his girlfriend Sharon's parent's owned. The company was located right down from the nursery off the highway. "Chesapeake is really going to become crowded now. Once a mall goes up, so does everything else around it. Neighborhoods, restaurants, strip malls." He continued naming off possible businesses until we heard Neana yelling from the bathroom.

"Wait in my bedroom, Junie!"

She was probably getting out of the shower.

"Okay!" I yelled back.

"Quiet out there!" I heard her father's voice coming from the master bedroom. It wasn't uncommon for their parents to sleep in until 2:00 or so in the afternoon. They were night owls. I headed into Neana's room as Paul left to go to work. As I passed by Paul and Jake's bedroom, I saw Jake playing on the floor. Their room had bunk beds against the wall, and a desk in between two windows that faced the front yard. Jake was playing with Matchbox cars, racing them and making little engine sounds. I went in and sat on the dark green-and-black-speckled carpet next to him.

I picked up one of the cars. "Neato," I said holding up the red sports car with a white stripe.

"Check this one out!" he said, proudly holding up a black sports car with a gold eagle painted on its hood. "Do you know what kind this is?"

"No." I thought that the toy looked like a car Mick and I had seen go past one day, a black Trans Am. "That's a *bad* car there," Mick had said as we watched in awe. We had never seen a car like that before. Mick and I both liked sports cars. His favorites were black Corvettes.

"It's a Trans Am," Jake said before making *vroom, vroom* noises. Neana came out of the bathroom with wet hair. She was always slow, taking her time doing whatever that needed to be done as if there weren't any clocks or passing time.

"Hi, Junie!"

"Hi," I said, getting up to go into her room.

"Don't you want to play cars with me?" Jake asked.

"No maybe later."

"Okay," he said, sounding disappointed.

"Guess what?" I said to Neana.

"What?"

"They're building a shopping mall up off Military Highway out in the nursery!"

"Really? That's *neat*," Neana said, holding her head to the side to carefully put in a stud earring.

"Do you think your mom will let you ride your bike up there with me?"

"I don't know, but I'll ask." Neana went down the hall to knock on her parents' bedroom door. I stood not far from her. "Mom, Dad, can I ride my bike with Junie to see the new mall being built?"

"What mall?" I heard her dad ask, sounding annoyed.

"It's up across the highway where the nursery is."

"No. You are not to cross that highway, and not even Providence Road, for that matter!"

Neana stepped away from their door with tears building up in her eyes.

"Don't worry, we'll see it another time," I said.

We spent the morning riding around the neighborhood, and then had lunch at my house at noon. My mom had made us bologna sandwiches with slices of her garden tomatoes. Neana loved my mom's sweet iced tea. Her mom was diabetic, and didn't add a lot of sugar to their desserts or drinks along with their being Jewish and eating kosher foods (which I happened to like). Neana preferred to eat at our house. We ate on the back patio. The thought of the new mall left my mind, and I began to worry about junior high school.

"I'm nervous about going to the junior high in a few days," I said.

"Why?"

"I heard there are a lot of rough kids in the school. Also, it's so much bigger than my old school. What if I get lost?"

"Paul liked it when he went there. Doesn't your old friend Kim go there, the one that went to St. Matthew's with you?"

"Oh yeah, I forgot about her. Thanks for reminding me about her. I think I still have her phone number."

Later, as we stood twirling our batons in my room listening to my *Xanadu* album, we discussed what we would wear on the first day of school. My mom had bought some dresses that I had picked out because they resembled the costumes of the character Kira from *Xanadu*. They were different pastel colors—lavender, pink, and blue. The wispy cotton dresses had ruffles around their hems, which fell around my knees. The mid-length sleeves had ruffles too. I thought the ribbon and lace trimmings around the V-necks looked romantic . I bought hair clips with silky ribbons dangling from them. Hopefully I would meet a nice, handsome guy who looked like Michael Beck, who played in the movie *Xanadu*. I envisioned going skating together or attending dances. Going to public junior high didn't seem so intimidating.

After Neana went home, I asked my mom if she still had Mrs. Demarco's phone number.

"It's still in the address booklet," she said.

I pulled out the drawer in the kitchen hutch and found the address booklet. After copying down Kim's phone number on a small piece of paper, I went into my room for privacy. Kim lived on Whitehaven Crescent, which was the first street on the right when entering George Town.

"Hello?" a familiar voice answered. It was Kim.

"Hi, Kim. It's Junie from St. Matthew's. Do you remember me?"

She was silent for a moment before responding. "Oh Junie! Yeah, I remember you!" She sounded excited to hear from me.

Kim was always so nice, I thought, suddenly realizing that I had missed her.

"Guess what?" I said.

"What?"

"I've decided to go to the junior high this year."

"Oh, that's so cool. We can walk together, if you want. You'll like the school so much more than St. Matthew's."

"I've been wondering about that. It's *so* much bigger."

"Actually, it will be open tomorrow for students to walk around to find their classes and lockers. Why don't we head up there?"

"Sounds great. Thanks, Kim."

"Come over tomorrow afternoon and I'll show you around."

"Okay."

Junior High School

I met Kim at her house. She seemed jovial when she answered the door, looking at me through her black-rimmed glasses. She still had shoulder-length black hair and a pale face, just how I had remembered her. I brought with me the list of classrooms and teachers that I had received in the mail two weeks back. We compared our lists to see if we had any classes together. To our disappointment, we didn't.

As we entered Indian River Junior High, I noticed instantly how much wider and longer the main hall was compared to St. Matthew's. The layout of the school was simple, which made it easy to find my classes. There were five corridors to the right of the main hallway, and the cafeteria, gym, and auditorium were to the left.

"What's this?" I asked Kim pointing to my schedule. "It says 'gym class in annex building.'"

"Oh yuck," Kim said, wrinkling up her nose. "I had that last year. There is a detached building right off Providence Road that only has two long corridors and an old gym. It used to be the junior high, but as the population increased, they built a bigger one, the one we're in. C'mon, I'll show you." We walked down one of the corridors out onto the bus ramp.

"This is a five-minute walk Junie which *sucks* because after gym class is over and you change out of your gym clothes, you'll be *late* for your next class if you don't *run*. There are only three minutes between classes. Don't worry about it, though," Kim said with a reassuring smile.

I guess she had noticed my worried expression. I didn't like the annex building. It had dim lighting and seemed spooky, almost haunted. We headed out the door and walked back to the main building to find my

English classroom. My locker was right next to it. Kim already knew exactly where her classes would be.

We left the school, taking the back way home past the baseball field and over the little bridge that divided Indian River Lake. We jumped over a ditch, making our way through a thicket that led to a large field that belonged to one of the churches on Providence Road. When we finally made it into George Town and stood in front of Kim's street, she asked if I wanted a ride on the first day of school.

"My mom is driving me. We can come pick you up if you want."

"Okay, that would be nice," I said thinking I wouldn't look like the obvious new kid in school if I walked in with Kim. "Thanks again, Kim."

"Oh, no problem. We'll pick you up at 7:45."

Mrs. Demarco pulled up into the driveway at 7:45 sharp. I had on a lavender blouse and white skirt with wedge-heel white sandals.

"Good luck," my mom called as I headed out the door.

"Thanks."

I brought money for lunch in my new lavender purse, along with pens and pencils. I carried a clipboard full of paper.

Kim and I went separate ways in the main hall, a busy madhouse of students going in every direction. Some girls wore dresses, but most were in jeans and T-shirts just like most of the boys. I recognized lots of kids that I had gone to elementary school with. I found my first class. *Math, yuck. At least I'll get it over with first*, I thought. My teacher's name was Mrs. Thompson. She had a round face, and wasn't very tall, even though she had on high heels. She had shoulder-length blond hair and wore large round glasses. I recognized the girl sitting next to me from George Town. We had never spoken before, although I'd seen her around the neighborhood. She lived over on a street that intersected with Crown Crescent. She was skinny like me, with flaxen blond hair that was cut really short. I couldn't help but notice her large round nose, which gave her a quirky look. She wasn't pretty, but she seemed nice enough.

When Mrs. Thompson called roll and asked for Cindy Evans, the blond girl answered "Here." So Cindy was her name. Then Mrs. Thompson called out someone named John. I didn't catch the last name.

When I turned to see who answered, my eyes widened. He resembled the actor Michael Beck from *Xanadu*. *He's gorgeous*, I thought. I turned back around in my seat and stared at my paper. I hoped he hadn't seen me staring at him.

The morning classes passed quickly. I looked around for Kim in the cafeteria, feeling awkward that I didn't know anyone else well enough to approach them. I saw Kim standing in the long lunch line and quickly made my way over to her.

"Hey Kim. How's it going?"

"Hi, Junie. How's it going for *you*?"

"Not too bad."

A lot of the faces were familiar, but it had been a few years since I'd seen those kids back in elementary school. I wondered if anyone would recognize me.

"What's for lunch today?" I asked, famished because I had skipped breakfast.

"Chicken chow mein."

That would do, I thought. Saucy chicken and vegetables poured over some steamy white rice would be filling as well as tasting good. Lunch usually came with applesauce, with a choice of regular or chocolate milk to drink. I always chose the chocolate. I didn't like regular milk unless it was poured over cereal. A lot of the kids stood in groups, chatting and laughing loudly amongst themselves. I didn't see any cute boys in the cafeteria. I was hoping to see John from math class. I felt odd wearing a dress with so many of the students wearing jeans and T-shirts. I followed Kim over to a lunch table. We sat next to a group of girls Kim knew.

"Do you know Ellen? She lives in George Town too."

Ellen was another girl who I had seen around George Town but didn't know.

"No. Hi Ellen. I'm Junie."

"Where do you live?"

"I live on Crown Crescent."

"Oh, I know exactly where that is. I live across from the old farm house."

"I know exactly where that is too. I like that old house."

"Isn't it cool?" Ellen was wearing a dress too, which made me feel less self-conscious. She was somewhat chubby, with long, straight, light-brown hair, big brown eyes, and a round face. Kim had on blue jeans with a pink I-zod shirt, which had a little alligator emblem on the breast.

"Hi, y'all," a voice said. The new arrival sat right next to me. I recognized Cindy from math class right away, thanks to her green chinos and pink shirt.

"So how do you like Mrs. Thompson?" Cindy asked.

"She's okay. Seems like a regular math teacher." I answered.

"Yeah, she does." Cindy replied with a smile.

"This is Michele," Cindy said as a short girl with wide hips joined our table. I noticed Michele was dressed casually too, wearing a red-and-blue plaid button-up blouse with blue jeans. I noticed as she sat down that her eyes were wider apart than most people's, and one eye seemed to stray to the side a little bit. She had thin lips and braces. I noticed Cindy had braces, as did Kim.

"What school did you come from?" Michele asked me.

"A private school called St. Matthew's."

"Where's that?"

"It's a Catholic school in Virginia Beach."

"Are you Catholic?"

"No. I thought it would be a nicer school to go to, but I ended up not liking it very much. We had to wear uniforms, and there weren't many students there."

"Oooh," Cindy replied, scrunching her up face. "I wouldn't like that either."

"I think I would. You would never have to worry about what to wear to school each day," Michele said before biting into her peanut-butter-and-jelly sandwich. It was a pleasant surprise to be chatting with a new group of girls on the first day. I had worried about winding up eating alone outside on the school's steps or something.

"Who's that cute guy in our math class with the long brown hair?" I asked trying to keep up conversation.

"I think his name is John." Cindy said after swallowing a bite of her bologna sandwich. "He's a little older. He failed a grade or two. He already has a steady girlfriend, though."

I wasn't surprised about him having a girlfriend. He was way too cute. When the lunch bell rang, everybody jumped up, threw their trash away, and headed out the side doors. I had gym class next, so I had to sprint to the annex building. It was a hot day, and the annex building didn't have air conditioning, which added to the list of things I didn't like about it. We had two gym teachers, Mr. Fein and Mr. Latier.

Mr. Fein introduced himself and his co-teacher to us. "We typically divide our class into several groups. You'll be expected to wear the school's P.E. uniform, or points will be deducted off your grade. If you still need to purchase a uniform, the office can provide you with one for $10." I remembered seeing Joanie and Morris wearing the same P.E. uniforms. The T-shirt was light blue with "I.R." stamped on the front of it, and the shorts were dark blue.

"I don't want any of you at any time going near the first hall here. That's where the emotionally upset kids attend school, and they can be dangerous," Mr. Fein told us.

The building was spooky enough. And now we were close to mental students. *Great*, I thought. There was an element of excitement to it all, a ghostly aura.

After fourth class, I sprinted to fifth, barely making it on time. My English teacher, Mrs. Smith, didn't seem very friendly, especially when she said "I don't care if you are coming from the Annex building or not. I don't tolerate tardy students. If any of you are tardy three times in one week, I will give you an F for the day."

This was going to be fun, I told myself, full of sarcasm. I sat, trying to appear astute and proper. I didn't want to draw any unwanted attention my way. Mrs. Smith pointed her finger as she spoke to the class. She was kind of short, like Mrs. Thompson, and had shoulder-length sandy blond hair.

I met up with Kim after school on the bus ramp as we had planned. Cindy and Michele caught up to us, along with Ellen. We walked along Providence Road before crossing it right where my friend Randy had been struck and killed by a car all those years back, a tragedy I'll never forget. *Randy, you would probably be walking with me right now if you were still alive*, I thought to myself, waiting to cross the road.

A car went screaming by with some guys, probably from the high school, yelling out the windows. "Arf, arf! Look at the dogs!"

We ignored them, but their comments left me feeling extremely self-conscious. I followed along behind the girls as they took a different route that was new to me. We walked along a dirt trail that wrapped behind George Town. Down below us was a clear, sandy-bottomed stream. There was a space between two chain-link fences that ran parallel to one another that we could squeeze through, and that lead us out onto a cul-de-sac in George Town.

"What a nice short cut," I said to Ellen as we carried our heavy textbooks.

We all said good-bye to Kim when she turned to go down her street. When we reached Crown Crescent, I went left, Michele and Ellen went right, and Cindy started to go straight.

"Hey, you live down there near Mick Ceaver," Cindy called to me.

"Yeah, he lives across the street from me. We grew up together."

"Oh … well, I heard he's *bad news*. My mom used to cut his hair. She's a hairdresser, you know. I heard he started doing *drugs* and got kicked out of school!"

"Yeah, he has a bad side to him, I guess," I said, feeling guilty for gossiping about my friend. "We've always been friends. He's harmless."

"My mom said I can't have anything to do with him. He's *so* cute though."

"I understand. My mom isn't too comfortable with me being friends with him either, but he's like part of the family."

"So do you smoke pot too?" I didn't like Cindy's candidness.

"Just because I know someone who does doesn't mean I do it too."

"See ya at school tomorrow," Cindy said, smiling as she turned to walk away. I couldn't tell if she was smiling or smirking. I headed down my street, passing Joanie and Morris's house and missing them. I wondered how they liked high school. Neana was still going to the middle school. Next year she would be in the junior high with me. *We could walk together*, I thought.

It was nice to get out of my high-heeled sandals and skirt and into my comfortable shorts. I didn't have any homework, which was nice. I put on my little white tennis shoes and bobby socks before sprinting down to Neana's. Paul answered the door. He was on his way to work, leaving in a hurry.

"Neana's in her room," he said as he brushed by me toward his light blue Ford Escort.

"Hi, Neana. How was your first day at school?"

Neana's eyes lit up as she told me she had joined band. "Guess what?"

"What?"

"I'm going to play the clarinet!"

"Wow, good for you." I never had known she had an interest in playing musical instruments.

"So how was junior high?" Mrs. Simons asked from the doorway.

"Oh, it was fine."

"Junie, will you be free Friday night? I need a babysitter."

"Sure." I hadn't made any plans. Plus, Neana and I had fun hanging out together.

The school week went by fast. We were given lots of homework assignments, which kept me busy after school. I ended up being late three times for English class. I had to fidget around with my lock a while before I could get it opened. The stupid thing didn't work right, which made it stressful to get my books out of my locker. I had never had a combination lock before. This one would get jammed, slowing me down and making me late for English class, which wasn't helped by the long walk from the annex. Ray, whose locker was next to mine, would usually help me open mine if he was there, but he usually wasn't. I got an F for a test grade for my first week! *What a bitch!* I thought as Mrs. Smith shook her head, marking down my tardiness in her grade book.

Sometimes it was embarrassing walking down the main hall. A lot of the guys made sounds as I walked by. I would usually hear imitations of a dog's woof being thrown in my direction. I started wearing jeans and T-shirts to fit in, but no one seemed to notice. At fourteen, I was a geek with skinny legs, braces, and fine, limp hair that would frizz in the humidity. I eventually made it into my first bra, size A.

I showed up at 7:00 on the dot to babysit at the Simons'. After the Simons' weekly movie and dinner, they liked to have cocktails down at the local Jolly Fox until midnight or later. Mr. Simons was a car salesman. He was a friendly guy and funny, always finding a joke in everything. Neana's whole family had a sense of humor. I will forever remember the image of Mr. Simons holding a tumbler full of rum and Coke and smoking a large cigar. He pointed with the drink and cigar in the same hand as he spoke. Mrs. Simons didn't work outside of the home. She was a good saleslady, always selling Tupperware, Avon, and Amway products. My mom would buy from her every now and then.

After Neana and Jake went to bed, I sat in their comfortable rocking recliner, turned on the side table lamp, and started my homework. When I was finished, I put my books back in my school bag. Before getting up to turn on the TV, I noticed a basket on the floor at the foot of the sofa that was full of fashion magazines. I picked up a few browsing, through the pages of *Vogue, Marie Claire* and *Glamour.* I was amazed at how perfect-looking the women in the magazine were. I was shocked to see how some were dressed scantily, in lacy black bras and panty hose with high heels. Their makeup was flawless. There were advertisements for makeup, eyeliner, and mascara. *Wow, I wish I had some of the dresses they were wearing. If I wore those to school, no one would make fun of me.* When Mr. and Mrs. Simons finally came in, I was flipping through a *Glamour* magazine.

"You can take some of those home with you if you want Junie. They're starting to clutter up my living room, and I've been thinking about throwing them out."

"Oh, thanks" I said, thinking about using the magazines for ideas of how to style my hair and makeup.

It was a good thing that I sat in the front of the class during math; otherwise I would have just stared at John during our lectures. The math class seemed a little easier after St. Matthew's, where our subjects were ahead of public school by a year. As Mrs. Thompson went over rounding decimals, I thought about John sitting behind me in the back of the class. He was one of the best-looking guys in school, and the least conceited. John was friendly toward me as we passed in the halls. He would usually smile and say hello, with me sheepishly saying the same in return. I liked how different John was from the boys who made fun of me. I felt so self-conscious that I began to avoid walking down the main hall.

I would hear girls laugh at me as I walked past their cliques in the main hall. They thought they were so perfect, flipping their big hair, applying lipstick, and making negative comments at others walking by.

One such girl pointed at me one day and said "Hey, check out Railroad-mouth Beanpole."

I just kept walking, acting like I hadn't heard anything, even though I'm sure my face was red from embarrassment.

John was a quiet guy who kept to himself. His girlfriend was average looking, with short black hair, a little heavy in the hips. Her name was Natalie, I found out one day from Kim, who was in the same geography class as her.

When I saw Natalie and John walking down the corridors together holding hands, they seemed to be in love. Something about the way they looked at each other told me that.

"If the identified digit is five or more, increase it by one," I heard Mrs. Thompson say as she handed out worksheets for us to complete in class. Every day was the same in her class. We would sit there, and she would lecture, and then hand out worksheets before writing the homework assignment on the board. *Rounding, Fraction and Decimal Conversions, page 188. Do all,* I copied off the chalkboard so I wouldn't forget.

After school let out, Ellen, Cindy, Kim and I walked home, taking the usual trail along the creek behind George Town. I felt tired and hungry after a long day. The books I was carrying seemed heavier than usual, and the walk seemed longer. When I looked up I was taken aback to see Michele light up a joint.

"Yeah, I smoke one every now and then," she said when she saw my surprised expression. "Don't tell my parents, though."

"Don't worry about it. I have friends that smoke. I don't, though."

"Want one?"

"No thanks." I thought about Mick and Morris, who both always had a cigarette in their hand whenever I saw them. Mick was the one who smoked pot. I remembered Joanie telling me how she would smoke one every now and then. That was when the Normans lived in the neighborhood. That's when pot came into the neighborhood. I was glad that Cindy and Kim didn't smoke cigarettes or pot.

When I finally got home I plopped my books on my desk and realized the house was empty. My mom was probably at the grocery store. I went into the kitchen and placed a saucepan on the stove to boil a hot dog. I was starving and decided to put another one in the pan.

The water came to a rapid boil and steam started rising. I held my face over the pan to feel the warmth. I liked how the steam made the tiny hairs of my eyebrows feel like they were curling up. I stabbed one hot dog with a fork once it changed colors and shrank a little. I plopped it on a bun and loaded it with mustard, grabbed a bottle of Coke out of the refrigerator, and headed back to my room. I wasn't supposed to eat in my room but my dad wasn't home from work yet. My mom didn't really care as long as I didn't leave dishes lying around when I was done. I sat at my desk eating while flipping to page 188 of my math book. *This should be easy enough,* I thought, pulling out my blue spiral notebook and pencil. I knew if I didn't get it done now I never would. I only had to finish answering two questions in my geography homework, because I had finished the other eight during class. It had been dark in the classroom, but I could still see with the light from the projector showing a boring film about topography. English was the same—just needed to finish up some questions at the end of the story we were reading about King Louis XIV of France and I would be all through.

I heard my mom come in through the utility room's door and the rattling sound of paper bags being dropped on the kitchen table.

"I could use some help in here!" she yelled, sounding frustrated.

I went into the kitchen, pulled out a gallon of milk from the paper bags, and put it in the refrigerator.

"What's for dinner tonight?" I asked as I grabbed some cans of food and put them away.

"Steaks, I guess."

"Sounds good." I loved steak and potatoes, which we ate a couple nights a week.

I went back to my room and laid down on my bed. I fell into a deep sleep. I dreamt of the train I could always hear but never saw. It appeared ominous, speeding along, running straight through houses, knocking over trees. It seemed so powerful that nothing could stop it. I couldn't move, trapped in my bed. I could see the black engine coming toward my bedroom window, tearing up our lawn and blowing its loud whistle. The train came crashing through my bedroom wall and ran over me, beheading me. It was odd. I felt no pain, only numbness. Then the train was gone, leaving silence. I opened my eyes, feeling nothing below my chin. *It was only a dream, wasn't it?* I wondered, half-awake. I looked at my bedroom wall; it was still intact. I looked up out my bedroom window. There was only the orange glow of the sun setting behind the pine trees and the neighbor's rooftop. I felt at peace. My body was still paralyzed from such a deep sleep. *What time is it?* I wondered. I turned my head to see my clock. Its orange glowing numbers read 6:00. Was it 6:00 AM or 6:00 PM? I was still disoriented, but the smell of the steaks sizzling on the stove in the kitchen brought me back to reality. What a welcoming sound and smell. I listened as my parents chatted about their days. *Thank God it's evening*, I thought. I was too groggy to think of having to go to school. I felt silly when I sat up to go to dinner. I was still in my school clothes, not my nightgown. Dreams are strange.

The days dragged by and we headed into December. Cindy and Michele would usually stop by my house in the morning, and my mom would drive us to school after picking up Kim. I wasn't happy. Missing Joanie and Morris was a dark cloud over my head. I thought I would forget about them and move on, but I missed them and needed them more and more. There were so many things I wanted to tell Joanie, so many things I wanted to ask her. I missed joking around with Morris and I missed all of us going on outings after church while listening to Mrs. Ainsworth speak passionately about her students' upcoming plays or the latest novels she was reading. Shaun. Where was he? How was he enjoying junior high wherever he was? I pushed thoughts of him out of my head which wasn't hard to do when I saw John first thing every day in math class.

I cheered up some when Michele invited me over for a sleepover one Saturday afternoon. "We have to go to bed early though, because we have to go to Sunday school and church the next day," she told me over the phone.

"I'll call you back, Michele. Let me get permission from my parents, okay?"

"Sure."

Michele lived all the way down at the end of Crown Crescent in a cul-de-sac. The houses were much larger down on that end. My parents didn't mind me spending the night at her place, so I called her back to let her know I would be over later. Her house was two stories high, with five bedrooms and three-and-a-half bathrooms. Her backyard was large, with a big in-ground swimming pool that had glass-like tiles on its bottom.

"That must look so cool in the summertime while swimming," I said looking down out of her bedroom window. "Can you see yourself in the tiles?"

"Yeah, it looks like you're flying over them."

Later when we had to go to bed, Michele fell right asleep. I lay wide awake as usual. Sometimes I would just lay awake almost all night. I didn't know why. Michele's room was small for being in such a big house. It was even smaller than my room. She had two single beds with a nightstand in between them. I turned on her radio, keeping its volume low to not wake her. I listened to the top ten count down. My favorite song, "Urgent" by Foreigner, was the number one hit. K-94 also played "I Love Rock 'n' Roll" by Joan Jett & The Blackhearts, another one of my favorites.

When morning came, I had to drag myself out of bed. I sat up. My head was spinning. I could have fallen back to sleep so easily. I was not used to being an early bird on the weekend, especially not after staying up half the night. There was no way I was going to make it through Sunday school and church service.

"Michele, I'm not feeling so well," I half-lied. "I'm sorry, but I think I better go on home."

"Oh, you don't? I'm sorry, Junie."

"No I don't feel well." *I just need another six hours of sleep*, I thought.

"Okay, we'll just drop you off at home on the way out."

"Thanks. I am sorry."

"Don't worry about it."

Her family stopped in front of my house to let me off.

"Maybe next time!" her mom shouted to me after I stepped out of the minivan and was about to close the door.

"Bye!" I said, waving as they pulled away from the curb.

I felt bad for Michele having to get up so early every Sunday. It was like having a one-day weekend. At least when I went to church with my mom, we didn't have to be there until 11:00 AM, which wasn't terribly early, nor did we go *every* Sunday. I walked across the brown lawn, which winter had taken its toll on, shuddering as I looked up at the gray skies. It was a quiet morning. The only sounds to be heard were a distant train's moaning horn and the cold breeze blowing in the pine trees.

"Shit." I turned the door knob. It was locked. I had forgotten my house key. I walked around to the side of the garage, trying the other door. Of course it was locked. I tried the utility room door. Locked. I went over the den door. Locked. "Damn it," I said, getting frustrated. I felt so impatient. I started knocking on the door. I was shivering now, with goose bumps on my arms. It wasn't like my dad to be asleep at 7:30 AM. He usually got up at 5:00 AM, regardless of whether it was a weekend. I hoped everything was okay. I hoped they hadn't gotten into a huge fight or something hurting one another. Finally, I saw my dad pull back the white sheer curtain; his bare chest was just as white as the curtain. I definitely took after him when it came to my fair skin.

"What the hell are you doing home?" he yelled. Typical.

"I'm just trying to get in. It's *so* cold out, and I'm *so* tired."

He let me in.

"What's she doing home?" I heard my mom yell from the bedroom. "Why didn't you go to church with them? How rude!"

I felt tension rising in me as I headed back to my bedroom.

"Get on the phone and call them to come get you," my dad said, much to my alarm.

"They already left!" I snapped. I quickly softened my tone to avoid trouble. "I was going to go, but I don't feel well and I'm really sleepy."

"You're not sleepy, you're just plum lazy!" my mom yelled.

I felt bad. I needed to lie down a while. I would be fine after that. *That wasn't lazy, was it?* I wondered as I set my sleepover bag on my desk chair and took off my shoes before pulling back the covers. I could hear my dad getting dressed.

"This is why you're a loser at everything you do," my mom said.

I was confused. *How was I a loser? What did I do?*

"You've just lost your friend," I heard my dad say from in the kitchen. "She'll never call you again; just wait and see."

I pulled the covers up to my chin, finally feeling warm. My parents would be in a better mood once they finished yelling at me. *How typical,* I thought. I slowly exhaled, and fell into a deep sleep.

I awoke to the sound of the vacuum cleaner. I looked at my clock.

It was 10:30. I was ready to get up. As my mom vacuumed my room, I pulled out a clean pink velour top and a pair of jeans from the closet. I went into the bathroom, turned on the shower, and got in when the water was nice and warm. Nothing was more revitalizing than a warm shower. I brushed my teeth when I got out, and then blow-dried my hair. As I looked in the mirror, I thought I looked so bland and pale. I remembered Joanie and how she had made up my face that one time, making me pretty. *What had she used?* I thought about the ads in the magazines. *Oh yeah, I remember. I need base makeup, eye shadow, eyeliner, and lipstick.* I mentally took an inventory so that when I went to the drugstore with my mom, I could buy what I needed. My mom usually went to the Revco drugstore on Sunday afternoons. I rarely spent my allowance. That plus the money I had saved from babysitting would give me more than enough to buy what I needed.

As we walked around Revco, I experienced new fondness for the makeup aisle. I had always loathed waiting for my mom to look at all the makeup on that aisle. But suddenly I felt like a kid in a candy shop looking at all the different kinds of eye shadows and lipsticks. I discovered clear bottles that read *Kissing Potion* across them. They came in all sorts of flavors. There was cherry, strawberry, peach, and bubble gum. I chose bubble gum and placed it in the shopping basket I carried. Picking out the right color of liquid base was tricky. I held the bottles next to my arm, trying to match the color with my skin. I was so pale. I picked one out called "Nude" by Maybelline.

"I didn't know you were interested in wearing makeup," my mom said when she found me in the cosmetics aisle.

I was staring at light pink blush colors. "Well, some of the girls at school wear makeup."

"Don't get *too* dark of colors," my mom told me.

I was glad she didn't object to my buying makeup in general. I was even happier when she paid for my purchases.

"Thanks," I said.

It took me a little longer to get ready for school the next morning. I accidentally spilled some of the liquid base on the collar of my pink blouse and had to change.

"Junie, you need to blend it in," Kim said at school as we walked down the hall.

"What do you mean?"

"The makeup on your face is much darker than on your neck. You're two different colors."

When I went into the bathroom and saw myself in the mirror, I realized she was right. *Oh great*, I thought. *I made myself look worse.* The next day I blended in the base down my neck, which gave me a more natural look.

Michele and Cindy loved my Kissing Potion, so I let them borrow it.

"It smells exactly like bubble gum!" Michele said, sniffing it. "Where can I buy this?"

"Revco."

"Well, I'm going to go there."

I felt excited when my mom told me to invite all my girlfriends over for a Mary Kay makeup party one Friday night.

"Really?"

"Yeah, I think you and the girls your age would like something like that. I'll speak with their moms about it too."

My dad was going to be working aboard ship over the weekend, so we had the house to ourselves.

I was surprised to see that the moms came along too. We all sat around the kitchen table with tiny, light pink Mary Kay sample bottles and white cotton balls in front of us. Mrs. Ayton had long, flaxen blond hair which looked odd to me, because it didn't match her face. Mrs. Ayton was our Mary Kay representative, and seemed very nice. She explained how we should always keep our skin clean by using an astringent and then applying lotion.

"Never go to bed with makeup on," she explained. "Also, when applying base makeup, rub it on in an upward motion."

I was proud of my mom setting up the whole thing for me and my friends. I was shocked to see the prices of everything. Just one lip liner pencil was $10! Seeing as my mom was the host of the party, she got a discount and I ended up with everything I needed. We learned that with our different skin tones, we all needed different colors and astringents.

"That was really nice of your mom, Junie," Michele told me before she left the party. I had invited Cindy, Kim, and Ellen as well. I wish I could have invited Joanie, although she probably could have instructed the class herself. I had invited Neana just to be nice, expecting her mom would only say she was too young for makeup, which Mrs. Simons did.

One night not long after the Mary Kay party, I was lying on my bed reading *The Outsiders* by S. E. Hinton when the phone rang. I snatched up the receiver.

"Hello?"

"Junie?" It was Michele.

"Yeah, hi, it's me."

"Guess what?"

"What?"

"The mall is now open to the public!"

"Wow! I didn't think it was open already!" I said, surprised.

"I didn't either, but when we drove by it today, we saw that it was open. My mom said they probably didn't want to make a big announcement because it would cause too much commotion. I asked my mom if she would take us there, but she said no."

Michele's mom also had two small children, fraternal twins, a boy and girl, who were two years old. The young kids kept her busy.

"I bet my mom would take us. Let me ask her and get back to you," I said, hearing the little ones squealing in the background at Michele's house.

"Okay, but when do you think we can go?"

"Probably tonight after dinner. Ask your mom if you can go with me."

We were all so thrilled to have a mall so close, especially during the winter months. We would now have an indoor place to spend our time. It would help pass the cold, drizzly, dark winter days. The other day I had noticed that the road leading to the mall was now paved when we turned on Military Highway to go to the gas station.

My mom was just as excited as we were when I told her that Greenbrier Mall was now open. My mom pulled out a heavy cast-iron skillet and set it on the stove. She pulled out steaks from the refrigerator. My dad would be home soon, so I started setting the table for dinner.

My mom opened the oven door to check the aluminum-foil-wrapped baked potatoes.

"Can Cindy and Ellen come too?" I asked as an afterthought.

"I don't care, as long as they all show up here no later than 6:30."

The phone rang again. It was Michele. "My mom doesn't mind if I go with you, but we can't be out past 9:00."

"That's fine. We wouldn't be out that late anyway."

"Tell her to be here no later than 6:30," my mom said, overhearing my conversation.

"I heard that," Michele told me before we hung up.

By the time 6:30 rolled around, we were done with dinner and the dishes. My dad was settled as usual on the couch, watching the news. The girls showed up on my doorstep not a minute too late. The three of them piled in the back seat and I sat up front with my mom driving. I turned on the radio. My mom didn't mind my rock 'n' roll music if it wasn't turned up too loud. The song "Don't Stop Believin'" by Journey was playing. I thought that the lead singer for Journey, Steve Perry, had the most unique voice. I could pick his voice out immediately. As we pulled into the mall's large parking lot, brightly lit by yellow streetlights, I thought it was odd that this had been all country just one year back. There were many other cars parked. The mall was T-shaped, with two floors. There was a glassed-in elevator that took us to the second floor. On the outside of the elevator was a wall with water cascading down its sides, giving the illusion of moving through a waterfall. There were green ferns set in large flower pots throughout the corridors. Greenbrier Mall was so clean, light, and airy.

"Okay, let's all meet by the water fountain no later than 8:00," my mom said. We agreed and went our separate ways. I knew my mom was going to enjoy herself browsing. The food court was upstairs. It seemed bright and cheery as we walked through checking out what they had. The walls were mirrored, with neon lights reflecting off them, giving a warm glow. We found a Chick-fil-A, a Taco Bell, a pizza place, an Orange Julius, a Dairy Queen, and a McDonald's. The main department stores were Miller & Rhoads, Sears, and JCPenney. The lower level had a cinema.

"Totally awesome!" Cindy said when she saw the theater. "We can watch movies here too!"

Finally, we came across the video arcade, the land of teens. This would be *the* place to hang out during our high school years. A teenager in the 1980s would have been lost without video games. Teens plopped quarters in those machines like gamblers at Las Vegas slot machines.

The Power of Fashion

Back at school, the snooty main hall girls still laughed at me as I walked down by them each morning. "Ha ha, hey, look at Pink Lips with that *grody* blouse and leg warmers. *Ooh, gag me with a spoon.*" Some of the boys laughed along with them. I passed by, still pretending not to hear. I was always relieved when I walked into math class to see my handsome John sitting there in the back, looking up to say "Hi" to *me*, Pink Lips with that grody blouse and leg warmers. I found it ironic that the cutest guy in the school didn't make any rude comments about me.

But as I entered math class one day, to my dismay, his seat was empty. *It was earlier than usual so maybe he would just show up later.* I sat at my desk as the kids came filing in. Still no John.

"Hi Junie! Wasn't that fun at the mall?" Cindy asked.

"Yeah, we'll have to go again this weekend!"

"We should see a movie too."

I was still looking back in case I'd missed John coming in. The next day was the same: no John. It was getting close to the Christmas holidays. I would have to wait an entire week to see if he would return. When the bell rang and the students left hurriedly to get to their next class, I went up to Mrs. Thompson's desk, where she was writing in her attendance book. She looked up at me.

"Yes Junie?"

"I have an off-the-wall question?"

"What's that?"

"Do you know where John has been?"

"Why, is he a friend of yours?"

"Yeah kind of."

"Unfortunately, he dropped out of school when he turned sixteen last week. I tried talking him out of it, but he was determined."

"Oh, ah, yes thank you." That was all I could manage to say. I felt a weight of disappointment pulling down my emotions. *Why?* I asked myself. *Why did he have to drop out? Why would he?* I wished I could ask him.

I closed my bedroom door the first Saturday of Christmas vacation. It was cold and drizzly outside, matching my mood. I turned on the radio and heard thunder. *Was that the radio? Or was it thundering outside?* When I realized it was coming from the radio, I turned it up a little to hear Jim Morrison of the Doors singing "Riders on the Storm." Lying on my stomach across my bed, I opened up a *Vogue* magazine. There was a picture of a girl walking down a sidewalk in Paris. The model was walking down along a cobblestone sidewalk next to a black wrought-iron gate. She was holding a black umbrella and wearing a raincoat like none I had seen before. It was black, with tiny red, yellow, white, green, and blue stars all over it. Her long brown hair and bright red lipstick enhanced her perfect face. Her gloves were red leather, matching her red stilettos. *Someday I'll go there*, I told myself. I pictured myself walking along the cobblestone streets dressed in high fashion, looking like the model in the magazine. *Maybe I could find John and we could go together. He wouldn't mind boarding a jet with me if I looked like her. We could get a flat together.* I had heard about Europe and how they call their apartments flats. The magazine also had a picture of a model standing in a large room with tall windows reaching the ceiling. I could see out the windows at the gray, drizzly skies. All of a sudden, I didn't mind the weather so much. It made me think of visiting faraway Europe dressed in *style*. It gave me hope.

Later in the evening, as I lay in bed looking up out my bedroom window at the tiny lights from jets going by soundlessly, I chuckled to myself. I imagined myself flying on a jet, going to France, England, or Italy. *Someday I'll be pretty and no one will laugh at me*, I thought. *Hey, I know. I'll try to find fashions of my own similar to the ones in the magazine. Then when the snooty main hall students laugh at me, I would know they didn't know what they were laughing at. Vogue isn't funny, it's high fashion.* I would just laugh back. *They don't know what high fashion is!*

During the holidays, I threw lots of hints toward my mom about certain clothes that I liked. Greenbrier Mall was only a five minute drive from our house, but I found its selection of clothes lacking. We headed over to our old stomping ground, Military Circle Mall.

Military Circle Mall, even though it was further away, was still my favorite. It was a home away from home for my mom and I. We had been going there since I was in a stroller. My mom would always give me a dime or a nickel to throw into the water fountains near Spencer's. I loved the sound of the rushing water cascading over dark gray tiles. I also loved the fountain's lights, which would slowly change colors—yellow, red, blue, and then green. Spencer's was my favorite store, because in the back they sold black lights and lava lamps. The display cast a mysterious glow on the psychedelic posters. There was always incense burning on the cashier's counter, giving off a small stream of blue smoke. I never really caught on to the pot-leaf symbols or other drug paraphernalia that was on display. If my mom did, she didn't comment on it. I bought a black light to put in one of my dresser lamps. I liked how it made me look like I had a tan at night.

This Christmas is definitely lacking in excitement, I thought as we drove home from the mall along the wet surface of Military highway. It was another cold, gray, drizzly winter's day in Virginia. It was cold enough to wear a jacket, hat, and gloves, but not cold enough to snow. How I longed for a white Christmas.

Once we pulled up into the driveway, I went dashing into the house. I went into the guest bedroom, where the Christmas paper was kept. I picked out a shiny gold-colored Christmas wrap and cut just the right size to wrap the beige-and-brown bathrobe I had gotten for my mom. I had bought her the robe while she was browsing in the panty hose aisle in JCPenney. I had also bought her a purse, also beige and brown, which were her favorite colors.

Dad was hard to shop for. If he didn't like what he got, he would say so and return it. I never understood my mom's fixation on buying him a shirt every year. He never liked them. Every year she would painstakingly pick out a shirt, one he would never like. My dad always knew exactly what to get me, and saved the big gift for last. Christmas

1981 was the year he bought me an Atari. Atari was a video game that hooked up to the TV like *Pong*, but it was much more advanced than *Pong*. My dad even bought me a twenty-four-inch color TV so I could play video games in my room.

"Thanks, Dad," I said with a smile, picturing myself watching TV when I couldn't sleep at night, as well as playing video games with my friends. We played so much that we literally had blisters on our fingers.

Even though I no longer believed in Santa, I still hung my stocking on my bed post. My mom would still stuff it on Christmas Eve. She put in makeup and Love's Baby Soft perfume, which smelled like cotton candy.

The Ceavers were gone for the holidays, more than likely on the farm down in Carolina visiting Mrs. Ceaver's parents. The Ainsworths' house stood empty, with them being gone so much, which made me sad. Joanie, Morris, and I always had exchanged gifts on Christmas. *This was just plain wrong*, I thought. I wanted my friends back. My mom missed her friend, Mrs. Ainsworth. When she mentioned this, to my dad he told her "Well, if she comes down and apologizes, *then* I'll give her another chance." I didn't like how my dad ruled my mom's life. I also didn't like how she let him.

Neana and I started our own custom of giving each other holiday cards. Hers read *Happy Christmas, from Neana*, and mine said *Merry Hanukkah, from Junie.*

After the holidays were over and we were back to school, the long, gloomy, cold days seem to drag. I missed seeing John sitting in the back of my math class. Even though we only ever said "Hi" to each other, he had been a small ray of sunshine that lifted my spirits.

Life was dull, the same old routine of getting up, going to school, trying to remember to write the correct date at the top of my papers. "1982, not 1981," I'd tell myself. And there were the never-ending walks home, the homework, dinner, bed. Not a thrill in the world. I didn't like walking home each day in the cold with Michele, who smoked cigarettes the whole time and complained about something in her cynical tone. Cindy bragged every day about what a terrific singer she was. Kim stayed after school for band practice most days. I slowly began to realize I didn't like Cindy or Michele. Cindy was snooty, and

Michele was a drag who talked behind everybody's back, making me wonder what she had to say about me. I tolerated them, though. They gave me someone to walk around the mall with or to go to the movies with. Ellen moved over the holidays. Nobody knew where. Her family just up and left over night.

I was saddened to hear that Kim was moving out at the end of March, another move due to someone's dad being reassigned to another base. Kim's dad was being transferred to San Diego. I thought about Krissy and how sad I had been when she had moved. She and I still wrote one another, but after the latest picture of herself that she had sent, I felt uncomfortable. Krissy looked like she was sixteen, with her beautiful long brown hair, tan skin, pearly white teeth, and what was probably a D-cup bra. I felt that if she still lived in George Town, she would be out of my league. She sounded so outgoing in her letters, having boyfriends, being a cheerleader, and winning beauty pageants in her school. I was fourteen, looked thirteen, and still had braces. Krissy and I drifted out of touch with one another.

It was Monday, St. Patrick's Day. I had on my green chinos with a baby pink blouse and white sleeveless undershirt. I had put the outfit together based on a model I had seen in the pages of the latest *Seventeen* magazine. The weather was warm enough for me to wear my open-toed pink high-heeled sandals. Students were used to me wearing my own styles instead of just jeans and T-shirts. Some of the girls actually started copying me. As I stood in front of my locker getting books out for my next class, I noticed someone familiar out of the corner of my eye.

"Mick! Whatcha doin' here?"

"I have to get some papers from the office so I can start on my GED," he said. Students had flooded the hall, and some were staring at Mick not recognizing him.

"Oh, well, it's good to see you, it's been a while."

"Yeah, it has. Whatcha been up to?"

"Just school, nothing exciting."

"Nothing exciting, huh? Well, at least you're keeping busy with school. I better let you go so you're not late for your next class," Mick said noticing students starting to pick up their pace to get to class. He gave me a hug and headed down the corridor. Cindy stood with her jaw dropped, staring at us. *What was that supposed to be about?* I wondered.

I remembered Cindy saying how she thought Mick was cute. *Could she be jealous?*

As the three of us made our way along the stream behind George Town after school, Cindy started complaining about Mick. "My mom said he does *drugs* Junie. You shouldn't be friends with him."

"Cindy, first of all, Michele smokes pot and that's a drug. Second, I've known Mick and his family since I was six. Drugs or no drugs, he doesn't *push* them on me. He's just a friend."

"Yeah, that's why you guys were *hugging* in the middle of the school!" Michele said, to my astonishment.

I felt even more defensive; they didn't understand. "Hey, look," I began. "My parents are friends with his parents and have been for years. We're like *family*! We weren't hugging in the middle of school! We gave each other a hug, just like you would hug an aunt or and uncle. We've done that since we've known each other."

The three of us made our way to where the chain-link fences didn't quite meet. Cindy and Michele had smirks on their faces. They *knew* Mick was just a friend of mine, whom I didn't even hang out with that much. We just lived across the street from one another and had for our whole lives. They *knew* that, they just wanted to stir up trouble. Kim and Ellen were gone now, which made me a third wheel in their sad, boring lives.

"So what does your mom think of Michele smoking cigarettes, Cindy?" I asked rhetorically.

"She doesn't know, and if she did, she wouldn't let me hang out with Michele."

"See? Same thing."

"No, it's not the same. Michele isn't a boy and we didn't hug! If you hug in public like that, then something more is going on!"

"Get over the goddamned *hug* thing already! Are you *jealous?*" I yelled.

Cindy turned and got in my face. I just stood there. I was taller than her and dared her to try something. She turned away from me.

"Bitch," she said.

I couldn't believe her audacity! It infuriated me. Michele seemed amused.

I shoved Cindy, causing her to drop her books. She turned and shoved me back, but I hardly budged.

RRRT!

Out of nowhere, the familiar green duster with the black stripe was stopped next to us in the middle of Whitehaven. "Get in!" Morris yelled at me through the window of his car. He always drove with his windows down. I knew that look on his face. If I didn't get in, he would probably get out and *put* me in his car. I got in, slamming the door. I didn't look back as he sped off.

"W-w-what was going on?"

"They are a couple of snobs trying to start trouble with me. Thanks for picking me up like that. I really appreciate it."

"N-no problem." We were silent for a few moments, staring out the windshield.

"I sure do miss you guys," I said, wondering what would have happened if Morris hadn't broken up the fight.

He glanced over at me with his big brown eyes. "We miss you t-t-too. Y-you know how my m-m-mom is," he said, rolling his eyes.

"You know how my dad is," I said, rolling my eyes back.

We laughed. He stopped on the corner of Crown Crescent and Longdale to let me out. We still weren't supposed to be friends.

"Hey, my dad said he would let us all be friends again if your mom apologizes. I hope your mom understands I wasn't trying to start trouble last summer. I just didn't know how to handle jealousy."

"I know. You don't have to explain. I'll talk to my mom. I-I-I'll talk her into it. She misses you all too."

"See ya," I said, closing the door, relieved to be talking with him again.

"S-see ya." He drove off, leaving me to walk the rest of the way so my mom couldn't see me getting out of his car if she happened to be looking.

Spring Flowers, Gardens, and Friends

I woke up one Saturday morning with warm rays of sun pouring through my window onto my bed. I stretched my arms and legs out and relaxed, listening to the cheerful sound of birds outside. It was spring. *Chirp, chirp. Tweet, tweet.* I think those little birds actually have little conversations among themselves. *They must be happy, because it's springtime,* I thought. I could see blue sky as I looked up through my bedroom window. *Maybe it would be warm enough for a bike ride?* I wondered. Usually April mornings were a bit too cool for riding. *If I put on a light jacket, I'll probably be warm enough,* I thought.

I pulled out jeans and a long-sleeved pink blouse from my dresser and carried them into the bathroom to start my usual routine of showering and teeth brushing. *I think I'll go get Neana today and see if she wants to go for a bike ride,* I thought as I blow-dried my hair. The birds' cheery sound had put me in a cheery mood.

When I came out of the bathroom, I heard voices coming from the entry hall. *Was someone crying?* I heard a familiar voice, an *emotional* voice. I stopped just around the corner to listen in. My mom was speaking to Mrs. Ainsworth through the screen door my dad always put up during the spring and summer months.

"I miss you, I really, really do, and Junie, all of you," Mrs. Ainsworth said.

"I know," my mom said, looking down a moment. "I miss you too, but you know how Dennis is. He'll want an apology. Come back later, Beatrice, when Dennis is home. He went to the package store on base. He'll be back by noon."

"Okay. Will do," Mrs. Ainsworth said, not sounding as sad.

I was pleasantly surprised to hear how strongly she missed us. If I had known that, I would have gone over myself and spoken to her. I pictured Mr. Ainsworth not having anything to say about us not being friends for the past nine months. He probably just sat with his small smile listening to Mrs. Ainsworth complain or cry over the whole matter.

As soon as my dad came walking in, placing a case of wine on the kitchen table and pulling out a receipt from his pocket to look over, my mom announced Mrs. Ainsworth would be stopping over to apologize.

"Oh?" my dad said. "Well, we will see." He picked up the case of wine and carried it into the garage. "Make sure she knows she needs to learn to get her emotional side under control!" I heard him shout from the garage.

When Mrs. Ainsworth came over to apologize; we all sat in the den.

"I love you all," she said. I felt her emotions as well.

"Well, we'll have to get together for a barbecue with the nice weather approaching," my dad said, his way of accepting her apology and lightening the tension in the room.

I heard the doorbell ring and got up to answer. It was Joanie!

"Is my mom here?" she asked with a concerned look.

"Yeah," I said, holding the door open for her to come in. "C'mon in." I tried to sound as friendly as I could. I wanted her to feel welcome.

"I'm talking right now Joanie. Go visit with Junie awhile," Mrs. Ainsworth said when Joanie went into the den.

"Okay."

Joanie followed me to my room.

"Have a seat," I said, gesturing toward my vanity table bench with the dark blue satin cushion. I sat in my desk chair.

"So how have you been?" Joanie asked.

"Okay, I guess." I didn't want to jump into the details of how I hated my first year in junior high school, and how Michele and Cindy had stabbed me in the back after Kim moved. I had so much to tell her, but it had been so long since we'd talked.

"Hey, remember that guy I was starting to date?"

"Yeah" I said, vaguely remembering. I had never actually met the guy. She had told me he was from North Carolina and had moved to a farm out in Chesapeake the last time we had talked, all those months ago.

"He passed away."

"What?"

"Yeah, he got killed a couple of months ago."

"Oh Joanie, I'm so sorry." I really was. I thought how trivial I had been, feeling sad just because a guy I never even had an actual conversation with quit school. Now here was Joanie, mourning the death of an ex-boyfriend.

"How are you doing now?"

"I'm okay, but sometimes I just cry. Why did he have to die? I don't know why God took him away like that."

I remember my mom saying once how God does things we can't understand. We have to trust him anyway. That's all I could think to tell Joanie. I was glad she had opened up like that. It seemed to break the ice and put our friendship back on track. I had to be there for her now.

"How did he die?"

"He was walking along a dark country road in Carolina. It was late at night and he was hit by a car. He was missing for a couple of days then they found his body in a ditch, where he had been thrown by the car."

I tried to picture Darren, tall with bronze skin and sandy blond hair, the way Joanie had described him. I pictured him lying dead in a ditch, but quickly pushed the thought out of my head.

"We were going to get married, you know."

"Really?" Joanie was seventeen, which seemed too young to marry.

"Yeah, when I turned eighteen we were going to get married. I know I used to say I would never get married. But *love* changes you."

"How old was he?"

"Darren was twenty. He worked for his dad."

"*Joanie?*" I heard Mrs. Ainsworth call from the hallway.

"Yeah?" Joanie answered.

"I'm leaving now. Do you want to stay and visit?"

"Yeah, I'll stay a while!"

"Okay then." We heard Mrs. Ainsworth and my mom exchange

warm farewells. "Let's get together next weekend," Mrs. Ainsworth said as she walked out.

I exhaled happily at the thought of things getting back to normal. I was glad I could help Joanie get over her loss. She looked much more mature now. Her red hair no longer hung straight without any style, but had been cut shoulder-length and feathered back on the sides.

"So how is school going for you?" she asked, changing the subject.

"It's been a long year."

"Oh?"

"Yeah, long and *boring*. I was friends with some girls, but when one moved away, the other two thought it would be funny to make me the odd man out. I think most of it stemmed from Cindy being jealous of my being friends with Mick."

"That's so ignorant," Joanie said, shaking her head. "I think you'll like high school much better."

"I wish our high school included ninth grade, like most others do." Indian River High school only enrolled sophomores, juniors, and seniors.

"One more year and you'll be there."

Later I went for a bike ride alone to think. I felt so relieved having Joanie and Morris back. It was sad to think of how Joanie must have reacted when she found out she had lost her fiancé. *Would I ever have a fiancé? No. I never want to get married. I would like a nice house of my own right on the beach. Actually I would like to stay right here in George Town.* I was glad the weather was warming up. Beach season was right around the corner. I suddenly realized I had already ridden around the block twice. That was typical of me when I was deep in thought on my bike.

I turned left onto my street, and saw Keith in his garage, waxing one of his beautiful surfboards. Keith loved surfing, maybe even more than I did. My dad wouldn't let me have a surfboard because he didn't want surf racks on top of the car. The few times I was able to surf, I had to rent a board. I mostly boogie-boarded. Keith had several boards hanging up in his garage. Some were a pinkish coral color, others a pearly yellow. I was envious. Keith was out in his garage every Saturday morning with the big door up, his radio blasting Devo or the B-52 s. He was either waxing his surfboards or out surfing. Even during the winter months he would surf; he would just wear a wet suit.

Keith had changed from a cute kid into a handsome young man. He was tall and muscular, with broad shoulders and a strong jaw line framed with blond shoulder-length hair feathered in the back. *He could easily become a pro wrestler,* I thought. Keith really loved watching wrestling, as did I. I always got a kick out of hearing Keith imitate Randy "The Macho Man" Savage, trying to sound tough and speaking with a deep voice. He would also imitate North Carolina's Roddy Piper. My favorite wrestlers were Hulk Hogan and the oh-so-gorgeous Ricky "The Dragon" Steamboat.

Keith and I never hung out together. I would only see him if he was with the guys hanging out in Mick's garage. I didn't really like Keith that much. He had become even more arrogant than when he was a kid. I'll never forget one time, when the Normans still lived in George Town, and we were hanging out in their garage one rainy afternoon. Keith dared me to try a taste of beer. When I took a sip from the Budweiser can, I realized he had urinated in it. I spit it out at him, and he jumped back, laughing.

"You're such a dork, Junie."

I went home after calling him a damn jerk.

After my bike ride, my mom told me that Mrs. Ainsworth had called, asking us to join them the next day at the new Baptist church she had joined. It was called DeBaun Memorial Baptist. So on Sunday morning, I got up and put on my summery white skirt, a pastel striped blouse, hose, and pale pink pumps. I sat poised and studious as the preacher gave his sermon. Sitting obediently was something that was instilled in me at St. Matthew's. Some parts of the sermon I could understand and other parts I couldn't.

"It is not for you to know the times or the seasons, which the Father hath put in his own power," the preacher read from the Bible. *Why did they use words like* hath *and* giveth? I thought. I was somewhat relieved when church let out. I was looking forward to going out with the Ainsworths afterward, just like old times. They always had something planned after church, whether it was just lunch or an outing. Mom and I had missed our outings with the Ainsworths, which were so much more fun than just going home to watch TV like my dad did on weekends. He never attended church or any of the outings we went on afterward. Looking back, my dad missed out on a lot, although I know he preferred it that way. Having the house to himself after a long work week was his way to unwind.

That Sunday's outing after lunch at McDonalds would be the six of us going to the Norfolk Botanical Gardens. Mr. Ainsworth drove us there, letting us out of the station wagon before he would go park and take a nap in the car. We went through the lobby to pay our admission fee and picked up a map showing all fifty-five acres of the various gardens. There was a Japanese garden, an enchanted forest, a nature trail, the colonial herb garden and a bicentennial rose garden, just to name a few. We had our choice of taking a boat, riding a tram, or just walking. Of course, Mrs. Ainsworth and my mom took the tram. With Mrs. Ainsworth being overweight, the tram was easier for her. Morris decided to go with them. Joanie and I followed the map on foot starting with what was called the Boarder walk. The walkway was lined with a variety of flowering shrubs, some white hibiscus and a backdrop of mixed perennials and annuals.

"Everything smells so good," I said as we walked along, using all of our senses to take in the surrounding flowers.

"I wish Darren could be here with me to see all of this," Joanie said somberly.

"Hey, look what's next—the colonial herb garden," I said, reading the sign cheerily, hoping to take her mind off Darren. There was a white picket fence around the garden with red roses running the length of it. A small brass sign read "Heirloom roses." A white gazebo with a small canal running behind it sat toward the back. This was a romantic place. No wonder Joanie kept thinking of Darren. As we walked through the enchanted forest section of the garden, I read the little signs posted along the way. I read them out loud to keep Joanie's mind occupied.

"This is oak," I read. "And these are azaleas. Yep. Azaleas."

The paved trail was lined with pink, red, and white flowers. Yellow daffodils sprawled along the front of the azaleas, only adding to their beauty. Flowery scents wafted in the air. It was simply intoxicating. Joanie and I were getting tired from the long walk, so we decided to head down to get on the tour boat. It was relaxing taking in the beauty while floating along. The tour guide pointed out the bald cypresses that lined the canal before it entered Lake Whithurst. Some of the other people in the boat were leaning across one another to snap pictures along the way. We were intrigued at how many turtles there were. They looked cute with their little heads bobbing along the water before quickly disappearing back into the dark green brackish water. Joanie and I counted four turtles resting on one log. She cheered up, laughing and saying how cute the turtles were.

As we headed back home in the station wagon, Joanie sounded like her old self again. I laughed as she whispered perverted things about the male statues in various parts of the gardens into my ear.

It was the spring of 1982. When my mom took me down to the local Cut & Curl, I had my hair washed, cut, and styled into a mullet. I was satisfied with my hair for the first time. It was short in the front and easy to manage, but in the back it reached all the way down to my waist. It was shiny and healthy looking, making me look and feel attractive. When we left Cut & Curl, we drove over to Bradlees to buy new summer clothes, because they had the latest fashions and the lowest prices. I picked out several miniskirts with tops to match. One good thing about a blue jean miniskirt was that anything would go with it. I bought polka-dotted tops, striped tops, and a variety of pastel short-sleeve shirts. That spring's latest summer style was pastel-colored tennis shoes with bobby socks to match. I never knew that shopping could be so much fun.

To top everything off, I finally had my braces removed. I sported a lovely smile with perfectly straight teeth. I remembered when they first took off the brackets and wires. I was amazed at how light my jaw felt. I could chew gum again, and was surprised at the extremely smooth texture of my teeth when I ran my tongue over them.

School was almost over for the year, which was nice. However, to my dismay, I found out that I had flunked English because of my perpetual tardiness. I found that idea hard to take. *She was actually going to flunk those of us who did all of our work and participated in class because we were* late? I would have to make it up in *summer school*? Mrs. Smith was such an ogress. I had explained to her several times that it wasn't my fault that the gym class was too far away. It was hopeless. Whenever I tried explaining my situation, Mrs. Smith just sat in her chair, staring at me with her big, cold, blue eyes as if I was boring her. I should have said something to the principal, but I found doing so too intimidating. I could have told my dad, but he would only embarrass me by yelling at the principal.

"Hello?"

"Hey Mick? It's me, Junie."

"What's up?" It was late at night, around 11:30. I had been lying in bed, looking up out my bedroom window at the tiny stars, when my mind became flooded with worrisome thoughts. I needed someone to talk to and Mick was the only person I could think of that would still be up. I pictured him watching TV like he typically did this time of the night, if he wasn't out partying somewhere. I had my bedroom door shut as usual to drown out sounds from the living room, but also to drown out my voice on the phone. My dad would yell at me if he knew I was on the phone after 9:00 PM. That was the rule. No phone calls in or out after 9:00 PM. I had my radio turned down low. The song "Jackie Blue" was playing.

"I just thought I'd call and see what you're up to."

"Not too much, I'm a little tired," Mick said, yawning.

I heard him turn the volume down on his TV, walk into the kitchen, open the refrigerator door, and pour his usual glass of sweet iced tea.

"Why can't you sleep? Is somethin at school botherin ya?" Mick could be very intuitive at times.

"Yeah. I flunked English and will have to make it up in summer school."

"How'd you flunk English?"

"Remember me telling you about Mrs. Smith and how she gave out Fs for test grades if you are late to class?"

"Yeah. You never worked that out?"

"I tried, but she wouldn't listen."

"Hmm, that's no good there. Well, look on the bright side. Summer school is fun."

"Really?"

"I had to go once, and we had a blast. It's real laid-back. Plus all of the high school and junior high summer students are mixed together, so you'll get to meet new people. Where are they having it this summer?"

"Just up at Indian River."

"See, girl. You can simply walk and not worry about taking a bus. You are also allowed to wear shorts, I think. What's four hours a day? You'll be home by 12:30 in the afternoon."

"Yeah, I guess you're right."

"When have you ever known me to be wrong?" he said with a chuckle that made me laugh. The Steve Miller Band's "The Joker" was playing on the radio.

"Hey, turn that up, that's a bad song there."

"I can't turn it too loud."

"Oh, that's right, your dad might hear."

"Yeah." I let out a big yawn.

"I feel the same way," Mick said, yawning himself. "I've been roofin'."

"Roofin'?"

"Yeah, laying tar on top of buildings. Do you know how hot and tiring that gets?"

"No, not really."

"We're up on the roof all day in the hot sun, laying tar, which is super hot. I'm completely worn out when I get home."

"So why do you do it?"

"It pays good."

"Oh," I said, picturing Mick on a roof laying tar.

"Well, my eyelids are fightin' me here. I'm gonna have to let you go."

"Okay, Mick. Goodnight."

"Yeah, goodnight."

The Black Rose

I slept soundly that night and had a dream that I would never forget. It wasn't a nightmare, nor was it a typical dream, where everything and everybody was jumbled. In this dream, I could *feel* the warm air and *smell* roses. I opened my eyes in a bedroom that wasn't mine. I rose from the bed and walked across the colorless room to an open window. White curtains blew in the warm breeze. As I reached the window, I realized it was a door. I opened it, finding myself gliding down a flight of stairs that ran alongside a house. I now was standing in a yard. Sun shone down in rays of pink and yellow. I could *feel* the light's *warmth*. There were roses everywhere, pink, white, yellow, and red. Their aroma smelled heavy in the early morning's humid air. Out of the corner of my eye, I could tell a dark figure was standing in the yard. I turned my head to focus and saw that it was a young man wearing black pants, a black shirt, and a black leather jacket. Even his short hair, parted on the side, was black. His arm was outstretched, and his hand held a black object. I turned to run, sensing something foreboding about him. Was he holding a gun? No, wait. It wasn't a gun. I stopped. Something alluring, exotic, and yet peaceful pulled me back. My fear faded into anxiety as I turned. I desperately wanted to absorb him with my eyes. Time slowed. I couldn't turn fast enough. When I was able to see him finally, I gazed at his friendly, peaceful, infallible face. His eyelashes were black, framing immaculate, captivating, deep blue eyes. The bluest eyes I had ever seen. His skin was flawless. He was beautiful. As I looked down to see the black object he was holding, I drew in my breath. It was a beautiful, perfect black rose, with the morning's dew sprinkled across its delicate petals. It was intoxicating.

I wasn't myself after waking up from that dream. I felt bewildered and tried to make sense out of it. I only felt peace, and a notion that my life was going to take a turn for the better. My life wasn't bad, but it was missing something. I would never forget the face of the young man in that dream.

Summer was upon us. I had only two weeks of freedom before summer school began. My dad volunteered me to go in his and my mom's place on a sailing excursion with an old navy friend. Mr. and Mrs. Dupree's boat only had room for two extra people. My dad declined Mr. Dupree's invitation, saying he saw enough of the ocean, but mentioned that I might want to go.

"They have a forty-seven-foot sailboat," my dad told me. "And I'll think you'll enjoy it."

Sailing was something I'd never considered doing. But I did enjoy watching sailboats whenever I sat on the sandy shores of the Chesapeake Bay. I loved how the white sails seemed to fly out, gracefully catching the wind. I called Joanie right away when I found out that I could bring a friend.

"My dad will drop us off at the boat pier on Sunday and we'll be out all day."

"Should I bring anything?"

"My dad said we'll need to wear tennis shoes that don't slip, a sun visor, and suntan lotion. We'll have to get up early, about 6:00 AM. If you want, you can spend the night."

"Let me call you back!" Joanie said excitedly.

Ten minutes later the phone rang. "So can you go?"

"Yeah!"

It was hard for us to get out of bed at 6:00 AM sharp, especially after Joanie and I had stayed up half the night talking about weird dreams.

"I dream about Darren all the time," she had said. "Sometimes I wish I didn't have to wake up so I can be with him longer."

I told Joanie about my strange black rose dream. "What do you think it means?" I asked.

"It means you were handed a death sentence," Joanie said with a smile and small chuckle.

"Naw. Really?"

"I don't know. I've heard of black roses being a symbol of death. But it could also mean peace."

"Well, I think it means peace, because that's what I felt in the dream. Are there such a thing as black roses?"

"I've never seen one. I think they might have 'em in Holland."

"The black rose was so beautiful. Just as beautiful as the guy's eyes and face."

"Sounds dee-deee …" Joanie said, never finishing the word "deep" because she had drifted off to sleep. I never understood how she could fall asleep in the middle of a conversation. As long as I was talking, I was awake.

I turned on my radio, keeping the volume low. "Moonlight Feels Right" by Starbuck was playing. After tossing and turning, I finally fell into a dreamless sleep.

I was surprised to find out how laid-back and friendly Mr. and Mrs. Dupree were. They both greeted me with friendly smiles, each taking turns to shake my hand, then Joanie's, when my dad introduced us. They had come up from the sailboat's cabin and crossed over onto the dock to greet us. Mrs. Dupree was probably in her forties. She had shoulder-length wavy blond hair; her face was nicely tanned but weather-beaten. Mr. Dupree had short brown hair with the same tanned face. It was a mark of their love of sailing and sunshine. One thing I had learned growing up in a city filled with navy folk was that they were either extremely rigid or just plain casual. Mr. and Mrs. Dupree were the casual kind. I was feeling quiet and shy, and was extra glad Joanie was with me. She wasn't afraid to talk, and knew how to ask intelligent questions to keep a conversation going.

The bay was beautiful with the morning's pink sun reflecting off the water. Joanie and I sat up on top of the deck taking in the scenery as we pulled out with Mr. Dupree at the wheel. There were many fishing boats and sailboats heading out toward the Atlantic Ocean. Seagulls screeched above us in the air as if to say welcome, flapping their wings playfully before gliding freely through the blue summer sky. I envied their being able to fly, especially when they swooped down and skimmed along the water. I bet they did that just for fun when they weren't searching for fish.

"Hang on tight to the side railings when we make our turns!" Mrs. Dupree shouted over the wind and the sound of the water against the hull. "My husband will call out right beforehand!"

Joanie and I nodded our heads, letting them know we understood.

"Hoooh!" Mr. Dupree shouted as the sail caught the wind, making the boat turn sharply toward the ocean. It was a little scary at first. Joanie and I looked at each other, understanding the need to grasp hold of the railings. The boat was nearly on its side. *We would slide right off into the water if we let go*, I thought. I would have to tread water until they came back to get me if I slipped off. My mom would be terrified if she found out. Then I pictured my mom sliding off into the water if she were there. I would have to jump in after her, because she couldn't swim. It was a good thing we had on life vests. I wasn't afraid of the water; I felt one with it.

Once the boat straightened back out, it was smooth sailing.

"Can I sit up in the front?" I asked.

"Sure, just keep hold of the railing!" Mr. Dupree replied.

I scooted up instead of attempting to walk. I let my legs hang off the front of the boat and resting my arms on the railing. With the wind blowing through my hair, I felt free from everything, as if I was in another world.

It's true what Christopher Cross had sung in one of my favorite songs of the time. *Sailing, take me away. It's not far to Never Never Land, no reason to pretend, and if the wind is right, you can find the joy of innocence again.* I tried to hear Christopher Cross's smooth voice in my head as we started sailing gracefully up over waves before swooshing down, dipping my feet into the water. Up again, then down. *Swoosh. Nothing could be more thrilling than this*, I thought. I laughed out loud. I felt like I was riding a horse as we swooshed down and back up again, going airborne over a wave. *This is like riding a giant sea horse*, I imagined. *If I ever get a sail boat that's what I'd name it:* My Sea Horse.

Further out into the Atlantic, the water was much calmer. I slid back onto the deck beside Joanie. The front of my body was wet from the sea spray.

"That was *so much fun*," I told Joanie. I almost suggested she try riding in the front when we headed back, but I stopped myself, remembering her not being able to get her wooden leg wet.

Joanie was leaning back with her hands behind her head, basking in the sun. I never understood how fair-skinned, redheaded Joanie could tan better than me. I always had to suffer a burn or two before getting a halfway decent tan.

Mr. and Mrs. Dupree, Joanie, and I were utterly exhausted by the time the sun started setting, melting into the water and streaking it with pink. My skin was burned from being in the sun all day, but not *too* bad. I was glad I had remembered to apply suntan lotion and put on my visor, or else I would have suffered a severe burn like I had many times before. There were times my sunburns were so severe that I had water blisters develop on my shoulders. Such blisters made even the softest breeze blowing on my sunburn excruciating. My mom had once bought Noxzema to cool my skin, but it only dried it out causing it to peel and bleed in some areas. The only thing that had worked was putting an Oil of Olay lotion bottle in the refrigerator to chill before applying. It turned out to be really soothing.

Mr. Dupree had the sails down and the motor on as we slowly cruised through the marina toward the dock. I could see my dad's green pickup truck parked, with him waiting inside.

"Thank you so much," I said after the boat was tied to the dock and we were ready to leave.

"Yeah, thank you," Joanie said.

"We enjoyed having you kids come along," Mrs. Dupree said with a wide smile.

"You'll have to come along again sometime," Mr. Dupree told us.

My dad had come over to meet us. "How did it go?" he asked.

"Oh, they fell overboard a couple of times, but they survived," Mr. Dupree teased. "No, it really went well."

"We had so much fun," I said.

"Well, hey, thanks. I really appreciate it," my dad said, shaking Mr. Dupree's hand.

"Sure anytime."

Joanie and I fell asleep on the way home. What was a thirty-minute drive seemed like three minutes. I opened my eyes as we pulled up in front of the house.

"Thanks for inviting me, Junie. I'll see you tomorrow," Joanie said sleepily.

"Bye."

I walked up the steps and into the cool air-conditioned house, heading straight for my room. I quickly changed into my light summer nightgown and got into bed.

My mom came in and sat on the foot of my bed. "Did you have fun?"

"Yeah, the best time ever."

"Do you want dinner?"

"No, we ate when Mr. Dupree anchored the boat once we were on smooth waters. I'm just really sleepy right now. I'll sleep *good* tonight."

"I bet you will," my mom said as she got up. "See you in the morning," she whispered before gently closing my door.

There I was again: warm breezes caressing my skin as I breathed in the intoxicating aroma of roses that surrounded me. I knew somehow that I was dreaming. I didn't want to wake up. I wanted to find *him*. I rose from my bed and walked across the same colorless bedroom from the first time. I descended the stairs that led outside. My heart jumped in my chest as I looked down in awe at a rose bush filled with black roses. They had all elegantly blossomed. Their hypnotic smells made me want to stare at them. I looked away only because I wanted to find *him*, to stare into his beauteous blue eyes. I didnt like standing alone. I wondered where he was. I looked all around, seeing only a blurred vision of greenery until ... there he was behind me. I felt instant warmth and peace before he started fading away, leaving me disappointed as I woke up.

"No," I said out loud when I saw I was indeed awake and looking at the familiar blue walls of my room. It was morning. I had slept straight through the night. My clock read 9:00 AM.

First Love

When I got up to get dressed, I wasn't happy with the gray skies looming outside. I never liked waking up to gray skies. I could hear thunder rolling. *A thunderstorm is coming*, I thought as I peered out my bedroom window and saw the tips of our pine trees starting to sway. Hail pelted the lawn before huge raindrops started coming down, soon turning into a torrential downfall. Sheets of rain blew across the lawn. It was over in just five minutes. I looked at my clock which read 9:05 AM Not uncommon in the Southeast. The sun came out, streaming the sky with a rainbow.

I went into the kitchen and poured a glass of tea after nuking a hot dog in our new microwave oven. My mom came into the kitchen. I heard the familiar sound of her slippers dragging on the floor.

"I'm going for a bike ride," I said, setting my half-drunk glass of tea back in the refrigerator. On mornings when my dad was at work, my mom and I went about our own separate routines.

The grass was wet, and parts of the yard were saturated from the morning's summer shower. I rode my bike across the lawn and coasted down the driveway onto the wet street. The gutters were filled with rain water that ran down to a drain at the corner of my yard. Steam rose from the street and the sun felt hotter than usual. *The rain seemed to have washed away whatever was in the air that might have blocked the rays*, I figured. It was disappointing thinking about not being able to go down to Florida or to spend the days at the beach because of summer school. This was truly going to be the worst summer ever, even worse than last summer, when I had almost lost my friendship with Joanie over my jealousy. *I'll never see Shaun again.* It seemed so long ago since he'd lived next door. My feelings for him had diminished quite a bit since last summer. It was puppy love, or a crush. After riding around the neighborhood, I decided to head back home after hearing thunder threatening overhead.

It rained off and on every day for the whole of the last week before summer school started. We couldn't plan long days at the beach with the unexpected rain showers constantly passing through. Lightning was a real threat during a thunderstorm at the beach. We couldn't have campouts in my backyard with the ground so drenched. It seemed our whole summer was thrown off-track. Morris, Joanie, and I were in the doldrums. We decided to spend Friday afternoon going to a matinee. *Summer Lovers* was playing. We decided on that movie because of the tropical scenery advertised on the lobby poster. It was filmed in Santorini, Greece. The movie was rated R, but the theater employees never paid attention to the fact I was under sixteen. I thought it was strange how the central couple in the movie let a third party in their relationship. I would have thrown that other girl over the edge of one of those cliffs. The ocean was pretty in the movie, and it took my mind off the gray skies outside. After the movie was over, Morris dropped me off at home. I thanked him and Joanie for the invite after stepping out of his car.

"Come over later, Joanie," I said as I closed the car door.

I walked up my sidewalk and into the house. I changed out of my jeans and put on shorts and flip flops, because it was still hot outside. *Why do they always keep the air so cold in theaters?* I wondered. Not long after, Joanie rang the doorbell. I stepped outside, closing the door behind me.

"Do you wanna go for a walk?" she asked.

"Sure" I answered, feeling bored myself. It was nice seeing a movie today but we still had the late afternoon to kill.

"Hey, I'm thinking about helping out a friend who will be teaching rifles up at the high school. So maybe I'll see you around," Joanie told me as we headed down our street.

As we rounded the corner onto Dunbarton, I saw a guy walking in our direction. He was only wearing cut-off jean shorts, and I couldn't help but notice his perfect physique.

"He seems kind of cute," I said to Joanie.

"Is that ... *Blockhead*?" she said.

"What?" I asked in confusion.

"It is! Hey *Blockhead*!" Joanie called out.

"Blockhead? Won't he get mad if you call him that?"

"No, he was a new guy in school last year, and likes joking around. He doesn't mind."

"What's up?" I heard the boy say as we got closer.

Oh God, hes so familiar, too familiar, hes ... I was at a loss for words. I felt my face burning. My heart started racing along with my thoughts. *How can this be? Hes ... thats ... oh my God, its* him! My mind was screaming. *Have I met him before?* I had to have. *I had to have seen him around before, not just in my dreams. That wasn't possible. No. I would never forget a guy this handsome if I had seen him in person before! When we get closer to him, if he has those blue eyes, I'll know. Take a deep breath, Junie. Don't be a dork.*

"Introduce me to him, Joanie," I whispered excitedly.

"Shh, I will, I will," Joanie said, looking at me strangely, like something was wrong with me.

There was *something wrong with me. I know this guy even though I had never met him before.*

"Hey, Richard, how's it goin'?" Joanie said.

"All right, except for all this rain. I don't like gray skies."

"This is my friend Junie."

"Hey," he said, nodding at me. His eyes were a deep blue.

Don't mess it up, don't mess it up, I thought. *Don't say anything stupid.*

"Hi," I said, trying to sound friendly.

"Richard moved here in March," Joanie said.

"How do you like George Town?"

"It's okay, I guess. Not like Carolina, though." His Southern accent made him sound warm and friendly.

"Where were you heading?" Joanie asked.

"I'm trying to find my little sister Penny. Do you know where a street called George Town Colony is?"

Something inside me clicked like a light switch. I had somehow defeated my shyness. I took control. "Oh, that's not a street" I said, happy to help. "It's another neighborhood on the other side of Providence Road. I'll show you."

He walked next to me as I guided him in the right direction. I usually was quiet and shy around guys I had just met, but there was something different about this guy. There was something, I didn't know what, but whatever it was, we were meant to be. He seemed so down-to-earth, so easy to talk to. I tried keeping my eyes off him. I didn't want to get caught gawking at him. We crossed Providence Road and headed toward a group of kids playing in a flooded yard. The water in the yard had to have been two or three feet deep. Someone's lawn was ruined.

"Penny!" Richard called.

"Yeah?" a short, chubby, sandy-blond-haired girl answered. She had stopped kicking and splashing around in the flooded yard.

"Mom says you have to go home," Richard said.

"No!" Penny shouted, kicking water up and spraying all three of us.

Richard darted after her and picked her up to carry her out, but three of the other boys, who looked to be about eight or nine years old, jumped on Richard, trying to pull him into the water.

Joanie started laughing but backed away from the water. Richard was laughing at this point and dunked Penny under the water.

"Ahhh, I'm telling Mom!" she yelled when he let her up.

Richard laughed. "Yeah, go ahead and tell her where I found you!" he yelled as she ran home. Richard turned to the boys that had tried pulling him down. "Okay, who's next?"

The boys started kicking and splashing water at him, so he picked up the largest boy and dunked him too. The little blond boy broke free of Richard's arms and tried to drag the older boy down but couldn't. Now all the kids jumped in along, finally pulling Richard down into the water. I started laughing along with Joanie, Richard, and the other kids. They started splashing us, getting me soaked. I went after them, slipping on the soft, mushy grass below the water, landing on my rear. Richard started laughing at me.

"Well, at least I didn't get my hair wet" I said.

"Oh, is that right?" He picked me up and dunked me completely under. When he lifted me back up, I tried pulling him down but couldn't budge him. His neck was so strong. He dunked me again before lifting me back up.

"Had enough?" he asked teasingly.

"I can't be any more soaked than I am," I said.

I laughed to myself as the three of us started walking back to George Town, leaving the kids to play. *I can't believe I just wrestled this amazing, special guy that I had just met. It all seems so strange.* I didn't understand. It was so crazy but I didn't care. I didn't care that I was drenched either, I felt so carefree. When we reached Whitehaven, he told me which house his family had moved into.

"Hey, you moved into Kim's old house. She was a friend of mine."

"Hope to see you around," he said as he walked back to his house.

"You too," I said with a wave.

Joanie talked the whole way back to our street, but I didn't hear anything she said.

"I better go in and shower," I said as we approached my house.

"Yeah, you better," Joanie told me with one last laugh on account of my drenched clothes. "I'll see ya."

"See ya."

I went straight to my room, pulled out dry clothes, and placed them on the bathroom counter. *That couldn't be him from my dreams. It's not possible.* I waited for the water to get warm. I was chilled from being wet and standing in an air-conditioned house. No, it was him; there was no denying it. *Was it possible to meet someone after dreaming about them first?* I wondered. *I guess so. But to be in love with them, too?*

I felt a weight lifting off me. I didn't have any reservations or insecurities. They all seemed to have left me that one hot, muggy, rainy afternoon. I knew what I wanted in life now. Somehow everything that I'd been feeling insecure about fell into place. School was now a priority. It was important, just like my parents always had told me. I didn't want to mess up the course of my life by making mistakes. I had a focus now. *Him.* Richard lived in George Town. I would definitely get to know him and become friends. I would take things slow, play it cool, like my mom sometimes said. I could see things so clearly.

Summer school became something I took seriously. Before the first day, I went through my desk drawer and gathered paper, clipboard, pens, and pencils. I organized everything just right in my book bag so I would be completely prepared on Monday morning. I went to my closet and stared at each article of clothing. I pulled out everything and reorganized my clothes. I put all of my white pants in a row, then the pastel blouses, starting with the pink ones. It was the summer of '82. The hip style was all about pastel colors, with shoes, shirts, purses, and junk jewelry in matching colors. I laid out a short-sleeved turquoise blouse with sandals to match. I was all set for summer school. Next was figuring out how to make myself a presence in Richard's life. I would start by taking strolls past his house on occasion. If I saw him, I would chat or wave.

I couldn't get the image of his blue eyes out of my head as I stared out my bedroom window at a breathtaking, hot pink sunset. As the sun set, the sky turned a lighter shade of pink before transforming into a deep purplish gray, a passionate color, I thought. Maybe this was why the rose was black in my dreams. It symbolized passion and peace.

Mick was right. Summer school was a lot more laid-back than regular school. We could wear shorts, as long as they were no more than two inches above the knee. "No Daisy Dukes," our teacher said with a smile as she went over the rules on the first morning air.

There were only eight of us in the summer English class. Ms. Mandeville told us we were to read a short story each morning, the page number of which was written on the chalkboard. We were to answer ten questions at the end of our reading assignments and hand them in before lunch period. Class began at 7:45 AM and lunch was from 9:45 to 10:15. After lunch our job was to return to class, check the board for our afternoon writing assignments, and then make sure they were completed before turning them in at 12:45. *Not bad*, I thought. If we weren't in summer school, we would all just be sleeping the morning away for the most part, being typical teenagers. So summer school wasn't going to be a nuisance after all. I would be home no later than 1:00 each afternoon, leaving plenty of time to head out to the beach. I wished I was attending just to get ahead on credits, instead of making them up. We had to get an A in the class to average it out to a C, because the school combined our Fs in with our final makeup grades. But this seemed easy compared to juggling six classes a day plus having to make that mad dash each day from the annex building to English class.

Joanie borrowed her mom's red station wagon each morning to drive us to school. She had decided to help with the rifle twirling class, which was only a two-hour practice and meant she would leave earlier than me. I would have to walk home. No big deal, though; it was nice walking home under the hot sunny skies.

Ms. Mandeville came over from another school district to teach summer classes. She didn't give homework assignments. She simply told us to make sure our class work was handed in at the end of the day. If we had problems with assignments, we were to make sure they were turned in no later than the end of the week. Even though she resembled my previous English teacher with her shoulder-length hair and icy blue eyes, she was kind and understanding, and not an ogress.

Day two of summer school was another lovely, sunny day. Joanie picked me up. We headed over to the McDonald's drive-through and then headed to school. Even though the temperature was in the nineties, I wore a thick wool button-up sweater over my summer clothes because the school's air conditioning was turned down so low. As I entered the classroom I looked at the assignment on the board which said *Read pages 126-156, "Finding your way," "Across the Level Farm Lands," and "In a Great City." Answer questions at the end of each.*

This is so easy, I thought. The short stories were only a couple of pages long. I finished answering all the questions on loose leaf paper and set my assignment on Ms. Mandeville's desk. I quietly returned to my desk to wait for the lunch bell to ring. The classroom was freezing. As I sat, I glanced around the room at everybody still working diligently on their assignments. I noticed they all had brought along some sort of light jacket or sweater to wear. We would all go to the vending machines when the bell rang before heading outside to thaw out in the warm weather.

"Hi, I'm Kelly. What's your name?" a short girl with long, curly, sandy-blond hair asked me. We were standing in line at the soda machine.

"I'm Junie."

"Which high school do you go to?"

"Indian River, except I'm a freshman, which means I still have another year in the junior high."

"Oh yeah, I've heard some high schools do that. My high school is freshman through seniors."

"What high school do you go to?" I asked, not having seen Kelly before.

"Hickory. It's just on the border of North Carolina and Virginia. I live in North Carolina."

"Really? Wow, you must have a long drive each morning."

"Yeah, tell me about it. I have to get up at 5:00 every morning to wait for the bus."

I could see that Kelly wasn't from around here. She had on jeans and cowboy boots, which was not an acceptable style in Virginia's coastal beach cities, topped off with a plaid shirt. I liked how she looked. Carolina people were so friendly and down-to-earth. Mick and James Ceaver were from Carolina originally, and they were friendly, down-to-earth guys.

Kelly put her quarters in the machine and pressed the Mountain Dew button. She used her foot to hold open the flap where the soda can rolled. I found that odd, especially for a girl. When I bought my Pepsi, I simply used my hand to push back the flap before grabbing the can. *Was that a Carolina thing too?* I wondered.

"Do you want to go outside?" I asked, feeling the goose bumps on my arms despite my sweater.

"Sure. Why do they keep it so cold in here?"

"I don't know, but it feels like winter in here."

The blazing sun felt welcoming. We sat on the steps in front of the school. We opened our bags of Funyons and Munchos chips and washed them down with soda.

Some guy from another school walked by and mussed Kelly's hair, making a funny bird call sound before heading inside. Kelly's face turned red as she brushed him off.

"Who's that?" I asked, thinking the boy was goofy looking. He had acne and was kind of short, like Kelly, with the same color hair as Kelly.

"He's some stupid guy I know who rides my bus. He goes to Hickory High School also."

"Oh."

The bell rang, so we headed in for the second part of our class.

"I'll see you tomorrow," Kelly said as we went separate ways.

I stopped before going back to my class. I felt something, a presence that gave me a yearning feeling. I turned, already knowing who it was. I was right. It was *him.*

"Whatcha doin' here?"

I was filled with instant excitement, looking at the face that I couldn't fathom living without.

"Hi! I'm taking an English class. What about you?" I asked, suddenly oblivious to anything or anyone around us. I felt almost as if I was levitating with joy.

"I'm making up credits for trigonometry class. I lost some credits when I moved here from Carolina."

"Oh, thats good. I mean, not good that you've got to make up credits, but..."

"Yeah, I know what you're saying. I didn't want to have to come to summer school. I'll see you after school to walk home," he said to my surprise.

"Sure see you then" I said as we parted ways. I should have been back in class earlier. I made it just in time stepping in the door as the bell rang. *Whoa,* I thought as I walked over to my desk, the feelings of levitating and elation still running through my veins. I didn't feel embarrassment as everyone stared at me. Nothing could penetrate my excitement. I didn't even realize it was freezing cold in the class until right before the last bell rang, making me remember I had left my sweater outside during lunch. I hurriedly dodged out of class to retrieve my sweater, making sure I didn't miss meeting up with Richard. I found him in the main corridor, leaning against the wall, holding his books against his thigh with his heel propped up behind him on the wall. I slowed my pace. I didn't want to seem too excited to be walking home with him. He looked so handsome with his long-sleeved red button-up shirt, Wrangler jeans, and cowboy boots. It was an outfit that none of the boys in the school would be caught wearing, unless they were from Carolina. The way he was dressed reminded me of John Travolta from the movie *Urban Cowboy,* a style that until then I would have made fun of as well. All the other boys were wearing jeans, white or checkered tennis shoes, and pastel O.P. surfer T-shirts. They irritated me with the way they walked around, noses in the air, their fake-blond surfer-dude hair spiked in the back and parted on the side, a lock hanging down over one eye. Neana always made me laugh when she put her hand over her eye and teasingly said "I'm a surfer dude, blind in one eye."

Another part of me was drawn to the surfer boys. No one loved the ocean and surfing as much as I did, I was willing to bet.

"Hey," Richard said, his deep voice melting me.

"Hi! Do you mind if we head out this way? I left my sweater out there," I asked, gesturing toward the set of doors that led to the front of the school.

"Of course not."

Richard opened the door for me as we walked out. *He fits me like a glove*, I thought. He reached down and picked up the abandoned wool sweater on the steps and handed it to me.

"Thanks."

As we headed toward George Town, I walked slowly because it was only a ten-minute walk to his street.

"So what class did you say you were taking?"

"English."

I went on to tell him about my struggles with Mrs. Smith. Our conversation moved on with him telling me how he had had a teacher like that once back in Carolina.

"I miss Carolina though. This place is just too goddamned fast for me."

"Oh?" I thought that was interesting. I had never pictured Chesapeake as a big, fast place.

"Yeah, North Carolina is laid-back, serene."

I had once heard Mick describe Carolina the same way. "A friend of mine said that too," I told him.

I felt bad. Richard was homesick.

"Hey, you should go to the beach some time. Looking out over the ocean is the most serene thing I have ever done."

"I just might do that." Richard slowed his pace down to a stop as we approached Whitehaven. "Well, I guess I'll see you around."

"Yeah, see you tomorrow," I said.

I wanted to scream *Hey, let's hang out all the time, before school, after school and in between!* I didn't, of course. I didn't want to sound like the overzealous person I was, wanting to be his friend and someday something more. *Take it slow, play it cool,* I told myself. *Someday I'll play my ace, once I figure out what it is.*

As I walked the rest of the way home alone, I started noticing things that I'd never paid attention to before. Love had changed me. I'd noticed pine trees with their brown pinecones and the roughness of their bark. I'd noticed flowers and green lawns, blue skies with billowy white clouds. I'd noticed sunsets, and on occasion, sunrises but I had never noticed the true beauty of it all until then. It was as if my senses were clearer. I'd heard my mom use the phrase "looking at life through rose-colored glasses," but I felt as if I had taken off the colored glasses and was looking at the world as if I had been reborn. *Maybe that's what the black rose meant. Maybe the old me died and now I was reborn.* The preacher always talked about accepting Jesus into our hearts, how we would be given life anew. I had always felt I gave my heart to Christianity while spending all those Sundays in church. *I guess the preacher would consider Richard a Godsend,* I thought.

By the time I approached my front door, I was covered in sweat. It was high noon, and the humidity was thick in the air making it hard to breath. I felt instant relief when I walked into the coolness of the air conditioned house. I went to my room to put on shorts and take off my sandals, and enjoyed feeling the soft carpet on my bare feet. I turned on the radio and heard "Hard to Say I'm Sorry" by Chicago. It sounded familiar, but I couldn't place where I had heard it before until Joanie called to invite me to the beach with her and her mom.

"That song was played in the movie *Summer Lovers,*" she said.

"Oh! I thought it sounded familiar."

"So can you go to the beach with us? Ask your momma if she wants to come too."

"Okay, hold on."

I put the receiver down on my bed to go find my mom. *Where is she? The house is so quiet.* I went from room to room searching while calling out "Mom?" I peered out the kitchen window and saw my mom weeding in the tomato garden. I opened the utility room door.

"Mom?"

"Yeah?"

"Joanie and Mrs. Ainsworth want to know if we'd like to go the beach with them today."

"No, I'm busy with the garden; maybe another day. You can go if you want."

"Okay."

I ran through the house and picked up the phone. "Yep, I can go, but my mom wants to do yard work today."

"Okay. We'll be by in half an hour. See ya."

"See ya."

I hung up and got into my new bathing suit. I grabbed the beach bag my mom always kept packed and went out to sit on the front porch. I was glad we didn't have homework in summer school. *What a drag that would be on such a nice summer day like today.*

The first two weeks of summer school passed like the blink of an eye. I'd wake up, Joanie and I would go to school, and I would spend lunch period with Richard or with Kelly if Richard wasn't there. I would head home and turn on the radio, and always find "Hard to Say I'm Sorry" playing.

Kelly gave me her phone number one afternoon when Richard was absent. We were sitting on the front steps of the school, thawing out from the freezing building and having chips and sodas. I called her later, even though it was long distance—she lived in North Carolina.

"I can't recall the last time I really had it bad for a guy, the way you do for Richard."

"I've had a crush on a guy before, but I know I really love this one. He makes my heart flutter with every breath I take."

"Why don't you tell him?"

"No. It's *too* soon. We're too young. He only seems to see me as a friend. But the right time will come."

"Wow, you really *do* love this guy!" Kelly said, sounding excited for me.

"I hope you won't tell anyone, Kelly."

"Oh, I won't. I have a secret to share with you too."

"Oh, what's that?"

"I'm pregnant."

"*Really?*" I was shocked. *Kelly, pregnant?* "Who's the father? I didn't know you had a boyfriend."

"Remember the guy who came by messing my hair up that one day when we were sitting on the steps outside?"

"Yeah," I said, picturing the dorky guy with acne. I had seen it in his eyes how he adored Kelly, but I had no idea they were seeing each other. "Yeah, we've been dating on and off for a couple of years."

"I had no idea, Kelly."

"I know. We keep it a secret because our families don't like each other and we live in a small town."

"What are you going to do now?"

"I'm going to have a baby without telling my parents who the father is."

"Good luck with that," I said, already seeing problems for Kelly.

"I'll be okay."

"I hope so."

Days passed. Waking up each morning, I looked forward to seeing Richard. I was truly happy. 1982 was a memorable summer for me. My generation would have been lost without video games and video arcades. It was all the craze, with teens flocking to the arcades that seemed to be popping up on every corner. The shopping malls had video arcades as well, full of beeping, bopping, bells and whistles, their sounds luring teenagers in. Games like *Pac-Man, Ms. Pac-Man, Joust, Centipede, Burger Time, Donkey Kong, Moon Patrol*, and *Asteroids*, just to name a few, were quite popular. They helped take my mind off Richard on the weekends.

Richard's father was the head foreman for a construction company, and he had Richard working weekends. Fridays were disappointing for me, because I would have to go the entire weekend without seeing Richard. He worked at least eight hours on both Saturdays and Sundays. On Saturday mornings, my dad would get me up at 9:00 AM to mow and edge the lawn. My mom would usually help me do some of the edging before we swept the grass off the sidewalk and driveway. I used to challenge myself to get rid of any grass, dried leaves, or rubbish the wind brought in during the week. I prided myself on keeping our gutter perfectly clean. Afterward, I would just stand in the shower, letting it cool me after working under the sun-parched sky. It would be close to noon when I was all done. I'd call Joanie so we could ride our bikes up to the 7-Eleven on Military Highway. Unlike other 7-Elevens, this one had a *Ms. Pac-Man* machine! We would buy large Cokes and strawberry-flavored Bubble Yum. The man working behind the counter would be waiting for us to exchange our ten-dollar bills for quarters. We would spend the entire afternoon playing that silly video game. Joanie and I would challenge one another, seeing who could get to the last level, the "banana" level. Eventually we'd run out of quarters and go home, with blisters in between our forefingers and thumbs.

After playing *Ms. Pac-Man* we would hop on our bikes and head back to George Town. Usually we would pass a baseball game being played on the junior high's baseball diamond near Indian River Lake. I remembered watching Mick, Morris, and Paul play baseball on the same field when they were much younger.

One Saturday, Joanie and I parked our bikes behind the concession stand to watch the game for a while. Joanie knew all the ins and outs of baseball, and wasn't afraid to stand at the chain-link fence yelling "Hey batter, batter, batter!" I sat in the bleachers, pretending I knew what was going. I really only understood that the ball should be hit and the runners had to make it on base.

I was getting bored as usual and started bugging Joanie to leave. "No, hold on a minute. I just want to see this one guy hit," she would say after every batter. "Run, run, go, go, go!" she would shout.

I liked Indian River's baseball uniforms. They were dark blue and light blue, with a dark blue feather on some of the jerseys or a dark blue Indian head silhouette on the others. The ball field was dusty. Everyone covered their face every time a gust of wind blew across the diamond. "It looks like rain again," one of the moms sitting behind me in the bleachers said. We all looked up to see the dark clouds rolling in. "They're gonna have to stop the game, it looks like," another mom said back. Sure enough, the umpire called the game and everyone got up to leave as a fine mist blew over us.

"C'mon Joanie" I said. As we started for our bikes, thunder rolled.

We pedaled as fast as we could to get home, just escaping the heavy downpour. Fortunately, my dad had the big garage door up which helped us dodge the large drops now sweeping the streets, lawns, and rooftops. It was fun sitting in the garage watching the rain and lightning, something my dad thoroughly enjoyed. Joanie and I went into my room to play my Atari *Pac-Man* cartridge.

My mom had automatically set out an extra steak for Joanie. My dad pretty much took over the cooking on weekends. All of the kids in the neighborhood were like one big family. An invitation to stay over for dinner was almost automatic.

Before summer school had started, I had thought it would be a grueling ordeal. But with seeing Richard everyday and walking home after school with him, summer school passed by quickly. I would walk with him to his house and then cut through on an adjacent street, which made my walk home shorter *and* gave me an excuse to walk down Richard's street with him.

We got to know each other quite well, although it was mostly small talk. I did learn that Richard's parents were divorced. He lived with his dad and his dad's new wife, Doreen. I met his parents one afternoon and they were very friendly. I thought Richard's dad was handsome, resembling the movie star Sam Elliott. Penny, Richard's stepsister, reminded me of myself when I was her age, always playing Barbies or dress-up. Richard Matrix was a year older than me. His birthday was in January, which meant he was a Capricorn. I was a Leo; so we were supposed to be compatible. He didn't have a car, but he was building a motorcycle. I thought that was really cool. I always thought there was something sexy and masculine about a guy on a motorcycle. Richard had told me to stop by some time to see his motorcycle on one of our walks home.

I stopped by one evening while riding my bike, and was impressed with how complete the motorcycle was. He showed me all the different parts and told me their names. I pretended to be interested. I was interested in Richard, not his motorcycle. If any other guy showed me motorcycle parts, I would have been out of there.

"That's the carburetor, and that is the cylinder."

I was happy to be next to him, breathing the same air. Sometimes I would get caught up staring into his hypnotic blue eyes as he spoke, and wouldn't hear anything he was saying. It was hard not to stare at his picturesque physique, face, and eyes. His jaw line was strong, and his pearly white teeth were perfectly aligned, giving him a smile that made my heart pound. *Okay Junie, you've visited long enough. You need to go home before you overstay your welcome and ruin your masquerade.* I thought. I was only fourteen, almost fifteen; still too young to start a romance with him. We would have a better chance when we were a bit older. I wasn't going to do anything to blow it, I hoped. It was hard to control myself because of my passionate feelings. It was a constant battle in my head. *Stay calm! No, scream out your feelings! No! Someday, I'll tell him I'm in love with him; someday, but not now. I just have to figure out how to hold on.* Whenever I spoke with older people who were in a relationship, I would ask if they had been friends with their partner first. Most of them said that friendship in a relationship was very important, and being friends beforehand often made for a stronger relationship. I kept that in mind as I continued along the journey of the new life that had begun when I met Richard.

I received my summer school grade in the mail. It was a C, which meant I had earned my A. It was a shame they had to combine the A in with my initial F. I had one year left in the junior high before I would be able to attend high school with Richard. Joanie would be graduating next year, along with Morris, Paul, and Paul's girlfriend, Sharon. I wished Kelly would be attending Indian River. I would miss her. I wondered if she would continue with school while pregnant.

I felt a tear form in my eye when I turned on the radio and "Hard to Say I'm Sorry" was playing. The words made me think of Richard. *Couldn't stand to be kept away, not for a day, from your body, wouldn't want to be swept away, far away from the one that I love.* What perfect words for my emotions. I wanted to shout out to the world just who the one that I loved was. I, just like Kelly, had a secret to hold onto until the time was right. I couldn't imagine having to carry a secret like hers though.

My mom got a job working for Dutch Plants in Greenbrier Mall. I spent many afternoons walking around the mall shopping before settling down at a table in the food court to do my homework. Usually my mom would bring home carnations and place them in vases around the house. They smelled so fresh, and I found the variety of colors interesting. If my mom put blue dye in the vase water, the carnations would turn blue. I didn't find the black carnations as pretty as the black roses I had seen in my reoccurring dreams, though.

Joanie spent her after-school hours for rehearsing for school plays or practicing her clarinet for the high school's band. In the spring, many high school bands, even some from out of state, met on our football field for fierce marching band competitions. Morris worked after school to save money. Mick got his GED and was still laying tar on rooftops. Sometimes Neana and I would have sleepovers and listen to the latest songs on the radio. We laughed at "Valley Girl," trying to mimic the singing of Frank Zappa's daughter. When the movie *Valley Girl* came out starring Nicolas Cage, it defined styles we wore in the '80s. Cable TV became a must-have in George Town, and introduced teens to MTV. Teenagers of the '80s were obsessed with music television. MTV's first music video couldn't have been more appropriate—it was for the song "Video Killed the Radio Star."

I no longer minded the cold, gray, drizzly days of winter. I dreamt of Richard and I dancing in a glass gazebo, in the middle of a rainforest. Sometimes my dream was set in the middle of a snowy forest. The gazebo was always warm inside. I thought of winter as my "glass gazebo" months, picturing the gazebo inside a snow globe with us dancing in it. When spring arrived, the world became more romantic with the blooming of each new flower, with each rainbow and each soft breeze that caressed my face. Lionel Richie's song "Truly" captured my thoughts and made me realize there were others out there that felt the way I did.

I accepted invitations to school dances or to the latest movies from some boys. I never paid attention to how they looked or what they said. It didn't matter. Those dates were just a way to pass time. My main goals were Richard and getting my education. Ninth grade passed. Tenth grade passed rather quickly as well once I was in high school with Richard. We sat together on the floor of the main hall before the first bell of the day rang. Richard mentioned having girlfriends once or twice, but his dates were never from our school. I never saw him walking around with a girlfriend, nor did I care to find out more about those girls. I knew no one would ever love him as much as I did. I would just wait it out. Unfortunately, we didn't have classes or lunch period together, but we always waved to each other when we passed in the halls. We always walked home from school together. Sometimes after football games, which I only attended because I knew Richard would be there, we would walk home together.

One evening, we sat on my front porch talking until sunrise. My parents thought I had already come inside for the night. Richard and I talked about religious beliefs, North Carolina, ghosts, relatives, *everything*, except the fact that I was completely, unconditionally in love with him. We became close friends. There were times I would wake up in the night, sensing something was wrong. At school the following day, I would usually find Richard brooding about something. He argued with his dad a lot, just like I did with mine. Another time after I woke in the middle of the night sensing something was not right, I found Richard on the verge of tears the next day at school. His grandmother had passed away. If I was feeling down about something; Richard would walk right up to me and ask if I was okay.

We went to the movies a couple of times, and he gave me a ride home on the back of his silver motorcycle. He would give me a quick peck on the lips before heading home.

In the midst of all this, Joanie had packed her things and moved out of the house out of the blue one day. I wished she would have said something to me, or at least told me good-bye. I hated it when she kept things from me. I didn't understand how she could drop out of school just a few months before graduating to move to the bad side of town with a not-so-nice guy without telling me. I didn't even know she was getting serious with any particular guy. I always pictured Joanie as someone who would go far in life. She was a cheerleader and she was the best on the debate team. Joanie was the captain of the rifle girls in the band before she took up the clarinet. She usually held first chair in the high school band. Her grades never dropped below a B. *What happened, Joanie?* I thought.

Morris had graduated from high school and was attending a local community college. I didn't understand how he juggled work *and* college. Mrs. Ainsworth wrote continuous letters to military recruiters and even the president to help Morris get into the army. The army wouldn't accept him because he stuttered, which was a damn shame. He was so smart and in excellent shape, getting up to jog every morning before work.

Neana and I hung out more often once my older friends had moved on with their lives. Paul and Sharon became engaged after graduating and moved into their own apartment while attending college. Neana and I would ride our bikes up to the field a lot. One Saturday afternoon, we rode up there and climbed on top of the monkey bars, just like when we were little girls.

"You know, this is *our* neighborhood," she said as we sat on top of the bars, looking around at the houses across the field.

"Yeah, you're right." I understood what she meant.

"We've all grown up here, and seen the passing of seasons, and neighbors moving in and out."

"You're right, Neana. I think we should never leave."

I imagined Richard and I living in one of the brick ranch homes.

"I can't picture living anywhere else," Neana said, looking out with compassion in her eyes.

We knew our way around George Town. We knew every street, yard, and tree. We knew which neighbors had lived there the longest, and which were new. It was our home, and neither of us could fathom leaving and letting our memories just blow away like leaves on a windy autumn day.

With my mom working, we didn't see as much of our neighbors as we had in the past. After Joanie moved away and Morris became busy with work and college, the Ainsworths delved into their own world. I figured Joanie would eventually call me when the time was right. I hoped she knew she could. Mrs. Ceaver still invited my mom and I over for pineapple upside-down cake and coffee every now and then. She was often distraught that Mick still lived at home and spent his money from work on drugs. I would wave at Mick when I saw him hopping into his pickup truck. He was always on the move, it seemed. I heard rumors again that he was working for the Mob. James struggled to hold down a job. For years, it was the same old routine. He would get a job, move out, lose it, and move back in. Mr. Ceaver was hardly ever home. Being a truck driver kept him on the road out of town.

During the last week of school; Keith and I ended up walking home from school together. Richard had left for work right after school.

I thought I'd risk an actual conversation with smart-ass Keith. He could be very nice and polite at times, but other times he was a complete jerk.

"So what are your plans after high school?"

"I'm going to dental school. After I'm a dentist, I'll spend all my weekends surfing the waves. What about you, dork? Have you even thought about what you want to do after high school?"

Oops, I shouldn't have risked it.

"Of course, dummy."

"Yeah? Like what?"

"I've thought of lots of things, but haven't settled on anything in particular," I answered honestly. I had thought about teaching or psychology. I was interested in home design. I had considered going to the local community college until I could settle on a career plan.

"Ha! You call me a dummy? At least I can make up my mind."

He was really irritating me. "Keith, you are the most stuck-up guy I have ever met!"

"Well, I have a right to be. I'm good looking, smart, and can whip anybody's ass any day."

I couldn't tell if he was being serious or just trying to imitate a pro wrestler. After traffic cleared and we crossed Providence Road into George Town East, I went to the opposite side of the road from Keith, trying to make it obvious that I didn't want to walk next to him.

"What's wrong, Junes? You think you're too good for me?"

"Nope. Apparently, *you're* too good for me!"

"You'd better watch out, or I'll come over there and dance all over your face."

"Go ahead, ass wipe!" I was hoping he would. I would kick him right where it hurts most.

Keith picked up a rock and flung it at me, hitting me on the side of my head. I picked it back up and threw it as hard as I could, but it missed him.

"Ha! You can't even throw, moron."

We ignored each other the rest of the way home.

When I told Richard about Keith the next day, he became concerned.

"Don't worry, I'll take care of him," he said.

"Richard, don't worry about it. I've known Keith since we were little kids. He's either very nice or an ass. It's just his way."

"No one is going to call any friend of mine names or throw rocks at them. If he bothers you again, just let me know."

"Really, Richard, it's okay."

"All right," he said skeptically.

The Lost, Loyal Puppy Dog

It was hard for me to make up my mind about what I wanted to do after high school. Richard said he was going into the navy, like most guys in the area. The majority of the Tidewater population had military ties. It was normal to be surrounded by navy, marine, army, and air force families. We were surrounded by military bases. There was Oceana, Fort Story, Fort Monroe, Langley, and the Norfolk naval base, the biggest in the world. Our Norfolk base was the size of a city. Richard still had a year left to think about it. I never considered going into the military. I had two years of high school left to think about a career. I was somehow going to find a way to be with Richard.

During the summer months, Richard and I were like ships passing in the night. He worked long days including Saturdays, so we hung out on Sunday afternoons in the engine shop behind his house. I would sit on the workbench while he worked on his motorcycle. He was always adding or changing parts on the bike. I was deeply saddened when he announced he would be spending most of the summer after school let out in Carolina with his mother.

"Hey, stay in touch" was all I could say, trying not to let him see my disappointment.

He could see through me. Concern showed in his eyes. "I'll always keep in touch. You be good. Don't end up beating up Keith or anything," he teased, making me laugh.

That summer, I missed Richard, and I missed Joanie. I missed how Mrs. Ainsworth, my mom, Joanie, and I would get up early to go garage sale-ing or to do Meals on Wheels. My mom was still working, leaving me alone at home without a way to the beach. My dad said if I got a summer job and my driver's license, he would buy me a used car. I was intimidated by the driver's license thing. I knew how to drive and had even aced my driver's ed class in tenth grade. *So what was my problem?* I wondered. I would only have to go down to the DMV, show proof of insurance (which I had through my dad's insurance company), and then take a fifteen-question test. Due to passing driver's ed class with an A, I wouldn't even have to take a road test. I had to ponder over this decision for a few days.

On a beautiful, sunny day, I hopped on my bike and rode all the way to Greenbrier Mall. I parked my bike by the entry doors and went inside. The familiar sound of the fountains echoing throughout the mall sounded cool and refreshing, and made me crave a cool, bubbly soda. I decided to head over to the food court to buy one before visiting with my mom at the plant shop. The Pepsi tasted so good after that long bike ride. The temperature that day was in the mid-nineties. I rested my arms on the railing, looking out over the mall.

"Hi, Junie!"

I turned to see a familiar face. I remembered this girl from my Spanish class, but I couldn't think of her name. She had long brown hair like mine, but straighter. She was thin like me, but her face was bland. She didn't wear any makeup and had dark circles under her eyes.

"Hi," I said, still trying to remember her name. She had showed up during the middle of the school year from New York.

"So what are you doing this summa?"

"I'm actually thinking about getting a driver's license. My dad said he would buy me a car if I did."

"What are you waiting fah?" I suddenly remembered her name after hearing her New York accent. *Melanie.*

"I'm a little nervous about it."

"Yeah, so am I. I want to get mine but my motha, she won't let me."

"Why not?"

"She's still got that New Yawk mentality. You have to be eighteen in New Yawk to get one. Hey, do you know a guy named Harris Jenkins? He's got blond hair and was on the wrestling team?"

"Yeah, I've known him since the second grade."

"You must be pretty good friends then."

"No, he doesn't live in my neighborhood. I should say, we've gone to school together since second grade. I only know *of* him."

"I'm looking for him. He was supposed to meet me up heah by noon."

Right when Melanie said that, I saw Harris walking toward us with a guy I had never seen before. The new guy was taller than Harris, about six feet two, I guessed.

"Hey, Junie."

"Hi, Harris. How's it goin'?"

"Good. So do you know each other?" he asked, looking from me to Melanie.

"We met in Spanish class last year."

Harris had left Indian River at the end of the school year, transferring to our rival school, Great Bridge. Some people called Great Bridge the hick school, because it was in the country part of Chesapeake. Great Bridge was a nice high school. In fact, it was where most of the rich kids went.

"Who's your friend?" the tall guy with glasses asked, looking at me.

"Oh, this is Junie." Harris introduced us. "This is J. D. Bentley."

J. D. reached out to shake my hand. His palm was sweaty. *Gross*, I thought. He had broad, round shoulders and was a little chunky in the middle. He had small blue eyes behind his large, round glasses.

"Well, nice seeing you all," I said, turning to go visit with my mom.

"Hey, do you want to hang out with us?" Melanie asked.

I didn't want to be rude. As I didn't have any real plans for the day, I agreed to hang out with them. We headed over to the video arcade. When Harris and J. D. went to get tokens out of the machine, Melanie approached me.

"Hey, thanks for hanging out with us. I'm nervous about being alone with Harris. It's kind of a first date for Harris and me."

"Oh no problem. Harris is a nice guy. You have nothing to worry about. He's cute, too. You made a nice choice."

Melanie laughed. I think I eased her nerves.

"Why did he bring his friend?" I asked.

"I guess Harris is nervous too."

"How did you two meet?"

"We met in class right before Harris moved. He gave me his phone numba and we've been talking eva since."

I remembered I had some tokens in my purse from the last time I had played in the arcade. Somehow tokens seemed to end up in the bottom of my purse all the time. I dug one out and put it in the *Ms. Pac-Man* machine, which was my favorite video game.

"How come I've never seen you around before?" J. D. asked me.

"I hang out up here a lot. My mom works in the plant shop." It was hard concentrating on the game and having a conversation at the same time. "Damn; I'm dead," I said when Ms. Pac-Man ran into the red ghost. *Oh well, I've still got two lives left*, I thought.

"I don't really hang out here a lot. I work in my parent's store usually." He was already boring me. "S-so you go to Indian River?" He asked nervously.

"Yeah." Another ghost got my Ms. Pac Man. I was down to one life.

"I, uh, go to Great Bridge." I could see J. D. fidgeting with his glasses, constantly sliding them up his nose as they slipped back down. "So, err, um, do you like your school?"

"I like Indian River, but I don't like school. I honestly would rather spend my days at the beach."

"Oh, not me. I hate the beach. It's so sandy and the salt water seems slimy to me."

I let Ms. Pac Man die, running her into a ghost. The game ended. I turned to J. D. "Well, it was nice meeting you. I have to go now."

As I turned to leave, I saw Melanie and Harris playing air hockey. I swiftly made my way out of the arcade into the open, well-lit mall. There were skylights high above in the ceiling, giving plenty of light in the mall during the day. I stopped in front of a department store that had a table set out front. There were a variety of jelly shoes on sale. I started browsing, rummaging through them. *Let's see, I don't have a pink pair. Maybe I'll buy those, and a black pair because Richard likes black*, I thought before noticing J. D. had followed me. *My God, this guy was like a lost puppy*, I thought to myself as I looked at him.

"Uh, my friends kind of ditched me."

"I'm sorry. I'm sure they just want to be alone a while. They'll show up." I turned to dig through the piles of shoes.

"What a weird thing."

"What's weird?"

"*Jelly* shoes?" J. D. said, emphasizing the word jelly.

"I happen to be wearing a pair," I told him unable to hide the annoyance in my voice.

"Oh. Sorry. I just sort of meant it's interesting how they're made."

I walked toward my mom's shop. She was getting off work soon, and could give me a ride home as she had driven the pickup that day. I could put my bike in the back of the truck.

"Hi, Mom," I said as I walked into the plant shop.

"Oh hi!" she said enthusiastically. "Oh, I have to work another three hours today. Connie can't make it in."

"Okay," I said, disappointed. *Why did I have to ride my bike all the way up here today?* I asked myself.

"Who's your friend you brought with you?" she asked, smiling politely at J. D., who had followed me without my knowing it. *He's my lost little puppy dog*, I felt like saying.

"This is J. D. I just met him through another friend."

"How do you do?" J. D. said, extending his hand to shake my mom's.

"Well, I'm going to head back home now," I said.

"You be careful on that highway out there."

"I will, Mom."

I turned and walked out of the shop, heading toward the exit where I had parked my bike. J. D. followed.

When he saw I had ridden my bike, he said "Hey, if you don't mind, I can give you a ride home. I drove my parent's station wagon and it has plenty of room for a bike."

This was where I would normally say "Get lost," but I really didn't feel like pedaling all the way back in the summer heat.

"What about your friends?"

"They ditched *me*. Besides, Harris drove his own car."

"All right then. Thanks."

"It's, uh, no problem. It's my pleasure." J. D. was so polite—a little too polite. I told him how to get to my house. Once we pulled up in front, he helped me drag my bike out of the station wagon. I thanked him again.

"C-can I sort of ask you a question?"

"What's that?"

"Would it be all right, you don't have to if you don't want, but I was kind of wondering—"

"What, J. D.?" I had an idea of what he was going to ask me, and I wished he wouldn't.

"Can I have your phone number?" *How do I get out of this one?* I thought. Now I was the one fidgeting.

"I don't have anything to write it on."

"I do. Hold on." He went inside the car and found a piece of paper and a pen. *I guess I'll just let him have the number. It will be easy to ignore his phone calls later.*

I took the paper and wrote my number down. "Here," I said, handing it back.

"Thanks!" He said. "I'll call sometime."

"Thanks for the ride." I was relieved when he drove away.

I tried avoiding J. D.'s phone calls as much as possible. If my dad was home, he always made me answer the phone. If he picked it up and it was for me, he'd make me take the call.

"I'm not interested in talking to him, Dad," I would say.

"Then tell him not to call back!"

It wasn't that simple. J. D. was a very nice guy, and I didn't know how to let him down..

One day, Melanie called to invite me to go out with her, Harris, a couple of guys from Great Bridge, and J. D.

"He's really nice, Junie, and has neva been on a date before. He would make a loyal friend, if nothing else."

"Okay," I finally agreed. *All of my friends were moving on with their lives,* I thought. *Maybe it wouldn't hurt to hang out with a new group to pass time while Richard is away.*

We spent the summer going to different video arcades, Busch Gardens, Kings Dominion, and even the beach. Andy and Mike were a couple of really nice guys who hung out with the group. They were nerdy. Mike was short and fat with acne. Andy was short, skinny, and wore big round glasses like J. D.'s. The boys often bragged about spending Sunday afternoons inside playing Dungeons & Dragons, which was some board game that made up medieval characters to role-play. They were very intelligent guys, though. When they graduated high school, it would be with honors, I was sure of that. They even had universities picked out that they wanted to attend.

J. D. had played football and baseball but had injured his knee, which forced him to quit playing. I didn't like looking at his face at first. It took getting used to. He had a large nose that reminded me of a potato, tiny eyes, and large buck teeth. J. D. started to grow on me as a friend. Melanie was right; he made a good, loyal friend. J. D. was one of the most compassionate people I had ever met. He listened intently with sincerity. I found myself rambling on and on about growing up in George Town and how my parents bickered so much. I had never told anybody about that before. Our phone conversations grew longer, especially if I had a bad day or got in an argument with my parents.

J. D. was always there, a shoulder to cry on or someone to make me laugh. He even gave me the confidence to get my driver's license, driving me to the DMV himself. He drove me to my first job interview, giving me tips on what to say and what not to say. He had experience from watching his parents run their Mini K variety store. I started viewing J. D. not as a lost puppy following me around, but as my *anchor*.

My first job was in Greenbrier Mall clearing tables at Piccadilly Cafeteria. My dad had bought me my first car. It was a round, apple-red 1976 Pacer, in mint condition. Keith would point and laugh at me whenever I drove by his house, and I would flip him the bird. The paint job on my car was unique. It appeared completely orange under the streetlights in the parking lot at night. I had to remember to look for my *orange* Pacer instead of my *red* one whenever I left work at night.

When I checked the mailbox one morning before work, there was an envelope from Asheville, North Carolina. *Richard!* I opened it and read it standing next to the mailbox. It was the second letter I had received from him during the summer. This one said pretty much what the last one had said.

I'm still hanging out with old buddies fishing down at the pond, doing my mom's yard work, nothing exciting. I hope you're enjoying

*the beach along with your summer. I'm looking forward to seeing
you again.*

Take care!

Love,

Tex, The Warlord, Richard

He always signed his letters like that. Those were nicknames his
motorcycle-riding friends had given him. I didn't mind as long as they
didn't call him Blockhead. I wanted to write back and say *My dearest
one and only* or *I love you more than words can say.* But I didn't.

Hey Richard,

*I've made some new friends to hang out with over the summer, from
Great Bridge. I am actually driving now and working. We should
have lots to talk about when you get back.*

Always your friend,

Junie

Junior year started off with me driving to school instead of walking.
Richard always preferred to ride his motorcycle when I offered him a
ride in my Pacer. He needed his bike handy right when school let out
so that he could get to work on time. Even with his dad being the boss,
Richard wasn't cut any slack. I never saw him, except briefly in the
mornings before classes started.

Melanie and I shared our first class together, Spanish three. We were
halfway fluent in Spanish by now. This was Melanie's senior year, as
well as Richard's. If only I hadn't been held back in third grade, I would
graduate with them. *Next year I'll be all alone*, I thought.

My second class was business management. On the first day, we all
noticed a very tall guy walking into the classroom. He had to bow his
head to avoid hitting it on the door frame.

"Gosh, he should be a basketball player," I said to a boy sitting in
front of me.

"He is," Anthony told me. "Scouts are already watching him."

"What's his name?"

"Alonzo Mourning."

"I'll have to remember that. I can see him playing on TV one day."

"Oh, you will."

My third class was my favorite: creative writing. After writing class came lunch period. I didn't know anybody at lunch. I always hopped in my car to get a cheeseburger and Coke at McDonald's. It was nice having my own car; it gave me a sense of freedom.

J. D. usually called me when I got home after school. I was glad he didn't go to my school. I didn't think about him when I was with Richard. The months passed quickly, with school during the week, homework in the evenings, and work at Piccadilly Cafeteria on weekends. On Friday nights I went to the movies, the video arcade, or to Pizza Hut with Harris, J. D., Mike, and Andy. I felt bad for Melanie, who had to spend her Friday nights babysitting her younger twin sisters. Her parents were very strict. If she got any grade below a B on her report card, she would get grounded. I was happy that my parents let me hang out with friends as long as I was home by 11:00 PM. My group of nerdy friends and I spent most Saturday nights going to *The Rocky Horror Picture Show*, which started at eleven. My parents knew I wouldn't get home until after midnight because of that. I was a good kid, just like my friends. We were harmless. None of us drank, did drugs, or smoked. I liked how my friends were just interested in laughing, playing video games, and listening to music. We totally enjoyed Nina Blackwood and Martha Quinn on MTV and were generally obsessed with music videos. My friends and I were care-free. Most importantly, my Great Bridge friends were my distraction from Richard. They were like a dose of medicine to soothe the aches and pains in my life. Without them, I would become consumed with my feelings for Richard.

I became a little perturbed one afternoon when my mom said she had signed me up for a modeling class at the recreation center on Tuesday nights from 5:30 to 7:00. I had wished she had asked me first. But I did like the idea of a modeling class. I still loved fashion and the class sounded fun. I was even happier when I found out Neana's mom had signed her up too. We learned the proper way to sit, how to cross our legs while sitting, and how to gracefully enter and exit a room. We learned how to walk and turn wearing high heels. Cici; our modeling instructor, had been a model herself. I learned there was a difference between runway modeling and magazine models.

"Lots of runway models aren't photogenic, but have long thin bodies which show off clothes well," she told us. "Your job as a model is to make a ten-dollar pair of jeans look like a hundred-dollar pair of jeans. Anyone can do that by the way they hold their head up and walk, even if they're not model material."

Cici arranged for us to be in a fashion show at Greenbrier Mall's center court stage. Various stores in the mall lent us clothes, and we changed in and out of outfits in a dressing room just off the stage. The class turned out to be a good experience for me, Neana, and the other teen girls.

After the holidays passed, Melanie and Harris broke up and began dating other people. J. D. and his friends considered me his girlfriend. I considered myself his friend. I was only living a façade, still carrying a torch for Richard, waiting to play my ace. Even though Richard was busy with work after school and we hardly ever saw each other; he was still there, still in my school and living in George Town. We spoke on the phone every now and then. His voice and laugh swept me away to a safe and warm place.

I woke early one cold morning to a violet and gold sunrise. I had had another dream of descending stairs into the green garden with black roses. Richard and I were dancing around and around. It was like I was out of my body, looking down through the familiar glass gazebo at the two of us. He was wearing a black tuxedo with a white shirt. I wore a long, close-fitting purple velvet dress. I hated waking up after those recurring dreams.

My glass gazebo months passed again, leading us into March. Everyone was making plans for the upcoming prom. Some kids were going to the prom in groups as friends. Even some of the couples were going as friends. That way they wouldn't miss out on prom, even if they didn't have a girlfriend or boyfriend. *What a great idea*, I thought. *I could ask Richard to go.* We were good friends and he didn't have a date, I was sure of that. He didn't have time to date. *I'll just casually ask him.* Going to the prom would give me an excuse to dance with him, just like in my dreams.

I found him standing in front of his locker at school.

"Hey," he said when he saw me.

"Hey," I said. "So who are you going to the prom with?" I asked, trying to sound as matter-of-fact as possible.

"Prom? I haven't really thought about it."

"It's your senior year. You have to go."

"I don't know, prom seems kind of sissy to me."

"Well, I'll take you. As a senior it's your right to go." I added quickly, "You know me and fashion. I need a reason to buy and wear one of those beautiful dresses. You'll be doing me a favor, and someday you'll thank me because you did go."

"Ah, I see" he said, holding his head back and chuckling, showing his beautiful white teeth.

"Well, looks like we're going to the prom. I'd rather go with you than with any of these bubble headed bimbos around here," he said, closing his locker.

"All right, cool" I said, turning to go before he could see my face turn red and maybe even hear my heart throbbing. *Thud, thud, thud.* I could hear my heart pounding as I glided my way to class, unaware of anyone around me. It was just me and my loud heart. I sat in my chair trying to catch my breath.

"Are you all right?" I heard Melanie ask.

"Yeah. I just ran all the way to class that's all."

I wasn't going to tell anyone at school about Richard and I going to the prom. I didn't want to jinx it. I would tell my mom, though. She knew how I felt about Richard just from watching me, seeing my face light up whenever he called or stopped by.

I walked around the mall searching for the perfect dress. All the dresses I saw were pretty. Some were sleeveless with ruffles at the bottom. Others had sleeves made of lace. All the dresses were floor-length, but in pastel colors only. I wanted the one I wore in my dreams. I wanted a deep, dark purple velvet or a black satin one. Richard loved dark colors.

"Do you have any dark-colored dresses?" I asked a saleslady.

"No. Pastels are the thing this year. But there is a store in Military Circle Mall that carries unique dresses that would work as a prom dress."

"Really? Thank you, I'll have to check it out."

I left Greenbrier Mall and headed straight down the highway to Military Circle Mall, blasting my radio. Cyndi Lauper's song "Girls Just Want to Have Fun" was on. I had an idea which store the saleslady was talking about. Sure enough, there were rows and rows of dark dresses hanging on the racks. There were red ones, dark green ones, even polka-dotted dresses, but no dark purple velvet ones. There were so many dresses on the racks it was hard sifting through them all. I was about to give up when I came across the perfect one. It was made of black silk, with a crisscross back and slightly elasticized straps. No sleeves. It was my size. Its long front had ribbons tying at the bust line, right where a tiny black satin rose sat. The bottom flowed like silky scarves. I checked the price tag. *$125*! I could never afford that. I slammed the hanger back onto the rack.

"We have layaway," a sales lady said, noticing my frustration.

"Then it's all settled," I said with a smile, taking the dress back off the rack and handing it to her. I put $25 down on it. I had to come up with the other $100. With my job, I could afford that by April. I had a month. My mom would help too, I knew she would. Later, on the phone, I told Richard I had my dress on layaway. He was renting a black tux.

"Is that okay? You aren't expecting me to wear one of those white girly tuxes, are you?"

"No, Richard, of course not. I couldn't see you in one of those anyway. I put a black dress on layaway today."

"Sounds gorgeous."

"It is."

"Wait, it's on layaway? I'll buy it for you."

"No really, thanks though. I got it."

"All right then," he said.

Neana came over that Saturday morning. She sat on my bed and let out a big sigh. Her face was expressionless. "I have something to tell you," she said.

"What?" I sat on my desk chair and faced her, giving her my undivided attention.

"You're not going to believe this."

"Is something wrong?"

"My parents are getting a divorce." I was taken aback. The happiest couple in the neighborhood getting divorced? She was right; I didn't believe it. They were always smiling, laughing, telling jokes. They went out for dinner and drinks, just the two of them every Friday or Saturday night. I knew. I babysat a lot for them.

"How did this come about?"

"Yeah, I know everybody thinks my parents are all hunky-dory, but they're not."

"Apparently not," I agreed. "Neana, I'm shocked you never told me any of this before. I didn't know your parents didn't get along."

"I didn't know either, Junie."

"My mom was really good at keeping things from us." When she started crying, I sat next to her.

"I'm so sorry, Neana. I don't know what to say."

"My dad moved out. He had been having affairs off and on for years."

I could see how that was possible. He was out of town a lot, working down in Carolina.

"Neana, you can hang out over here as much as you want if things get too heavy at home, okay?"

She nodded her head yes, wiping her tears before she started laughing.

"Now what?" I asked. She covered her face with her hands, her shoulders shaking up and down.

"My parents are planning a big wedding too."

"What do you mean?"

She brought her hands down off her face. "My parents are getting divorced, and Paul and Sharon are getting married."

We both started laughing. We always found the humor in any situation.

"I'll be going to court one day and the next we'll be looking for wedding cakes and dresses," she said.

"Oh gosh," I finally said. "Your life is getting topsy-turvy."

Neana seemed to be feeling better. "Speaking of topsy-turvy, have you told Richard you true feelings yet?"

"No, not yet. Not until he's about to graduate."

Neana was the one person I could trust to keep my secrets. I had told her everything, all about J. D. and Richard. The other person who knew was Kelly. I had called her one day to see how she was doing. She had a baby boy and was still keeping the father's identity secret. Why was it that we all had secrets? Maybe everybody does.

One week before prom, as I sat in my math class, the last class of the day, I looked up to give my eyes a rest. The numbers on my paper were causing my head to hurt. To my surprise, I saw a familiar girl walking down the corridor by my classroom. It was Joanie! My teacher was preoccupied with reading something, so I started to wave to get Joanie's attention. Joanie had already seen me and was motioning for me to come out of the classroom.

I walked up to Mrs. Butler. "Mrs. Butler, may I be excused a minute? I need to go to the restroom."

She looked up at me and then at the clock on the wall. "Go ahead and leave for the day Junie. The bell is going to ring in five minutes and there's no homework assignment."

"Okay, thanks." I whispered back. I gathered my books and quickly walked out of the class. I was so excited to see Joanie. I hadn't seen her in almost a year! With her holding an infant girl and me holding my books, we managed to give each other a hug.

"How have you been?" she asked.

"Busy with school and stuff. I've missed you! Why haven't you called me?" I said, looking at the pretty baby with her black hair. "What's her name?"

"This is Katie, my daughter."

"Wow, she's so pretty." *Now I knew why she moved before graduating.* Joanie and I were walking out of the school toward the parking lot.

"This is my car," she said pointing to an old brown Pontiac. Joanie opened the door and set Katie down on the seat to change her diaper. "I'm sorry I haven't spoken to you in so long, Junie."

"I guess I can see why," I said, looking down at Katie. "Joanie, I can't believe you're a mom now. It seems like yesterday we were playing Barbie dolls."

"Let's go sit by the lake a minute," Joanie said, gathering up her pink baby bag. "Here, hold Katie a second." She shoved Katie into my arms. I was glad I had set my books on the top of the car. I'd never held a baby before. Katie was so light.

"Do you need to go anywhere?" Joanie asked.

"Nope, I'm done for the day. I have very little homework, it'll take no time at all."

We walked across the parking lot and behind the fenced-in tennis courts down to the green grass next to the lake. Joanie spread out a blanket from her baby bag. I set Katie gently on the pink blanket and sat next to her, while Joanie sat on the child's other side.

"I wanted to stop by and visit friends today, and explain everything that has gone on in my life over the past year. Last year, my mom and dad got mad and told me I couldn't see Raymond anymore. They didn't like him because he lives in a trailer in Norfolk. I just got so mad. Plus that's when I found out I was pregnant, so I moved in with Raymond and his sister. Raymond and I got married, so my last name is Hartsfield now," Joanie said, holding up her left hand to show me the gold band on her finger.

I was happy for her, but unhappy at the same time. How could she have kept all of this from me? I didn't want to say anything. I was glad to be talking with her again.

"You would have been proud of me Junie. I finished my high school credits in summer school. I got my diploma from Craddock. I know it wasn't Indian River, but all that matters now is that I have that piece of paper."

"I am proud of you, Joanie. But why didn't you ever call and tell me any of this?"

"I thought you would be mad at me."

"No, I was disappointed that you dropped out of school and moved away without telling me is all. I was worried."

"Oh, sorry. I just had a lot going on."

"It's okay, I understand," I told her. "I heard rumors that you were pregnant, but didn't know what to believe. We rarely ever see your family anymore. I miss them too."

"So what are you up to these days?" she asked changing the subject.

"I'm going to the prom with Richard Matrix." I felt I could confide in her.

"Really? Blockhead?"

"Yeah. Just as friends, though."

"I always thought you two would get together."

"Really?"

"Sure. Why not? You befriended him before anyone else did practically, and he's nice. I'm happy for you Junie. Raymond is learning how to become a mechanic," Joanie said, picking up Katie while reaching in the baby bag for a bottle.

"How do you like being a mom? You seem to really know what you're doing."

"I wouldn't have it *any other way*." Joanie seemed genuinely happy and looked well, even though she had gained a few pounds. The lake's surface glimmered under the blue sky. It was a beautiful afternoon. After Katie was fed and burped, I helped Joanie gather up everything and walked her back to her car.

"Please don't be a stranger," I said.

"Let me give you my phone number," she said, pulling out a pad and pen from her purse. "Here."

The last name *Hartsfield* would be hard to get used to. She put Katie safely in her car seat and gave me a hug.

"Bye," she said, waving her hand out the window as she drove off.

"Bye!" I waved back.

I drove home delighted about visiting with Joanie. I was elated over the fact that I was going to the prom with Richard. Life seemed to be on track again.

As soon as I walked in the door, the phone rang. I ran to answer it, hoping it was Richard, although I knew it wouldn't be because he was attending a funeral down in Ashton, North Carolina. He wouldn't be back until Friday.

"Hello?"

"Hi there." It was only J. D.

"Hi, J. D. What's up?"

"My prom is coming up Saturday. I was kind of hoping you would like to uh, to go with me?"

I'm sure he was. I had invited him to go to the ring dance with me in January. Richard had been out of town that weekend. Melanie had wanted me to go to the ring dance because she had a date, and J. D. was convenient. Now he was confident I'd go to his prom with him.

"Sorry J. D., I made plans for that night. I'm helping out a friend," I lied. I didn't want to hurt his feelings.

"Oh, uh, well, that's okay." I could hear the disappointment in his voice.

"I'm sorry," I said again before we hung up.

It would have made my dad's day if I went to the prom with J. D. He really liked J. D. What father wouldn't have? He was smart, polite, and came from a nice family with money. I liked J. D.'s family. They were nice, almost too nice. He had three brothers and a sister; all younger than J. D. They seemed to like me too, and were happy that J. D. had a female friend for a change. My mom understood my true feelings for Richard. My dad didn't like Richard, mainly because he rode a motorcycle.

The phone rang again. "Hello?"

"Ah, yes, hello. Is this Junie?"

"Yes, it is." The familiar female voice with the Southern accent had me curious.

"Hi, Junie, this is Mrs. Matrix. Richard wanted me to call you. He had a motorcycle accident down here in Ashton. He's in the hospital."

"Oh my God! Is he going to be all right?"

"Oh yes, yes. But he's banged up pretty good. The doctors want to keep him for a few days to keep an eye on his concussion. Don't worry, he'll be fine."

I felt panic running through me, but her calm voice soothed me.

"Thank you, Mrs. Matrix. Please tell him I'll be thinking of him."

"I have the hospital's number if you want to call him."

"What is it?" I asked, grabbing the pen and paper my mom kept by the telephone in the kitchen. As I wrote the info down, my eyes started tearing up. I hated the thought of my beautiful Richard banged up in a hospital bed.

"His father and I will be heading over to the hospital shortly Junie."

"Thanks, keep me posted."

"Will do. Good-bye now."

As soon as I hung up, the phone rang again.

"Hey." It was Richard; he sounded tired.

"How are you?"

"I'll live."

"Your mom just called and gave me your number. I was just about to call you. So what happened?"

"A truck pulled out in front of me when I was on the highway. When I swerved to miss running into it, I ended up in oncoming traffic, so I swerved again and hit a log on the side of the road. It sent me flying. I rolled several feet before stopping. You should see me." He chuckled a little. "I have the worst case of road rash in history. I wasn't wearing a shirt when I crashed."

"I wish I was there. I'm so sorry this happened to you."

"No! Now don't *you* apologize. I wanted to call to apologize to *you*."

"To me? For what?"

"I promised to take you to the prom and now I can't. I … am … really … *sorry* about that. I mean it."

"I don't care, Richard. As long as you're okay, it doesn't matter. I *mean* it. I should let you go; you probably need to rest."

"Yeah, I'm tough though. I'll see ya when I get back."

"Okay Richard. See ya." I hung up. He was okay, and that's all that mattered. I wondered if I should return the dress or just hold onto it. *No, I better return it. My mom paid so much for it.*

The phone rang again.

"Hello?"

"Hey, Junie. It's Harris. What's up?"

"Hi Harris. How are you?"

"Good. Hey, listen, I need to tell you something."

"What?"

"My good buddy J. D. is in tears over you."

"Why?"

"He's crazy about you. He just called me, and I have to admit, I've never heard him so upset before."

"Why? Because I can't go to the prom with him?"

"Yeah. I guess you could say that. You know how sentimental he is."

I felt sorry for J. D. all of a sudden. I pictured him in tears. No other girl would go to his prom with him.

"My plans have actually changed. I guess I am available to go to the prom after all."

"Oh, that is so cool. We are all going as a group. I asked a girl named Carol to go with me. Mike and Andy have dates. It will be fun."

"All right. Let me call J. D. and tell him I'll go with him."

"See ya Junes." I hated being called that. *Why do I have to be so nice?* I asked myself as I picked up the phone to dial J. D.'s number.

J. D. was thrilled when I said I could go to the prom with him after all. I went back and returned my black silk dress with the black satin rose sewn on the bust line. I needed the money I would receive back to get another prom dress.

Let's see, I thought as I looked at the modern dresses at Greenbrier Mall. Billy Idol's song "Eyes Without A Face" was playing on the radio. I wanted to wear the opposite of what I would have worn for Richard. I remembered liking the white dress that Sandy wore in the movie *Grease*. An all-white dress wouldn't be hard to find. Sure enough, I came across a floor-length sleeveless white dress with ruffles across the bottom half. It was only $40; I could pay back my mom some of the money with the difference between the two dresses. J. D. was going to wear a white tux with a pastel pink cummerbund and tie, so I decided to buy pale pink pumps. I remembered the elbow-length pink lace gloves I had worn during the fashion show that I still had at home. I would wear those as well. I might as well *try* to enjoy myself at this prom that I didn't really want to attend.

J. D. was right on time, showing up in a light blue Citation he had rented. My mom was excited, snapping pictures of us with a smile spread across her face. My dad was away working aboard a ship. I forced a smile, trying to look pretty and as if I was having fun. If Richard could have made it, he would have shown up in a limousine. He had talked about renting one. At least the weather was nice. George Town was beautiful this time of year, with the sprawling lawns a brilliant green color and the dogwood trees' little white flowers starting to bloom.

We all met at a seafood restaurant for dinner on the beach. I was glad we went as a group. The guys talked, making jokes and laughing while the girls talked about their dresses and the trouble they went through to get their hair as big as possible. It was hard to maintain big hair with the high humidity. Usually, I would bend over, let my hair hang down, and then spray massive amounts of Aqua Net hairspray on to keep my hair as fluffed out as possible.

I complemented the other girls' dresses even though I wasn't really paying attention to what they had on. My thoughts were on Richard. J. D. seemed elated and had a constant smile on his face. The restaurant had large windows all around, giving a panoramic view of the Atlantic Ocean. I stared out at the waves crashing on shore. I wanted to get out of my dress and dive into the ocean to swim as far as I could.

When we left the restaurant, we left in separate cars. We were headed to a high-rise hotel in Norfolk for their prom. There was a live band playing music, with the singer sounding just like Sade when covering "Smooth Operator." But the vocalist didn't sound much like Madonna when she sang "Like a Virgin." We all danced before sitting to eat cake and punch. Someone bumped into me, causing me to spill my red punch down the front of my dress. I was shocked to see that it simply ran off my dress onto the floor. Not a stain was left. *Awesome*, I thought, *a waterproof dress; the highlight of my night*.

"I have to be home by 11:00 PM," I lied to J. D., so we would leave early. My parents had said I could stay out longer if I wanted because it was prom night. I didn't tell J. D. that, of course. I was growing bored of the whole night and was worried about how Richard was doing in the hospital.

"Uh, um, okay," J. D. said.

Not long after, we said goodnight to his friends.

Harris gave me a hug. "You look beautiful tonight."

"Thanks, you look great yourself." Harris had flaxen blond hair and beautiful blue eyes. He was skinny but built well. Being a wrestler kept him in good shape. He looked great in his black tux and red tie.

When we finally reached my house, I turned my head away slightly as J. D. tried to kiss me goodnight.

"Thanks for taking me. I had a really good time," I told him hoping his night was special for him.

"I'll call later," he said as he left.

After he drove off, I sat on my porch hoping Richard was doing okay. I didn't want to go in yet. I looked around the neighborhood, which was illuminated by the moonlight. As I sat listening to the crickets; I could see that Mick was in his room. His bedroom light was on behind his red curtains. All of a sudden, a small car screeched to a halt in Mick's driveway. A lady got out, leaving her car door open and the headlights on. She stood in front of his window.

"*Mick*! I swear to God, if you don't come outside right now, I will run my car straight through that garage door!"

Holy shit! I thought. *Should I call the police? No, I don't want to cause trouble for Mick. But I will call if this gets out of hand.* I stood up when she got back in her car and revved up her engine. Mick came out dashing through his front door, jumped down all four of his front porch steps, and sprinted off down the road. The lady peeled out after him, leaving black skid marks in the road. The neighborhood was silent again. *What the hell is going on with him?*

Shortly after, someone came walking down the middle of the street. It was Mick.

"Hi, Junie!" he said, trying to sound casual. But I could hear in his voice that he was upset.

"She went that way," I said, pointing and letting him know I had seen everything.

He crossed my lawn and plopped down next to me on the steps.

"You're glowing in the moonlight."

"Huh?"

"Your dress."

"Oh yeah. I didn't feel like going inside."

"What the hell are you doing sittin out here all alone in your lovely prom dress?"

"I came home early. I don't like the guy."

"Why did you go with him?"

"To make him happy, he's a nice friend."

"Look at ya, all grown up into a beautiful young lady."

"Aw, thanks, Mick."

"What the hell is going on with you?"

He lit up a cigarette and leaned his elbows on the steps behind him. "Oh, that's Karen. The teacher I was dating."

"Are you still?"

"I *was*. I just broke up with her."

"She seems immature to me, Mick."

"Yeah, she is."

"Do you think she'll come back?"

"Probably. I better get going. Go inside, girl; it's getting late," he said as he headed across my lawn.

"See ya."

"See ya." He got in his truck and drove off.

I went inside, got into my nightgown, and went down the hall to the living room. I sat on the foot of the couch, where my mom had fallen asleep waiting up for me. The TV was still on. She opened her eyes when I called her.

"How did everything go?"

"It was a nice prom. We had dinner in that nice restaurant on the beach. I didn't stay long enough to get our prom pictures."

"I'm glad I took some here before you left, then," she said sleepily. She was big on taking pictures. I threw my prom dress in the bottom of my closet and went to bed.

I love you, Richard, I said to myself before falling asleep.

I couldn't help but give Richard a hug when he showed up on my door step a week later. But I was careful because, as he had said, he had the worst case of road rash I had ever seen. I liked how he gave me a strong hug back.

It was graduation night at Indian River High School. I stood back behind the chain-link fence watching crowds of people walking in different directions. The sun had set, and the bright football lights cast long shadows behind the pine trees. Indian River's seniors were lining up for their senior march onto the field. Richard looked so handsome, as he walked his usual bold, sturdy, and strong walk. He held his head up high as he walked in line with his graduating class. Melanie was in front with the rest of the honors grads. *Good for you, Melanie*, I thought as she walked by. She had decided to join the air force. I was so happy for everyone, but at the same time I felt sad. I was losing more friends.

Richard would be leaving for boot camp in a couple of weeks. I decided to write him a letter telling him my true feelings. I would let the cards fall where they may. I would remain his friend always, but my love for him would never die, either. Someday he would realize no one could ever love him like I did. I thought about what he had said during the nice dinner we had after he got out of the hospital. I had told him about my recurring dreams of someone handing me a black rose. I didn't tell him who it was in my dreams; he'd think I was nuts.

"Does a black rose mean danger for me?"

"No Junie, it doesn't."

"How do you know?"

"Because there is no such thing as a black rose. They don't grow naturally. How can there be any danger from something that doesn't exist?"

Then I knew. Black roses only existed in my mind. I decided it was a symbol of my love for Richard. It symbolized a love that was deep, bold, and strong. What other color could represent that kind of love? My love for Richard existed in my heart and in my mind. I had to tell him. After the speeches and the granting of diplomas, I waited by Richard's motorcycle. Eventually he would head over. When he saw me, he crouched down and playfully sprinted over to pick me up and swirl me around. I giggled.

"Thanks for coming," he said, putting me back down.

"Hey, way to go! Lucky, no more school for you."

He was so excited that I felt excited too.

"Let me give you a ride home before I head out. I've been invited out to a graduation party. Or do you want to come?" I had never been to a party before, at least not like the one he was going to. "I can't promise you a ride home though."

My parents would cause a big scene if I had to call them for a ride home. They would never let me go to a late-night party. That would be too embarrassing in front of Richard.

"Naw, go ahead. Have fun and don't you crash!"

He still had some red scars on his neck from his crash in North Carolina.

When he dropped me off, I looked at him. "Richard, I need to tell you something important, but not tonight."

"What? You can tell me."

"No. Just call me sometime."

"Okay. See ya," he said, revving up his engine and doing a wheelie as he drove away.

I sat at my desk with a pen and paper. How would I start off this letter? A song came on the radio that always made me think of Richard, "The Rose" by Bette Midler. There were lots of love songs that could bring tears at that time. When I was a little girl, I had thought love songs were mushy and stupid. Samantha jumped up in my lap. She was getting old and liked to stay warm by sitting on someone's lap. She purred when I rubbed the top of her head.

"Okay, Samantha, get down; I'm writing right now." I gave her a gentle push and she hopped down.

Dear Richard,

I've been wanting to tell you something for a long, long time, but haven't. I've been harboring a secret in fear of losing our friendship. With the way I feel and because I want to be completely honest with you; I'm going to tell you.

I, since the day I met you, have been truly, deeply, with all my heart, in love with you. I've loved you every minute in between and will forever. I'll always be here for you and of course will always be your friend.

Junie

I put the letter in an envelope and sealed it after reading over it twice. The next time I saw him, I would give it to him. I couldn't tell him face to face without my emotions turning into tears. If he were to become angry or embarrassed, the look on his face would have been too much for me to bear. So I would just give him the letter and wait for a response.

It was nice not having to deal with school for a whole three months. I had work, but only part time. One of the girls at work was my age and was somewhat new in town. She had moved down from Maine during the spring to live with her dad. Her name was Jeanie. I thought that if she had grown up in George Town, she would have been a J-Bird along with Joanie, Janie, and I. Jeanie's long red hair reminded me of Joanie. Jeanie was ecstatic over living in Chesapeake and being so close to the beach. She asked me one day how to get to the beach. I told her I would drive us. There was more than one beach to choose from, which could be confusing for a newcomer.

I picked Jeanie up at her father's condo, which was right behind

Greenbrier Mall. I drove us to the Fort Story beach, located on an army base. I had a military sticker on my windshield, so we could just drive right through the gate. I had an officer's sticker, and if I slowed my car, the soldier at the gate would have to salute me. I never did that, as I found it unnecessary.

"The beach is further in on the Chesapeake Bay, which leads out into the Atlantic Ocean," I explained to Jeanie as we drove down a two-lane road surrounded by pristine sand dunes and sea grass. I drove by the old lighthouse, and Jeanie snapped pictures with enthusiasm. She photographed everything in sight, snapping pictures of things I had always taken for granted. As always, the smell of the salty air blowing through our rolled-down windows gave me a sense of excitement. There was a new wooden walkway that led down to the beach. I remembered when I was little, and how we had to trudge through the burning hot sand. Jeanie was taking everything in with an expression of wonder and excitement on her face. She had wide eyes and a big smile. It was her first time on a warm, sandy beach. The only things she saw up in Maine were lakes, trees, and grassy fields, she later told me.

It was a sunny day and the beach was full of life. Boats and Jet Skis played upon the water, reminding me of children on a playground. There was laughter from children making sandcastles. Some of the kids were running back and forth in the waves crashing on shore. As I sat on my towel next to Jeanie, I pushed my hands under the warm sand and felt for tiny seashells, something I'd done since I was a small child.

"Are you ready to go in?" I asked her.

"Yeah, sure, Junie!"

We headed toward the water. People's heads turned as we walked. We both had on bikinis. Mine was black and white, and Jeanie had on a black and pink one.

"Okay, this is what you do!" I said just before diving headfirst through a wave and coming out on the other side.

I turned back to Jeanie, who was looking at the swells coming at us.

"The best way is to just dive through!" I yelled.

I was glad to see her actually dive through a wave.

"Wow, you're right! That does *seem like* the best way to get through a wave."

Soon we needed a rest from swimming. We laid out on our towels to work on our tans. I told Jeanie all about Richard and J. D.

"Why don't you just dump J. D.?"

"It's not that I don't like J. D. I really do; he's one of the best friends I've ever had. I find myself actually missing him when I don't see him for a few weeks. I feel like I need him around to lean on. I could *never* love him, though. Not as more than a friend."

"What would you do if Richard called you up asking to be more than friends?"

"I'd go to him, no questions asked."

"What if he just wants to remain friends?"

"I'll just stay friends with him then. I wrote him a letter telling him my feelings, but I haven't been brave enough to give it to him yet."

"I understand. I like this guy who lives in the apartment building that I live in, but I'm too embarrassed to say anything to him."

"I guess we both need to be a little braver, huh?"

"Yeah, I guess so."

Later, before Richard left for boot camp up in Great Lakes Naval Station, he came by to say good-bye. We sat privately in the formal living room. I was glad that my mom was working outside in her tomato garden and my dad was aboard ship.

"What was it you wanted to tell me?"

"Oh, just that I really hope we'll stay in touch. Please write me." I was such a wimp.

"You know I will, and you better write me too."

"Hey, good luck, Richard" was all I could say when he stood up to go. I couldn't bring myself to give him the envelope. *Just tell him to wait a minute, Junie, and go get the damn letter!* I was screaming inside my head. I had been playing the good old buddy role for so long that it came a little too naturally. I had to break out of that mold. I had to rip off the mask I'd been hiding behind for over three years.

"Are you okay?"

"Yeah, I'm just really going to miss you," I said. I let the love I felt for him pour out of my eyes for once. I was hoping he could see it.

"I'll miss you too. Make sure you write me." He gave me a tight hug before leaving. I watched him as he rode down my street on his silver motorcycle. A part of me left with him.

I went through the motions of life; but didn't really feel alive after the day Richard left. We wrote each other, with me still playing the good old buddy role. He told me all about boot camp. After boot camp, he would be going to school for electronics. My dad had started out doing the same thing.

I went to school during the week and spent all of my weekends with J. D., Andy, Mike, Harris, and whoever Harris' girlfriend of the week was. We went to the movies, Pizza Hut, and video arcades. We spent most Friday evenings cruising the strip that ran alongside the Virginia Beach boardwalk. Excitement was all around us, with hundreds of teens walking past all the tourist shops and hotels. The street was flooded with teens driving cars, honking at attractive pedestrians. Guys and gals made cat calls from their cars at one another.

Sometimes I had dinner over at J. D.'s house. I enjoyed the Bentleys' company. J. D.'s father reminded me of Mr. Rogers from the children's TV show. J. D.s mom was very prim and proper. They were goody-goodies, but easy to be around.

George Town wasn't the same without Richard. It wasn't the same without Neana. She moved away with her mom shortly after her parents divorced. It definitely wasn't the same without Joanie, either. The stress from my parents' constant bickering was eating away at my nerves. Life was harder to juggle with my friends being gone. Neana and Jake had moved with their mom to a small apartment in Virginia Beach. Mr. Simons moved out too, but I didn't know where. Sadly, Neana didn't know either. It had all happened so fast. Neana came over one day and said they were leaving by the end of that week. Neana hadn't even known she was moving until that very day. When she left for good, we hugged each other good-bye tearfully.

"How am I going to get along without you? I just don't know," I said. "We'll have to stay in touch. Give me your phone number and address as soon as you can."

"Okay Junie! Good-bye!" And that was that.

Joanie moved a second time without telling anyone where. She was only a memory now. Mick moved out. I would really miss our late-night phone conversations.

I missed the Ainsworths. They were always busy with work. Their busy jobs combined with the stress of Joanie disappearing made them antisocial. Morris was finally accepted into the army, which took him out of George Town. I was so happy for him.

"Good for you, Morris," I told him just before he left.

We gave each other a big hug.

"Y-y-you stay out of trouble," he said teasingly.

I felt sad, disappointed, and lost. The very fabric of my home was being ripped out. I was thankful for my Great Bridge friends, and clung to them for security as I once had relied on my George Town East friends. My sadness grew when I called Teddy Jeffries, hoping to hang out with him sometime. I hadn't seen him in so long. He told me he was moving with his parents to Key West by the end of summer.

Almost every Saturday, I had dinner with J. D.'s family. I would help his siblings set the dinner table, and then load the dishwasher when we were done eating. It was as if I was part of the family.

At work, Jeanie told me about how she had started dating a young man living in her condo building. We mostly spoke in between cleaning tables at work. We didn't have any classes together at school.

The meaningless days drifted by. Life was happening all around me, but I just wasn't living it. After the holidays, J. D. took me out to a nice Italian restaurant. As usual, I pictured Richard and me sitting in the restaurant, surrounded by the romantic décor. He was always on my mind, even with J. D. trying to amuse me or while hanging out with friends. I looked around the restaurant at the dark red velvety drapes. I looked at the statues and how they evoked a sense of romantic antiquity. I pictured myself becoming a statue in a garden, waiting forever for Richard. The lit fireplace was cozy and romantic.

"Junie?"

"Yeah?"

"I want to tell you, uh, I want to ask you something."

That hesitating tone is familiar. Was prom coming up? No, it wasn't for a few months still.

"What, J. D.?"

"I thought you should know that I love you. I really love you." He pushed his glasses up on his nose. *What did he say? He loved me?* I was jolted out of my deep thoughts about Richard and sucked back into my real, ugly world. *Oh God, not this.* He got down on one knee next to where I was sitting and pulled out a small blue, velvety box.

"Will you marry me?"

I stared down at the small, round diamond ring. The stone sparkled under the dim lights of the restaurant. People were staring. I was embarrassed.

"I don't know what to say. This is so nice; you are so nice, J. D. but ..."

"Just say yes. Even if you don't love me now, some day you will."

That's impossible! "J. D. ... I ..."

I didn't know how to decline. I felt put on the spot.

"I can make you happy."

"J. D., I can't," I said before getting up and running out.

I honestly didn't want to lose J. D.'s friendship. I for sure didn't love him. I was walking down the cold, wet sidewalk. It had been raining all evening. I heard footsteps coming up behind me. J. D. was running after me. I turned to face him.

"J. D., I am so sorry. I can't marry you. I don't love you and never will. *I love Richard.* We're too young."

I was bawling now. It had hit me just how much I missed Richard.

"Hey, it's okay. Just forget it. But if you ever change your mind, I'm here. Who's Richard?"

"I don't want to talk about it, okay?"

"Okay."

After a quiet ride home, we said good night. I went straight to my bedroom and pulled open the desk drawer where I kept the letter to Richard. I put a stamp on it, took it out to the mailbox, and put it in, even though it was 11:00 PM. *If I don't do it now, I never will*, I thought.

I was sick and tired of school. One afternoon, I came home and turned on the TV. Dan Rather was talking about how a space shuttle had blown up. I didn't believe it at first, but then they showed scenes of it over and over. I'll never forget the funny white cloud that the explosion left behind. It must have been traumatic for the families of the crew.

Thank God it was my senior year; only four months to go and I was out of school. But then what? Would Richard write back saying he loved me too? I didn't want to go to college right away. I was so burnt out from high school. I wasn't sure what kind of career I would pursue.

I didn't want to spend any more time living at home with my parents, either. I hated feeling so indecisive. I was sure that I would no longer be indecisive after as Richard told me where we stood.

As I waited for Richard's response letter, I continued to drift through the motions of life. Neana and I talked on the phone at least once a week. She was not happy with her new school, and had to share a room with Jake in their cramped two-bedroom apartment.

January passed with no letter. February passed; still no letter. Along with the insecurities of no longer having my George Town friends to run to, along with my parents bickering, the anxiety of *not knowing* roared in my mind, mixed with a roaring silence from Richard. All this caused my angst and sadness to grow. I decided to write another letter.

Dear Richard,

I hope you're not angry with me for keeping my feelings in all this time. I will always be just your friend, if that's what you want. I do ask that you respond. I need to know how you feel too.

Love always,

Junie

I mailed off the second letter with expectations of a response. March passed with no letter; April passed with no letter. My angst spiraled into a deep, dark depression after I stopped by Richard's house to ask his mom if she had heard from him. They had moved. The house stood empty.

I love you so much, I thought as I cried myself to sleep each night. My black rose dreams were now unpleasant. I tried not to sleep at night. Instead I studied my school books, reading assigned chapters over and over. When I was finished studying my assignments, I read unassigned chapters of history, sociology, and science. By the time May arrived, I was numb. I didn't care that I was graduating high school. I didn't care that summer was approaching. The air around me seemed thin, and I couldn't catch my breath.

I remembered the excitement of school letting out when I was a kid, the anticipation of hitting the beach. We were so happy then, playing hide-and-seek long after sunset. I missed those days of catching lightning bugs while getting bitten by mosquitoes, serenaded by the chorus of crickets chirping in the night. Life was easier as a kid. *Why did I have to grow up and fall in love?* I had to chuckle a little when the song "Love Stinks" played on the radio. It was true. Love did stink. I felt my depression slowly change into a burning anger, my attitude turning cynical. *If Richard was truly my friend, he would have responded to my letters by now, dammit!* I thought.

Graduation night came. My parents were *so* proud of me in my light blue cap and gown. As we lined up outside the fence that surrounded the football stadium, I began to sweat in the hot and humid night air, June 12. Some seniors were proud and held their heads high as we marched in to "Pomp and Circumstance." Some didn't seem to care, like me. We just wanted to get the ceremony over with. When the principal, Mr. Philips, began his speech, his first line made me start thinking about my future.

"This is the beginning of a new life. Your future is ahead of you. Go forth and flourish. You can fulfill your lives."

I was going to go forth and flourish, and eventually fulfill my life. I didn't know how, but I was. Obviously, Richard was never going to speak to me again. *Damn jerk! I ought to marry J. D., just to show Richard I could move on, and that he missed out. If he didn't love me back, fine. But to not write or call me after I had asked him to? He was no friend to leave me hanging like this, torturing me.* I was angry at everything. Angry at the fact my friends in George Town had moved away, how the house next door to me still stood empty, how Joanie moved again and left no phone number or address. Teddy Jeffries had moved and not left me a return address as well. I was angry at Richard's parents for moving and not telling me. I had no idea where they were. I was angry that I couldn't make up my mind about my future. I was lost without Richard. My anger slowly started to make me feel *better*. Being angry was easier than feeling the pain in my heart, the thorns my beautiful black rose had grown. When my name was called, I walked up, shook Mr. Philips' hand, received my diploma, and walked back around to my seat. Everything else was a blur. Just like in most of my dreams, my life was blurry, except my anger.

I thought about a song called "Let's Go Crazy," by Prince, where he sang "In this life, you're on your own and when the elevator tries to bring you down, go crazy, punch a higher floor."

Shotgun Wedding

My parents hugged me and congratulated me. I smiled at them. I didn't want them to know the agony I was in. They seemed so proud. I didn't want to ruin their joy. J. D. walked up, holding a bouquet of pink carnations.

"I'll see you later," I said to my mom and dad before turning to J. D. to thank him for coming. My parents thought the world of J. D. and never cared how much time I spent with him or how late I came home, as long as I was with him. They left swiftly to get out of the huge crowd that was forming. Mingling parents and students were flooding the area.

"Want to go to dinner?" J. D. asked.

"Sure J. D. Let's go." I pulled off the cap and gown and felt much cooler, tossing my graduation outfit into the back seat of his station wagon. The white cotton dress I had on underneath felt cool. My anger felt hot. I was going to flourish, all right. I was going to punch a higher floor. *If Richard wants to be a good friend or more, he would have to come after me and rescue me from what I was about to do*, I thought with a vengeance.

"J. D., take me back to that Italian restaurant. I liked that place. It was romantic."

"Okay," J. D. said with enthusiasm. When we were seated and handed menus, I put mine down and looked right at J. D.

"J. D.?"

"Yeah?" he said, setting down his menu too. He looked straight at me, listening intently.

"I'm sorry. I haven't been very nice to you lately. Let's go ahead and get married. I love you with all my heart," I lied. My anger made it so easy to lie. I didn't care whose feelings I hurt. I was tired of being the nice guy all the time. I was going to be the bad guy. I felt a newfound freedom.

"Really?" J. D. asked, his eyes wide, his face turning red.

"Yes. We'll have whatever kind of wedding you want."

"Really?" I thought he was going to faint.

"Is the offer still open?"

"Yes, of course."

"Good. Let's order up a bottle of champagne and celebrate," I said. Both J. D. and I looked much older than eighteen, and we didn't get carded.

My parents were thrilled when J. D. properly asked them for my hand in marriage. I would have asked Neana to be my maid of honor because she was a closer friend than Jeanie. This wasn't going to be a wedding I was going to take serious though. This was my version of a shotgun wedding, and Richard was holding the gun. It made me think of the song "White Wedding" by Billy Idol. The anger and vengeance in his voice when he sang made me wonder if he was singing to me. I couldn't get married without having Neana in my wedding. She would be hurt. So I called her up and asked her to be my bridesmaid.

"Junie, are you sure you want to get married so soon after graduation? I thought you loved Richard," Neana said.

"I do. That's why I'm marrying J. D. Richard will have to come get me if he cares about me. Besides, I'll get divorced once I make up my mind about my future."

"Okay, Junie. I'll be there, but I think you're making a huge mistake. You should sit back and wait."

I could have just continued on with my life, gone to college or worked. But I had a strong feeling pulling me, not letting me sit back and wait. All of a sudden, I realized I didn't want to *lose* J. D. I felt insecure when he wasn't around to help take my mind off Richard. No, I wasn't going to back out of the game. This was the hand I was stuck with, and I was going to gamble with the cards that were dealt.

"When is this wedding?"

"It's July 12." I had chosen the day one month after my graduation, the day when I had decided to let my anger give me strength, aggression, and vengeance. J. D. liked July 12 because it was one month to the day since we had gotten engaged. I only wore the engagement ring when J. D. was around.

Jeanie was honored that I asked her to be my maid of honor, but had the same doubts as Neana. I lied, assuring her that I was truly, deeply in love with J. D. My anger allowed my lies to sound so believable. Jeanie didn't take the role of maid of honor lightly. She picked out all of our wedding announcements, although I asked that there be no roses pictured on them.

"The latest colors for weddings are pink and white, so I decided to have the bridesmaids wear that," Jeanie told me. "I can wear my pastel-pink, lacy prom dress, which will be ideal. Is that okay, Junie?"

"Sounds perfect." I even asked her to pick out a wedding dress for me at JCPenney. I didn't want to pick one out.

My parents couldn't have been more thrilled that I was marrying J. D. His parents were filled with joy as well. The Bentleys had only been eighteen years old when they were married.

I could have cared less. I watched everybody's excitement regarding my shotgun wedding. I knew the marriage was a temporary thing. I figured I could get out of the house and into my own apartment long enough to figure out the next card I would play.

J. D.'s parents helped us find an apartment to move into, and even offered to pay the first month's rent. It was nicer than I expected, with two bedrooms and a swimming pool right out our back door. I had to get a full-time job. Cleaning tables at Piccadilly on weekends wouldn't cut it. I decided to interview for a job in a day care that I saw in the want ads. This job paid $2 more per hour than Piccadilly's, and was full-time, with weekends off. I liked babysitting, so I thought it would be an ideal job until I could decide when and where I would go to college. J. D., of course, could work in his parent's Mini K variety store.

The wedding plans were done in no time. Mike and Harris were to be groomsmen. Arnold, an old friend of J. D.'s like Teddy Jeffries was to me, would be best man. A couple of girls from work agreed to be bridesmaids, too. The shotgun wedding was to take place on a Saturday afternoon. I played the Prince album *Purple Rain* over and over. Its music matched my mood, sounding both sad and angry. I decided to write one more letter to Richard.

Dear Richard,

I haven't heard from you; so that gives me my answer. J. D. asked me to marry him. That's not what I want. I truly hope you have a nice fulfilling life, Richard.

Love always,

Junie

My brother and his family showed up the day before the wedding. They had their clothes picked out and were ready for my supposed big day. Mrs. Simons dropped off Neana to spend the night before my wedding.

"Junie?"

"Yeah?"

We were in our sleeping bags in the room over the garage. My brother and his wife were sleeping in my room, while my nephew Chris was sleeping in the guest bedroom.

"Remember when we were little and had sleepovers up here? We used to get scared of the attic door, and would try to put tape around it, so if monsters tried coming out we would have time to run down stairs."

I started laughing. Neana could always make me laugh, even during sad times. We stayed up half the night talking about the old times. We talked about playing Barbies, roller-skating, riding bikes, when we had first met, and our favorite songs from the movie *Xanadu*. We drifted off to sleep while singing some of those songs.

It was a joke, the whole entire event. What a joke. As I slowly made my way down the aisle holding my dad's arm—he looked handsome dressed in his white navy uniform with his sword attached to his side—I began to cry. I cried not out of joy, like everyone assumed. I cried because Richard wasn't coming in to crash the wedding and rescue me. I somehow had it in the back of my mind that he would.

J. D. looked like he was going to pass out when I glanced at him. I noticed Jeanie was crying also. Everything was a blur again. I repeated vows after the preacher said "Repeat after me." Vows? Meaningless words. I didn't write them. I didn't think them up. I didn't feel them. *This is only temporary, Junie,* I thought to myself as I looked down. *You'll get away for a while to think and plot how to get Richard back without being under Mom and Dad's roof and influence.* When the preacher asked

J. D. to repeat the vows, I looked into J. D.'s eyes. For the first time, I felt like I was going soft. He loved me. He really did. He was such a good friend. He was smart, intelligent, and for the first time, I thought he looked handsome. *Do I love him? Yes, I think I do. Not like Richard, but yes, there was something there.* I hadn't realized it until right then. *No, Junie; you're on a mission, don't stop now.*

I could hear and see everyone in the reception hall, even though I felt as if I was standing in a mist outside looking in. They were all eating and drinking merrily. The three-tiered wedding cake was beautiful, all white with lace frosting wreathing the edges. Jeanie did a good job picking it out. I held a frozen smile on my face the entire time, feeling nothing. I was relieved when it was time for us to head out of the church and drive off in the little white Citation that J. D.'s parents had bought for us. Mike, Harris, Arnold, and Andy had written *Just Married* all over the hood of the car with shaving cream, and tied old shoes and beer cans to the back of the car. It was so stupid, but everything happening was stupid.

Everyone followed us out of the parking lot, honking their horns and rejoicing. J. D. dropped me off at my house so I could change out of my hideous, puffy wedding dress with its eight-foot train. He was going to go back to his house to change before coming back for me. His parents had purchased us a vacation package in Hilton Head, South Carolina. *A great place for me to get away and think to plan out my future,* I thought. Another wave of confusion came over me. *Maybe I should hang on to J. D. He's perfect husband material, or at least everyone thinks so.* I sat at my kitchen table and took off my white pumps. My feet were swollen from the tight-fitting shoes and ninety-degree weather. Neana came in a few moments afterward and handed me the mail. She had stopped by my mailbox on the way in. In the stack of mail was a letter addressed to me. The handwriting was familiar. Here was my response from Richard. I stared at it a few seconds before opening it. My heart was racing and my palms were sweating.

Dear Junie,

I'm sorry, so sorry, that I haven't written you back in so long. I was in shock when I received your letter saying that you love me. First, I wondered how anyone could love me; especially the way you do. Now that I look back, I realize I was a fool. I thought I saw deep compassion in your eyes. I now realize that this was true love. You never said anything, so I figured you were just a really good friend. Then I had to think about my feelings for you. I didn't want to write you back until I was completely sure. Yes, Junie, I love you too. Someday I will come for you. Please write me back.

Love always,

Richard

Now I knew. I had my answer. *This would be the shortest marriage in history, or would it?* I had to tell J. D. that I couldn't continue. We would have to get an annulment. My dad would help me. He had told me once that I could always come back home if I was unhappy. *I had to remain in George Town until Richard came for me. Or did I?* Why was I thinking this way? I want Richard. But J. D.? I never gave him a genuine thought. The wall of anger that I was hiding behind was starting to crumble. *Maybe I should stay with J. D., at least until I can figure out my divided feelings.* When J. D. came in through the kitchen doorway to get me, I liked the elated look on his face. I tucked the letter from Richard deep down in my purse, smiled at J. D., and took his hand.

"Let's go."

"Call me!" Neana yelled out.

"I will. Tell everyone we left, and that I'll send them postcards!"

I didn't know if one could love two people at the same time. I would just go about my way with J. D. and Richard, and let fate decide where I would end up.

Looking back on my life in George Town East, I realize that it was an ideal way to grow up. Eventually I left George Town. I later left J. D., but we remained good friends for many years. Richard and I remained friends for a few years eventually drifting apart. Oh, the silly days of high school and growing up. I'm sure there are things we all wish we could have done differently, but that's life. The journey without love isn't life at all. I read somewhere that life can only be learned if lived forward and only understood if lived backward. I will always cherish my memories.

THE END